SAINTS, SINNERS, AND CHRISTIAN HISTORY

I0807311

SAINTS, SINNERS, AND CHRISTIAN HISTORY

The Contradictions of the Christian Past

JAMES S. PACKER

CFI
Springville, Utah

© 2008 James S. Packer

All rights reserved.

No part of this book may be reproduced in any form whatsoever, whether by graphic, visual, electronic, film, microfilm, tape recording, or any other means, without prior written permission of the publisher, except in the case of brief passages embodied in critical reviews and articles.

This is not an official publication of The Church of Jesus Christ of Latter-day Saints. The opinions and views expressed herein belong solely to the author and do not necessarily represent the opinions or views of Cedar Fort, Inc. Permission for the use of sources, graphics, and photos is also solely the responsibility of the author.

ISBN 13: 978-1-59955-137-1

Published by CFI, an imprint of Cedar Fort, Inc., 2373 W. 700 S., Springville, UT, 84663
Distributed by Cedar Fort, Inc., www.cedarfort.com

LIBRARY OF CONGRESS CATALOGING-IN-PUBLICATION DATA

Packer, James S.
Saints, sinners, and Christian history : the contradictions of the Christian past / James S. Packer.
p. cm.
ISBN 978-1-59955-137-1
1. Church history. 2. Christianity—Controversial literature. I. Title.
BR148.P28 2008
270—dc22

2007052185

Cover design by Jeremy Beal
Cover design © 2008 by Lyle Mortimer
Edited and typeset by Kimiko M. Hammari

Printed in the United States of America

10 9 8 7 6 5 4 3 2 1

Printed on acid-free paper

CONTENTS

PREFACE

This book is based on a simple conviction: The lives and teachings of those that lead Christian churches—as well as the church doctrine—should be compatible with the ethical, theological, and moral principles taught by Jesus and his followers in the New Testament, or at the very least should conform to even the very broadest of Christian morals. Through much of history, particularly during medieval times, that was not the case. Church leadership has been an unpleasant mixture of corruption, hunger for power, hedonism, simony, immorality, wars, bloodshed, political chicanery, deceit, hate, violence, and abusive fights over doctrine—all committed in the name of Christ. The immorality, behavior, and vindictive doctrinal infighting of Christian leaders and priests during parts of the last two thousand years stagger any imagination trying to picture such men as practicing Christians on any level, let alone leaders.

This history does not intend to denigrate the courageous epics and moral victories of Christianity; those have been lauded and attested to by many. It does, however, point out the many and curious incompatibilities between Christian traditions and historical fact; between the principles laid down by an unusual individual and his immediate followers two thousand years ago and the long train of supposedly divinely appointed leaders and doctrines since.

The flights from Christian standards are not figments of one's imagination (would that they were for the sake of conscience), but are the facts of history, and they are well attested to. It seems somehow obvious that such abuses cannot be reconciled with the morality of the New Testament Jesus. In addition, the ideas and principles taught by

Jesus are not, in many cases, the same as those taught by descendant churches. History therefore presents us with a gaping incompatibility.

Writers and scholars throughout history have commented on the striking and obvious impossibility of reconciling descendant Christian churches with Christ. Thousands of ordinary Christians have come to the same conclusions. Such painful discoveries generate different responses. Some give up faith; others embrace some form of modern Christianity as the best compromise available—believing the original message *in spite of* Christian history. Some insist on debunking Christianity altogether, taking the excesses and contradictions of descendant churches as evidence of the falsity of the whole message. Millions, ignorant of historical fact, accept to varying degrees the traditions handed to them through church organizations. Others simply ignore the evidence altogether.

This book details logical, historically valid alternatives to those above. That is, that the original ideals and organization laid down by Christ and his followers were indeed valid and good, but they simply did not survive long. The *remnants* of Christianity were then changed, molded, and warped by man through the ages, and subsequent organizations reflected the ideas and morals of their surrounding cultures. Seen in this light, the apparent contradictions of history are easily explained. The history of Christianity after AD 100 demonstrates the *normal* history of human enterprises, whether business, government, or politics, and not the original pattern laid down by Christ. Confirmation pours in steadily. Newly discovered manuscripts, more ancient than any found before, have forced the Christian world to recognize that the practices and doctrines of the original church were really quite different from those used today. From these new discoveries, authorities readily distinguish between two levels of Christianity, and some even suggest that an old, original Christianity was obliterated by new and invading forms.

Here we will explore the contradictions between what churches are today and what they were in the past, and compare this with what Jesus and his followers taught in the New Testament. It is not a pretty picture; by even the vaguest moral standards, the morality and theology of many Christian officials and leaders were appalling. Perhaps those with a highly emotional attachment to their church might best leave this history alone, since itemizing the Christian past is at times most unsightly and not apt to bolster confidence in descendant churches.

Why, then, look at all? First, because it is fascinating history. Second, like any other subject, tracing Christian history gives us a better conception of what the end products are. Third, and most important, early Christian history indicates that Christ and his followers knew that their teachings would be lost and perverted shortly after their own deaths. In spite of that seemingly dreary outlook on the future, they remained optimistic; because knowing the doctrine would be lost, they also believed and predicted it would be restored again, whole and intact, as had happened throughout history. The gospel, as the ancients understood, was not granted a single time only, but was, in a series of dispensations, given to mankind as it waxed and waned in its worthiness to receive it. So, for Christ and the apostles, there was great hope for the future, although they knew of the long, sad, dry spell during which the church would be lost and corrupted. They preached that in spite of the coming apostasy, future generations would again see the original church replaced intact.

CHAPTER 1

The Falling Away

"Of such is the kingdom of God . . . "

He was sacrilegious, vindictive, immoral, and treacherous; a drunkard and a gambler. His sexual hunger was insatiable, and he violated the innocent by force or freely took the offerings of courtesans. He casually betrayed emperors depending on his capricious judgment, and he was willing to trade virtually anything, instigating chaos, war, and suffering for thousands, as long as he could maintain his own high style and comfort. In mad rages he tortured his followers by castration, blinding, hacking off fingers or hands, or cutting out tongues. He was finally, fittingly, killed by an outraged cuckold who caught him red-handed and beat him so unmercifully he died soon after. He was a pope.[1]

Another was vain, hypocritical, intolerant, immoral, profligate, greedy for money and power, coarse, unscrupulous, syphilitic, and dishonest. With his unchallenged power, he killed and tortured all he suspected of disloyalty, ruling with blood, horror, and terror. He was a king.[2]

Ogres of history? Mad monsters whom the hand of God had never touched with enlightenment? Perhaps so, but not according to the individuals involved (and millions of their spiritual descendants today). They both protested just the opposite, claiming to be the sole authorized representatives of God on earth during their respective times. The first was Pope John XII and head of a church which has long claimed the one and only depository of God's truth on Earth. The second was King Henry VIII, who for very personal reasons claimed for himself—with the backing of political leaders—the only direct representation of heaven. Many prominent Protestant churches of today descend directly from the church he founded, the Church of England.

Both were equally misfit as men of God. In fact, from their lives most people might easily conclude that they worked for the other side! Were they exceptions, anomalies in the long history of Christian existence? Not at all. Similar sins appear often, in greater or lesser degree, in scores of the "sole representatives of God" and their associates through the first 1600 years or so of organized Christianity. Perhaps more important, even where leaders' lives have been more respectable, the doctrines and practices they espoused through the ages often clash with those preached in the original Christian church.

While writers and scholars throughout Christian history have seen and commented on this fundamental contradiction, such observations generally received cold reception among religious leaders and tended to be swept under the rug as strange aberrations of the past. No more. New discoveries of manuscripts more ancient than any ever found before have forced the Christian world to recognize that the practices and doctrines of the original church were quite different from those used today.[3, 4] These discoveries have popped across the sky of history in a series of bright constellations in recent years, and their final impact may eventually resemble an overwhelming cannonade.

These exciting discoveries of recent years enable scholars to piece together a more coherent picture of what happened to the original church. Quite early, apparently, the first literature of the church was lost and another substituted in its place, so that the modern student is now confronted with two distinct bodies of Christian teachings. "The original literature," wrote W. Schneemelcher, "was supplanted by another literature very strongly influenced by the non-Christian environment."[5] On the basis of the new manuscript discoveries, authorities can readily distinguish between the two levels of Christianity, and some even suggest that the old, original Christianity was destroyed by the new, invading forms. The new winners (which would eventually evolve into modern Christianity) naturally wiped out every trace they could find of their former rivals.[6]

These changes were gradual but simple and devastatingly effective.

In the confusing period after the deaths of the apostles there was no main "church," but rather a chaotic jumble of Christian churches, each scratching and clawing to nail down its claim as the sole authorized church of Jesus Christ. The heretic hunters of these churches, in their fierce and zealous fight to establish some central orthodoxy—now that the original guidelines had been lost—suppressed every saying of Jesus or doctrinal image that did not agree with their particular concept of orthodoxy.[7] Thus, descendant churches have inherited a payload of doctrine and practice often opposed to those taught in the original church.

So, how to explain this fundamental contradiction between the lives and doctrines supposedly blessed by Jesus but in reality foreign to what he taught? If we buy tradition, we are indoctrinated to collectively set back on our haunches in awe at the swift rise of Christianity from a tiny, outlawed sect to the world dominating heights of today. Naturally, we are not supposed to notice the current—or past—and strangely contradictory bickering among Christian "brothers" over who has the "true" Christian church. Nor, heaven forbid, should good members bring up the embarrassing facts of history and wonder about the other strange contradictions between modern Christianity and original Christianity, including the blotchy stains of immorality, corruption, mass confusion, name calling, and even bloodshed on the pages of Christian history and in the lives of its officers and priests.

The Christ of the New Testament at times seems completely incompatible with the Christianity described in history—and with good reason. They *are* incompatible. History provides the answer why. Pope John and King Henry were not the anomalies; they were part of the regular stream of history. The anomalies were Christ and his doctrines, which, in their pure and uncorrupted form, existed for only a few years.[8] The original teachings of Christ had tough sledding and never did appeal to many. They were, in fact, rather quickly lost and *did not* conquer the world. The original church of Jesus Christ did not survive past AD 100.

What's more, it was not expected to. Christ, the apostles, and the earliest church fathers knew that (1) the message would be rejected, (2) the light would depart and the world would choose darkness, and (3) the church and the gospel would be perverted and changed into new forms. In other words, they knew that the original church would not survive; such was part of their message.[9]

This thought, of course, stands directly in the path of a monstrous tidal wave of tradition that roars the opposite—of course Christianity survived. Otherwise, what are all these churches that exist?

What indeed? After the original church died, there was no orderly transfer to Rome or anywhere else. There were instead hundreds of Christian churches and doctrines squaring off in a brawling slugfest to determine who was going to be *the* Christian church. The fight was long, bitter, and often bloody. Then, "the beaten ones were not only covered with green sod, but with a great silence as well."[10] Historians agree that the eventual winners were only faintly related to original Christianity. Also, just as the apostles had predicted the loss of the original, they had in like manner foreseen the formation of these new groups. Something named Christianity would survive, but it wouldn't really be Christ's. In fact, the descendant churches seem to be purely human organizations and have freely mixed paganism, philosophy, legend, and their own thoughts into the original gospel. (So much so that some historians claim that Christ's influence on Christianity is actually minor!)

All this gnaws ferociously at tradition, of course, but tradition has ever been an unreliable guide to truth. Since the earliest Christian history (that of Eusebius in the fourth century), the emphasis in church history has been to describe the development of the church, rarely questioning its actual survival (so much so that when something *named* Christianity actually came through the early ages, surprised officials had to dance nimbly around previous prophecies that it wouldn't).[11] Nonetheless, a close study of history challenges any survival of the original church of Christ. What's more, the evidence of the loss has been lying freely all over the surface of Christian history for years. Churchmen and scholars have treated this topic like a lightweight would treat Muhammed Ali, not wanting to get close to something that dangerous. Most of those who have stumbled over it have either ignored it or hurriedly backed off from the abyss and thereafter avoided it. It is just too big, too awesome an idea to entertain, and its implications are devastating to the existing forms of Christianity that descended from the original. In spite of any intramural differences, Christian churches are agreed on one thing. The church *must* have survived, even if history and prophecy must be ignored or rearranged. Any other idea is appalling.

Nonetheless, we cannot ignore uncomfortable thoughts just because they are uncomfortable. Drastic changes in the early church did take place, and the historical evidence of the losses is consistent. Religious scholars have ever since, dug, weeded, and turned the garden of history, attempting to explain away the radical differences between Christ's original church and the existing copies.

Once one recognizes what actually happened, however, the overwhelming abundance of clues clarify 1900 years of religious history, facts drop into place, and light dawns. There was an apostasy—not *from* the church, but *of the* church—on such a grand scale that the original church disappeared! That original church did not descend by tradition into Catholicism and later resurface by reformation in Protestantism. These churches are strictly human organizations that marched out of the smoking ruins of the original church hundreds of years later.

Our emotion and reason may fight against such conclusions, but the evidence of history is clear. In the following chapters we will examine the evidence of the loss of Christianity and its replacement with the pseudo-Christianity that has reigned in its place for the last 1800 years or so.

Notes

1. Chamberlin, chapter 2.
2. Durant, *The Reformation*, chapters 23–25.
3. Nibley, *Since Cumorah*, 123.
4. Marshall and Taylor, 43.
5. W. Schneemelcher, "Neutestamentliche Apokryphen," in Nibley (c), 97.
6. Nibley, *Since Cumorah*, 67–68.
7. H. Koster, "Patrologia Orientalia, IX," in Nibley (c), 94.
8. Nibley, *The Passing of the Primitive Church*, 143.
9. Ibid., 131.
10. H. J. Schoeps, "Urgemeinde, Judentum, Gnosis," in Nibley (c), 86.
11. Nibley, *The Passing of the Primitive Church*, 145.

CHAPTER 2

Back to the Original Design

To understand just how far modern churches departed from the original idea of two thousand years ago, we must look briefly at that first model.

Jesus Christ established a body of doctrine and a church. We have only a small part of its history, constituting those few books and letters known as the New Testament. From this meager surviving evidence some theologians and scholars theorize that Christ gave his disciples not a complete doctrine, but a hazy philosophy, an unformed lump of clay if you will, that needed shaping and evolution. That theory might have originated when later churches found they understood little of Christ's original doctrine and had to explain why. A careful reading of biblical references, however, indicates the opposite was true. Apparently inexhaustible amounts of doctrine and advice were available to church leaders: "And there are also many other things which Jesus did, the which, if they should be written every one, I suppose that even the world itself could not contain the books that should be written" (John 21:25).

Apparently Christ thoroughly taught organization and doctrine to his leaders. After his death, for example, he showed himself to the apostles "being seen of them forty days and speaking of the things pertaining to the kingdom of God" (Acts 1:3). Churchmen have never cared much for this reference, since to profess that a special or a secret teaching that had since been lost (the churches don't have what Christ gave to the apostles on that occasion) would seriously undermine their claims as successors to Christ's original church. Many have therefore tried to pass off this forty-day period as a special social call or lingering farewell instead of the critical occasion for instruction it really was.[1]

Many apocryphal works have professed to illustrate the lessons of the forty days, but most scholars (again the reluctance to admit of special knowledge that didn't survive in church doctrines) have hastily condemned them. Significantly, however, "the favorite theme of the early apocrypha happens to be 'the teachings of the Lord to the Apostles after the Resurrection.' "[2] One consistent, standard teaching of those sessions—that simply pops up much too often to be explained away by coincidence—is the almost immediate corruption of the church, the falling away, and the long age of darkness without the true church. The apostolic fathers, coming along soon after these events, had the same knowledge. The overall theme of coming apostasy and sadness is too consistent; it had to be based on some original knowledge given to the apostles during the forty days.

The apostles, then, did indeed have access to an enormous wealth of information on the future, the gospel, and the running of the church. Strangely, however, they did not leave detailed instructions on organization and doctrine. The world has mourned the loss, supposing the apostles' failure to provide written instructions a tragedy. Such a blunder from *prophetic* men seems colossal indeed. Why didn't they leave more?

Churchmen and scholars, pondering this question for years, concluded that the apostles—and even Christ—believed the Second Coming was due any day, and therefore they took no thought for the future. This theory has the advantage of saving the church; that is, it explains that once the early members got over this misguided belief about the Second Coming, they could buckle down and build a church instead of waiting around for the end of the world. However, it doesn't do much for the reputation of the apostles, who had so miscalculated on their prophecies. And even Christ, in charge of the Second Coming, was confused and didn't know when it was! Scholars and churchmen arguing for this theory willingly accept all that, however—rather Christ and the apostles wrong than they.

But were Jesus and the apostles that foolish? Were they so befuddled they didn't understand the very events they preached about so vividly? They did talk about a Second Coming, the eschaton. They also predicted some imminent and dire event about to befall the church. But were these the same event? Was the coming catastrophe the end of the church in that generation and not the end of the world? Could the apostles have been right after all? Some scholars are now cautiously concluding that Christ may indeed have predicted some such eminent catastrophe (but not the Second Coming) and therefore did not intend to create a long-time church survival at all.[3]

Again, however, most churchmen have been reluctant to look at this conclusion and have determined that the church simply must have survived. They would prefer that Christ, the apostles, and the early church fathers appear as confused visionaries rather than accept anything else. Indeed, one way modern churchmen can salvage the world of *evolved* Christianity is to downgrade the apostles as unsophisticated locals who misunderstood prophecy, scriptures, and revelation, and somehow forgot to leave any instructions behind. The shoe may have been on the other foot. The apostles apparently knew the church would not endure beyond their generation and may not have taken any great thought for written instructions for the succeeding generations.[4] The same behavior was reflected by the early members.

So, the doctrine given to the apostles was complete, and they did not hesitate once the comforter came. They realized that though Christ was gone, he had left them with full instructions and authority to build up the church, even if it were to endure only for their generation. That they proceeded to do, first filling the vacancy left in the presiding officers, the Twelve Apostles. This they did by revelation, and chose Matthias as the new apostle, thus restoring the quorum (Acts 1:26).

The apostles and early church members knew, and the scriptures abundantly demonstrate, that this quorum of twelve apostles was the foundation of the church, the general presiding officers (Ephesians 2:20, 4:11–13; 1 Corinthians 12:28).

There was order in the church, from the top down; even the apostles had their presidency chosen from among the twelve.[5] The apostles, by revelation, received the doctrine from God to be given to the church. When the first great schism confronted the early church—the Judaizers in Antioch insisting on adherence to the law of Moses (Acts 15)—the church there did not try to resolve the question by calling a council of bishops. They knew that the right authorities must be consulted and decided that "Paul and Barnabas, and certain other of them, should go up to Jerusalem unto the apostles and elders about this question" (Acts 15:2).

Paul understood this principle well. He was no freelance artist out winging it on his own and formulating his own interpretations. In his travels he preached only that doctrine given by revelation to this inspired body of men: "And as they went through the cities, they delivered them the decrees for to keep, that were ordained of the apostles and elders which were at Jerusalem" (Acts 16:4).

Later apostles, such as Paul, and possibly Barnabas and others, were also pulled into the ranks as the need arose to keep the presiding council at full strength.

On the apostles Jesus bestowed all the authority, privileges, and keys necessary for organizing the church. Apostles were *general* officers with universal authority who traveled around the world, preaching, organizing local branches of the church, and ordaining local officers, always guided by the spirit and by direct revelation.[6]

They were the binding glue of the church. They gave their lives in defending it and the last surviving apostle, John, continued in the true order of organization until he too was finally gone.

> After the death of the tyrant, John passed from the island of Patmos to Ephesus, and used to go to the neighboring districts of the heathen, in some places to appoint bishops, in order to reconcile whole churches, and in others to ordain some one of those pointed out by the spirit.[7]

Finally, however, the world prevailed and by lashing out at the apostles, mortally wounded the church. One by one the apostles fell. No new ones were called. Revelation ceased. Without the presence of authorized and inspired presiding officers, the church quickly drifted into an irreversible and quite human evolution.

The Keys to the Church

To accomplish the overwhelming task of organization and inspiration of the church, the apostles possessed two indispensable gifts to which we have already alluded: the priesthood, or divine authority, and revelation.

The words *priest* and *priesthood* automatically trigger in our minds a firmly etched idea of a separate and managerial class of people, a minority professional group of clerics who have sole charge of all religious matters and who grant laymen only very limited participation—an idea and description that the apostles would never have recognized.

This modern concept is so thoroughly carved into our mental guidelines that it may be only with some difficulty that we can lay it aside and understand the original idea and nature of the divine authority settled upon the shoulders of early church leaders. But we must try.

First, no minority priestly class separate from laymen; no salaried ministers or priests; no powers to decide spiritual matters for all without revelation from God.

What then?

Ignatius, one of the early church fathers, wrote, "What is the presbytery (priesthood) but a sacred assembly, the counsellors and assessors of the bishop?"[8]

> Ireneaus [bishop of Lyons, AD 200] wrote that "all the righteous possess the rank of elder [a primary priesthood rank]."[9] No ruling clique here, but a shared possession. This startling thought clashes sharply with modern priesthood standards. Now Peter's words are clear when he wrote to "the strangers scattered throughout Pontus, Galatia, Cappadocia, Asia, and Bithynia . . . But ye are a chosen generation, a royal priesthood" (1 Peter 1:1; 1 Peter 2:9). This was no letter to only a few select bishops or a separate minority class, but one to all members of the church in the areas mentioned, describing the shared priesthood of the branches of the church. The members were apparently asked by the presiding authority to serve as counselors, advisors, or leaders of various kinds. All were laymen, and all held the priesthood. There were no professional clerics.[10] The early church clearly taught the universal priesthood of believers. There was no priesthood distinct from the general mass of Christianity.[11]

That original priesthood held in common by the general body of the church had many offices that the churches of today are hard put to explain. As a matter of fact, most churches simply overlook these offices since they can't account for them. Paul (as well as modern historians and writers of the Old Testament) wrote about different degrees of the priesthood, such as high priests and a "priesthood after the order of Melchizedek" (Hebrews 5:7). Strange items indeed, and certainly unknown entities in today's churches, along with apostles, prophets, and other officers described in the New Testament. There is no record that either Jesus or the apostles ever gave any instructions to change the order of things.

Priesthood authority alone, of course, was not enough to govern the divine church. One other important, necessary item was direct guidance from heaven. The very essence of the original church was constant and recurrent revelation.[12] It was *the* method used to run the original church, and the New Testament is replete with samples of revelation used to guide the apostles in their decisions.

In the book of John, Jesus specified that the spirit (or comforter) would guide them: "Howbeit when he, the Spirit of truth, is come, he will guide you into all truth: for he shall not speak of himself; but whatsoever he shall hear, that shall he speak: and he will shew you things to come" (16:13).

Examples abound, and a few more will suffice to illustrate the principle. When Paul paused in Caesarea before his trip to Jerusalem, a prophet named Agabus visited him with a warning. "And when he was come unto us, he took Paul's girdle, and bound his own hands and feet, and said, Thus saith the Holy Ghost, So shall the Jews at Jerusalem bind the man that owneth this girdle, and shall deliver him into the hands of the Gentiles" (Acts 21:11).

Paul testified to the saints in Galatia that the gospel he preached was not of man. "But I certify you, brethren, that the gospel which was preached of me is not after man. For I neither received it of man, neither was I taught it, but by the revelation of Jesus Christ" (Galatians 1:11–12).

He reminded those same members that on his first trip to Jerusalem as a General Authority of the church he "went up by revelation" (Galatians 2:2).

Peter, in his letter to a number of branches of the church, pointed out that prophets had always relied on the spirit of revelation (1 Peter 1:10–12). In his second such epistle he took care to warn that such prophecy came through holy men as they were moved upon by the Holy Ghost—it give instructions and scriptures to man. In a clear allusion to what was currently happening (and what would happen), he further warned that such scriptures and prophecies were not for *private* interpretation. The intimation is clear. Former prophecy, now scripture, could only be interpreted by those with like gifts of prophecy, as revelation (2 Peter 1:20–21).

(You can already see the problem that would present for future churchmen. If that was always the way in the past, wouldn't it also hold for the future? This uncomfortable question is strenuously avoided or hastily condemned by descendant churches, which deny any such thing as any revelation any time after the death of the apostles.)

Peter also pointed out just how apostasy took place before and how it would take place among the people he was writing to, members of the church; even the very elect. "But there were false prophets also among the people, even as there shall be false teachers among you, who privily shall bring in damnable heresies, even denying the word that bought them, and bring upon themselves swift destruction. And many shall follow their pernicious ways; by reason of whom the way of truth shall be evil spoken of" (2 Peter 2:1–2).

Philip received revelation to seek out and baptize the Ethiopian eunuch. "And the angel of the Lord spake unto Philip, saying, Arise, and go toward the south unto the way that goeth down from Jerusalem unto Gaza, which is desert. . . . Then the Spirit said unto Philip, Go near, and join thyself to this chariot" (Acts 8:26, 29).

Cornelius, in the city of Caesarea, received a revelation on how to obtain the gospel message. An angel visited him and told him to send for an authorized representative—in this case Peter (Acts 10:3–6). Peter, in turn, received his own vision to go and teach Cornelius—thus opening up the great dispensation of the gentiles (Acts 10).

The rest of the apostles in like fashion governed the church by direct revelation from heaven. No one was surprised at this. Quite the contrary. It was expected. That was the way Christ's church worked.

The early church fathers also knew of the importance of revelation, even while recognizing they weren't receiving any in their time. "The agreement of Ignatius, Clement, and John the apostle, writing at about the same time, is especially significant: (1) as to the prevalence of dissension and apostasy, (2) as to the constitution of the church, and (3) as to the importance of the gifts of the spirit and revelation."[13]

This constant stream of revelation guiding the apostles in directing the church came by various means: by the spirit (promptings to do this or that), by visions, by heavenly messengers, and in the person of Christ. Constantly, unchangingly, unendingly revelation *always* guided church leaders. The necessity of revelation for the church can hardly be emphasized enough.

The book of Revelation, written by John, the last surviving apostle, markedly demonstrates the way revelation worked in governing the church. John obviously had in his charge the various churches in Asia. In the first chapters of the book, John records some very specific revelations about the churches within his stewardship.

The revelation received for the Ephesians was conciliatory, congratulating them on resisting the already spreading apostasy (which even included apostolic impostors!). Even they, however, needed a gentle chiding. Then John received further instructions, and in writing about them was careful to specify that they were not *his* instructions, but direct revelations (Revelation 2:7, 9).

And so on down the list of the remaining active branches John was responsible for. It was the same with Peter, James, Paul, and the other apostles. They made no pretense of guiding the church on their own or from instructions from councils, but freely acknowledged their dependence on *direct,* divine intervention.

Notes

1. Nibley, *When the Lights Went Out*, 35.
2. Ibid., 37.
3. *Time* Magazine, Aug. 6, 1976, p. 54.
4. Nibley, *The Passing of the Primitive Church*, 137.
5. Eusebius, Book III, chapter XXIII.
6. Mourett, "Historie Generale de Peglise," in Barker, 99.
7. Eusebius, Book III, chapter XXIII.
8. Ignatius, Trallians, VII, Ante-Nicene Fathers.
9. Barker, 101.
10. Schaff, Vol. II, chapter 4.
11. Schaff, Vol. II, 124–25.
12. Barker, 84, 92.
13. Ibid., 21.

CHAPTER 3

The Apostasy—An Early Beginning

Here is the early church as the apostles knew it: church headquarters in Jerusalem; local branches soon forming nearby; the apostles (and men they called to the ministry) spreading out and preaching the word; more and more converts pledging their faith; and branches of the church soon springing up everywhere in the fertile grounds of the Mediterranean world. The apostles traveled and taught, organized and supervised the local branches, called and ordained local officers. "The first Christian communities . . . were established in the cities, one for each city."[1] Presidents of the local congregations were called bishops.[2] Elders, local priesthood holders, were sent out to care for smaller congregations, but "as soon as a village counts a sufficient number of Christians, a bishop is installed."[3] (It wasn't the same kind of bishop we know of today in descendant churches).

In these local branches controversy and discord wormed quickly into the woodwork of the gospel structure. Christianity, drawing its converts from a wide variety of pagan religions and Judaism, stirred a bubbling and troublesome cauldron of conflicting opinions, theories, and practices. Pagans were easily tempted to interpret Christian teachings in the light of their pagan experiences. For them it was a simple step backwards into pagan practice; many backstepped happily. Many of the Jews obdurately refused to accept gentiles as brothers and fought tenaciously to glue the law of Moses onto Christianity and frantically wriggling Christians.

In the first blush of conversion the differences were smoothed by common enthusiasm. As time, tempers, and patience wore on (and out), however, the local branches seethed with buried rumblings waiting to explode into argument, schisms, and apostasy. This was no time of tranquility, harmony, and unity. It was one of squabbling, disunity, and disorder. Questions exploded over doctrine and ceremonies. The apostles were few and far away and quick airmail answers were two thousand years in the future. How to proceed? How to interpret this particular scripture? Who has the answer to brother Flavius's questions? How do we interpret this particular ceremony? Should we change it? The mounting questions and puzzlement quickly became endless. The Christians in Antioch answered one way while those in Ephesus answered another. Even within the same branches divisions arose.[4]

Within a few hundred years, Christian writers, massively readjusting history, would wring out of these quarrelsome and bitter times a golden apostolic age, when Christians were purer and braver, the church united and undivided. It was a myth. There was indeed an apostolic age when the apostles received, by revelation, pure and unadulterated doctrines. There was not, however, a golden age of perfection. Even during the apostles' time, argument schism, and heresy, already set loose in their mission to destroy, ran rampant through the church.

In fact, the New Testament letters existed largely to correct these serious problems. The epistles were instructions written to help contemporary Christians cope with the desperate problems gnawing ferociously at their faith. Paul's letters exude warnings against false doctrines, and expressions of sorrow over the spreading stain of the Apostasy (he was not surprised to see it, only that it had come so soon). He pled with the Corinthians to avoid disputes and divisions. He condemned the formation of cliques into followers of Paul, Apollos, Cephas, and Christ, as the members were choosing up their personal favorites (1 Corinthians 1:12–15; 3:3; 2 Corinthians 12:20). The two letters to this branch of the church are poignant with Paul's warnings. The Corinthians were so divided that Paul warned them they couldn't even receive any advanced doctrine (1 Corinthians 3:2).

To Timothy Paul wrote that "all they which are in Asia be turned away from me" (2 Timothy 1:13–15); and that "some are already turned aside after Satan" (2 Timothy 5:15); and to avoid "profane and vain babblings, and oppositions of science falsely so called: which some professing have erred concerning the faith" (1 Timothy 6:20–21).

To the Galatians he wrote: "I marvel that ye are so soon removed from him that called you into the grace of Christ unto another gospel: Which is not another; but there be some that trouble you, and would pervert the gospel of Christ" (Galatians 1:6–7).

At a conference in Ephesus Paul warned the priesthood leaders and bishops of coming events. He flatly told them that even some of those present, the very leaders, would be the ones to pervert the church: "For I know this, that after my departing shall grievous wolves enter in among you, not sparing the flock. Also of your own selves shall men arise, speaking perverse things, to draw away disciples after them" (Acts 20:29–30).

(Moses possessed of the same power of revelation and prophecy and in a strikingly historical precedent had in like manner also predicted an apostasy after his [Moses'] death [Deuteronomy 31:29]).

The other apostles also issued warning after warning about the apostasy, already in full flower. Jude knew that the pure gospel once delivered to the church members was being perverted: "It was needful for me to write unto you, and exhort you that ye should earnestly contend for the faith which was once delivered unto the saints. For there are certain men crept in unawares . . . ungodly men, turning the grace of our God into lasciviousness" (Jude 1:3–4).

The apostle John warned about one church leader, Diotrephes, so far gone in apostasy that he excommunicated any that believed in the apostles (3 John 9–10). In 1 John 2:26, he wrote, "These things have I written unto you concerning them that seduce you."

The book of Revelation, the Apocalypse, sounded specific and dire warnings about apostasy to the churches under John's care. To the church at Ephesus he wrote, "Thou hast left thy first love. Remember therefore from whence thou art fallen, and repent and do the first works; or else I will come unto thee quickly, and will remove they candlestick out of his place, except thou repent" (Revelation 2:4–5).

John was commanded to denounce the false doctrines of certain sects and teachers that entered the church at Pergamos. The Laodiceans were roundly condemned.

No, this was no golden age of perfect Christians and peaceful harmony, but a brawling cat fight, a time of heartbreak and sorrow for the apostles as they strove in vain against the tidal wave of apostasy wrecking the church. They knew the next generation was lost, but they fought for those already converted. While alive they could barely rush from branch to branch erecting emergency breakwaters to hold back the worst; what would happen when they died?

A Church without Apostles

Persecution arose early in the church. Contrary to popular opinion, however, it was never widespread, and relatively few suffered the extremes of death and torture. The real danger of persecution was the dagger aimed directly against the leaders. In the fierce battles that now loomed up, the strong men of the church were the ones attacked—and the first to fall.

Obviously, the church could not lose its apostles (the very foundation of the church structure), many of its strongest bishops, and other dedicated leaders without being seriously weakened. After the apostles, revelation, and church headquarters were gone, what happened to the Church of Jesus Christ? Catholic historians would like us to believe in an immediate transfer of power to Rome and a gradual growth of the church through that power base. Many religious historians—pushing the claims of descendant churches—have presumed a simplistic interpretation of the transition years, summoning up a vision of a unified church, obedient to a single head; a church which was always recognized as the one true Christian church.

That simply wasn't so, and the false basis of that premise is quickly grasped by even the most casual perusal of the theological struggles that ripped and tore the churches after they were cast adrift. These festering sores of contention spread hate, bloodshed, and division through the Christian churches for hundreds of years. The Christian "church" was a madhouse of conflicting dogmas seeking dominance. With the fall of the strong, the disruptive elements in the church that the apostles had fought and warned against so fiercely found themselves free to expound their doctrines and undermine the structure of the church.

It may not always have been deliberate. With no qualified leaders to answer questions, those left had to muddle through as best they could. They supplied their own answers, colored by their own background, experience, or the votes of the branch in unison. Little wonder there was such a rainbow of differences in the post-apostolic churches instead of the unity Christ had taught.

Persecution did not cause the Apostasy, then; it merely aided it, accelerated it, as the church fell from within, not from without. Pagans are never mentioned as any source of real danger to Christianity. It was the believers, or professors of belief, who betrayed and destroyed the church.

The New Testament explodes with the warning signs. We read about betrayal, disobedience, corruptions, deceivers, perverters, traitors, wresting the scriptures, denying the gifts, quenching the spirit, turning love into hate, truth to fables, sheep to wolves, of embracing "another gospel," and so on. Who are the perpetrators of such infamies? The Christians themselves!

The Christian historian Eusebius recorded an eyewitness account (Hegisippus) of these momentous events that tore the church apart.

> The church continued until then as a pure and uncorrupt virgin; whilst if there were any at all, that attempted to pervert the sound doctrine of the saving gospel, they were yet sulking in dark retreats; but when the scared choir of apostles became extinct, and the generation of those that had been privileged to hear their inspired wisdom had passed away, then also the combination of impious error arose by the fraud and delusions of false teachers. These also, as there was none of the apostles left, henceforth attempted, without shame, to preach their false doctrine against the gospel of truth.[6]

Already, in these early writers, we see the attempts to create the apostolic golden age that never was. They write clearly enough about the apostasy breaking up the church, but try to create the impression it began only after the apostles died. It did not, but erupted at the very founding of the church and was an *expected* event. With the death of the apostles, of course, the problems confronting the church took a quantum leap; the two hard rock basic elements of the church, revelation and authority, careened into oblivion.

The Loss of Revelation

Once the apostles were gone, revelation ceased. Belief in it did not fade so rapidly. Individual members nourished it as a fundamental principle. They knew of its necessity and had numerous manifestations of it in their lives. One of the main tenents of the Montanist heresy, for example (around the middle of the second century), was the lack of revelation in the then existing churches. *The Teaching of the Apostles,* or *Didache,* an early document of the church probably written early in the second century, gives instructions on how to receive a prophet and how he is to be treated.

The churches at first clung desperately to the principle of revelation. Gradually, however, they decided that the heavens were sealed and that there would be no more communication from God. The reasons for this were probably twofold. First, revelation was being abused. Itinerant "prophets" wandered around the countryside took advantage of the gullible, lived off the donations of the humble, and passed out their "revelations" loosely and in great confusion.

> They displayed them at an improper season, presumptuously disturbed the service of the assembly, and by their pride or mistaken zeal they introduced . . . a long and melancholy train of disorders. As the institution of prophets became useless, and even pernicious, their powers were withdrawn, and their office abolished.[7]

Second, church leaders themselves, although at first recognizing the necessity of revelation, obviously did not have it themselves. That posed a pretty fundamental dilemma that somehow had to be explained away. One must feel sympathy for those early church leaders left on their own. They knew revelation, a requirement for the church, had disappeared. The confusion and abuses of self-proclaimed prophets, however, became too much. In order to stop the abuse they made what was perhaps a reluctant decision that would have wide ranging repercussions—and which would drastically influence the new "Christianity." They slammed shut the door between man and heaven. Gradually the idea became accepted, and then firmly fixed. As the Apostasy spread, the heavens became not only closed, but *forever* closed. All descendant Christian churches have inherited this doctrine.

Some even try to use the book of Revelation to prove that all revelation had ended at that point, since John wrote in chapter 22, "If any man shall add unto these things, God shall add him the plagues that are written in this book; And if any man shall take away from the words of the book of this prophecy, God shall take away his part out of the book of life" (vv. 18–19).

Curiously enough, there are similar warnings in the book of Deuteronomy (4:2, 12:32)—which if taken the same way would mean that all subsequent writings in the Bible would be cursed.

The meaning in all cases is clear. It is man that is not to add or subtract from the scriptures—no limit has been put on God. When John wrote "this book," he was referring only to the particular book of Revelation, not the New Testament. The New Testament did not even exist at that time as a book. What the prophets are saying in both cases is, "Don't monkey around with what I have said and try to rewrite it." The warning was practical and necessary, since forgeries were blossoming in uncontrollable numbers at the time. The multiplicity of these spurious gospels induced Luke to record his history of Christian events.

Revelation was part and parcel of that organization that represented Christ—it was *the* method used to run his church. For men to decide that revelation ceased seems presumptuous. It was one thing to recognize that authorized revelations were suspended—that is, that God was no longer talking to the then or current church leaders. It was quite another to limit God and say he could *never* speak again. Such pronouncements fly in the fact of the entire body of the word of God known as scriptures; that body itself being revelations given to prophets without which we would have no scripture at all.

The Loss of Priesthood

After the loss of the apostles, local priesthood authority perched precariously on the shoulders of branch leaders. As we shall see, later churches would retroactively try to nail this authority down more firmly and upgrade it into a claim for *General* Authortiy over the church (a very tough job, and the fact that it took several hundred years to accomplish speaks for the difficulty of trying to build a huge house on half a foundation). That local authority, or priesthood, was just that—local; it never had any power over the general church. It was so used later, but by men seeking to build a new church left over from the original. In addition, the local authority had been given by the general officers of the church to branch authorities. These latter could not pass it on to others—that was the prerogative of the apostles and their delegated assistants. Later churches would claim an assumed authority of their own making. Revelation and the authority of God were no longer present when remnants of the original church finally banded together again into a general church organization— this time called the Catholic Church—formed hundreds of years after the apostles had died.

The apostasy, or falling away, was a rebellion *within* the church and happened very quickly. The organizational shell continued intact for a short time and then began its long transformation into what we know today.

The Apostasy Was Predicted

One of the privileges of the apostleship was the gift of prophecy. By using their gift the apostles pulled the curtain of time to one side just widely enough to peek into the future—and wept at what they saw.[9] Their task, they knew, was to preach to a generation that would not listen. Even while fighting the Apostasy with every mental and spiritual weapon they could bring to bear, they knew apostasy would succeed and the church would die.

Paul warned of it in his letter to Timothy: "Preach the word; be instant in season, out of season, reprove, rebuke, exhort with all long suffering and doctrine; for the time will come when they will not endure sound doctrine, but after their own lusts shall they heap to themselves teachers having itching ears; and they shall turn away their ears from the truth, and shall be turned unto fables" (2 Timothy 4:1–4).

Prophetic words indeed. We have already mentioned Paul's poignant words to the bishop's conference at Ephesus, where he predicted that even some of those supposedly worthy leaders would direct the Apostasy (Acts 20:28–30).

When writing to Timothy again, Paul rehearsed the coming events of the Apostasy: "Now the spirit speaketh expressly, that in the latter times some shall depart from the faith, giving heed to seducing spirits, and doctrines of devils; Speaking lies in hypocrisy; having their conscience seared with a hot iron: Forbidding to marry, and commanding to abstain from meats, which God hath created to be received with thanksgiving of them which believe and know the truth" (1 Timothy 4:1–3).

Dr. Adam Clark, the noted biblical authority, explained in his *Bible Commentary* that "in the latter times "meant any time consequent to those in which the church then lived.[10]

In his first letter to the Thessalonians, Paul commended them. They somehow assumed from his letter that the Second Coming of Christ was about due and were figuratively in the backyard waiting for it. Paul grabbed pen and ink and fired off his second letter warning them not to be deceived, because the day wouldn't come until after the Apostasy was complete!

> Now we beseech you, brethren, by the coming of our Lord Jesus Christ, and by our gathering together unto him. That ye be not soon shaken in mind, or be troubled, neither by spirit, nor by word, nor by letter as from us, as that the day of Christ is at hand. Let no man deceive you by any means: for that day shall not come, except there come a falling away first. (2 Thessalonians 2:1–3)

The chief apostle, Peter, also warned of the apostasy hovering over the church ready to pounce. "But there were false prophets also among the people, even as there shall be false teachers among you, who privily shall bring in damnable heresies, even denying the Lord that brought them, and bring upon themselves swift destruction. And many shall follow their pernicious ways; by reason of whom the way of truth shall be evil spoken of" (2 Peter 2:1).

The apostasy, then, was real and well known, plainly predicted by the apostles. One of the most consistent themes of the resurrected Christ's forty-day instruction period was a predicted rejection of the apostles, their coming violent deaths, and of a quick end of the church. Since the apostles made no secret of this knowledge, the first members and leaders should also have known about it. Indeed, that is the case, and the apostolic fathers, those leaders closest to the apostles in time not only knew about it, but watched it happening.[11] "The final stumbling block (or source of danger) approaches. . . . We take ernest heed in these last days; for the whole (past) time of your faith will profit you nothing, unless now in this wicked time we also withstand coming sources of danger."[12]

These fathers saw the church, losing what headway it had made, about to fall into the trap Christ and the apostles had warned it to avoid.[13] They warned, pled, and cried for a change before it was too late[14] and finally saw that the church was being dismantled piece by piece, and the structure rebuilt on worldly standards, with second class materials and defective workmanship.[15]

They, like the apostles, knew the church would die. They apparently knew that the name of Christ and Christians would somehow be glued onto new structures, but this gave them little comfort, since those terms were already being freely and loosely used by all kinds of apostate groups and corrupters of doctrine.[16] "The Apostolic Fathers take their leave of a church not busily engaged in realizing the Kingdom, but fast falling asleep; the lights were going out."[17]

To us it may be disturbing to contemplate the hard fact that the gospel of Jesus Christ was rejected by man and withdrawn from the earth. Indeed, churchmen skitter away from this subject like water on a hot greased frying pan. Regardless of intra-church differences, all have had a very special interest in helping perpetuate the myth of church survival itself. The church *must* survive, they say, even if history has to be ignored or the prophetic predictions regarding the last days, restoration, and the Second Coming derided as fables.

"God would not allow his church to fail after investing so much in it," they argue. "Nonsense," roared back the Apostolic Fathers when the same argument was tried on them.[18] Those who plead in that vein overlook reality. If the very Son of God can be killed, who will venture to judge what will be allowed or not allowed. One of the early church fathers, John Chrysostum, wrote that "after the prophets came the false prophets, and after the Apostles the false apostles, and after the Christ the Antichrist."[19] The only step left out, which we can now supply, is after the church, a false church.

The people on the scene realized that Satan would gain the upper hand and would be left in clear possession of the field; "the days are evil, and Satan possesses the power of this world."[20]

Would the Gospel Return?

In all this dismal knowledge of coming events, one ray of hope brightened the future. Though most Christians have been taught that Jesus Christ on earth brought the first and only appearance of the gospel, that was a later idea hauled up onto thc bandwagon of the Apostasy.

The earliest church fathers who followed the apostles apparently knew something quite the opposite. That is, that there had been various "dispensations" of that same true and valid gospel Jesus taught. The gospel had been on earth during a number of different periods previous to the Christian era, lost for a time, and restored.[21] This knowledge is fundamental to understanding the Apostasy and what was promised to follow.

Irenaeus, an early bishop, wrote, "Thus they were perfected who knew one and the same God, who from beginning to end *was present with mankind in the various dispensations.*"[22]

Kirsopp Lake, in the introduction to his translation of Eusebius's "Ecclesiastical History," says that Eusebuis "maintains that the teaching of Christianity was neither new nor strange. . . . It had been followed centuries before by Abraham and Moses and later prophets; and the religion of the patriarchs was identical with that of the Christians. . . . The student of church history will have little difficulty in recognizing that this is in the direct line of Justin Martyr, Aristides, Clement of Alexandria and Cyprian."[23]

The actual words of Eusebius offer an early knowledge about "dispensations." He refers to Jesus' ministry as a dispensation of the gospel. He knew it had existed before, as he wrote: "By this method, at the same time, the antiquity and the divine dignity of the Christian name will be exhibited to those who suppose it a recent and foreign production, that sprung into existence but yesterday, and was never before known."[24]

He even gave clear evidence that Jesus Christ had appeared many times before.

> Then it was, that the first begotten wisdom of God, existing before all creatures, and the self-same pre-existing word, induced by his exceeding love of man, appeared at times to his servants, in visions of angels; at others, in his own person. As the salutary power of God, he was seen by one and the other of the pious in ancient times, in the shape of man, because it was impossible to appear in any other way.[25]

Look briefly at several more passages from Eusebius illustrating his understanding of this principle.

> And now, that no one may suppose his doctrine is new or strange, as if springing from one of recent origin, and in no respect differing from the rest of men, let us also briefly examine this point. . . . Should anyone, beginning from Abraham, and going back to the first man, pronounce those who have had the testimony of righteousness, Christians in fact, though not in name, he would not be far from the truth. . . . What, then should prevent us henceforth from acknowledging that there is one and the same principle of life and conduct, the same course of piety common to us, who have after Christ, with those pious men who lived in times long before. Whence it is evident that the religion delivered to us in the doctrine of Christ is not a new nor a strange doctrine.[26]

Various other early Christians wrote about this doctrine (Ambrose, Methodius, Jerome, and Lactantius), explaining that the church was "like the moon, a thing that disappears and reappears from time to time."[27]

Evidently these early church fathers were quite familiar with the idea of the gospel being taken away and restored from time to time. Later churches, although paying lip service to believing in what these early church fathers taught, contrive to ignore many of these troublesome points. Now churches teach only of one dispensation. This is necessary, of course, to validate their claims to representing the Church of Jesus Christ as it supposedly continued from his ministry down to modern times.

Now the serious readers must ask themselves an important question. The gospel had appeared at various times before Christ and was lost. It had come again with Christ and was then lost. If this has been the pattern of the past, would it not also be the pattern for the future? Might it not come again? That is apparently just what the apostles taught in Acts 3:19–21: "Repent ye therefore, and be converted, that your sins may be blotted out, when the times of refreshing shall come from the presence of the Lord; And he shall send Jesus Christ, which before was preached unto you: Whom the heaven must receive *until the times of restitution of all things,* which God hath spoken by the mouth of all his holy prophets since the world began" (italics added).

The gospel, appearing on earth many times before, would be restored once more. The clear fact of apostasy does not mean the end of hope. Momentous things would come again. The scriptures promised a restoration of "all things."

All of that, however, lay in the future. First must come the "falling away," the Apostasy. It took place and we will study it in the following pages. Remember through this at times depressing tale that the apostasy is temporary. Christ had promised that after the Apostasy truth would be brought back again—not by political power or some individual agency or ecumenical togetherness—but directly from heaven through prophets to be called and sent forth.

All that, the scriptures tell us, would come later. First, to the Apostasy.

Notes

1. Barker, 118.
2. Bardy, "La Theologie de l'Eglise de Irenne au Concile de Nicee," in Barker, 118.
3. *Loc. cit*
4. Mosheim, Cent. 1, Part II; chapter 3:11.
5. Talmage, 39.
6. Eusebius, Book III, chapter XXXII.
7. Gibbon, chapter 16.
8. Clarke, "Bible Commentary," in Talmage, 37.
9. Nibley, *The Passing of the Primitive Church*, 136–37.
10. Clark, "Bible Commentary," in Talmage, 37.
11. I Clement, III, Ante-Nicene Fathers.
12. Barnabas IV, Ante-Nicene Fathers.
13. Clement I, III, XXIV, XIX; Ignatius, Trallians, VII; Ephesians XVII, IX; Hermas, Vision, III; Ante-Nicene Fathers.
14. I Clement I, III, XIX, XLI, XLVII, LII, LXV; Barnabas II; Ignatius, Ephesians, XVII; Philadelphians, II; Hermas, Vision, II, III, IX; Ante-Nicene Fathers.
15. Hermas, Vision, III; Ante-Nicene Fathers.
16. I Clement XV, XXX; II Clement III, XVII; Barnabas, X; Ignatius, Ephesians, XV, VII; Magnesians, IV; Trallians, VI; Polycarp, Phillippians, X; Hermas, Vision, I; Ante-Nicene Fathers.
17. Nibley (a), 135.
18. Ibid., 144.
19. *Loc. cit*
20. Barnabas, II; Ante-Nicene Fathers.
21. Lyon, 30.
22. in Lyon, 31; italics added
23. *Loc. cit*
24. Eusebius, Book I, chapter II.
25. Loc. cit
26. Eusebius, Book I, chapter IV and V.
27. Nibley, *The Passing of the Primitive Church*, 145.

CHAPTER 4

Christian Churches without Christ

From Garden to Desert, the Apostolic Fathers

We have already seen and duly noted the enormous forces of dissension racking the church while the apostles lived. All too soon, however, the apostles were violently removed from the world. With their deaths, the church abruptly and precipitously lunged down onto the shoulders of ordinary human organizers—and became a human organization.

Nothing is more impressive in reading Christian history than this striking judgment on the abrupt change in character of the church after the apostles were gone. Philip Schaff writes:

> We now descend from the primitive apostolic church to the Graeco Roman . . . from the fountain of divine revelation to the stream of human development; from the inspirations of the apostles and prophets to the productions of enlightened but fallible teachers. The hand of God has drawn a bold line of demarcation between the century of miracles and the succeeding ages, to show, by the abrupt transition and the striking contrast, the difference between the work of God and the work of man. . . . There is no other transition in history so radical and sudden, and yet so silent and secret.[1]

A. Cleveland Coxe, in his introduction to the Ante-Nicene Fathers wrote much the same thing.

> Disappointment may be the first emotion of the student who comes down from the mount where he has dwelt in the tabernacles of evangelists and apostles; for these disciples are confessedly inferior to the masters; they speak with the voices of infirm and fallible men, and not like the New Testament writers, with the fiery tongues of the Holy Ghost.[2]

There was an abrupt change between the first church and the organizations that followed. Historians have noted the sharpness of its delineation, calling it by various names (the great gap, the lacuna, the eclipse, the void). No matter the words, the meaning is the same. A dramatic pause in history marked the end of the Church of Jesus Christ as a quite human organization picked up the pieces and patched together a new and totally different kind of organization. The great gap was real, radical, and abrupt; not a long drawn out line of evolution we would expect in a normal system. So abrupt, in fact, that it makes some scholars doubt there even was a primitive church at all.[3]

It turns out that the very worldly, and therefore normal, operations of the post-apostolic church meet the norms of history. It is the brief interlude of Christ and the apostles that are the strangers. The first Christian literature "had no literary predecessors and no successors, but appears as a completely alien intrusion into the classical tradition, an incongruous and unwelcome interruption, an indigestible lump which, however, disappears as suddenly as it came, leaving the schoolmen to resume operations as if nothing had happened."[4]

All this had been expected by Christ, the apostles, and the early church in general. The early members knew quite well of "the general apostasy which would precede the coming of the Messiah."[5]

The great gap was a jagged tear that could never again be matched up to the original truth, a precipitous drop from the lofty plains of the original Christian doctrine. It comes as no surprise once one realizes what happened; quite the contrary, it was to be expected under the conditions. Once the divinely inspired general officers of the church were gone, all that were left were the local leaders of each church. They, not being apostles, were barren of apostolic authority and right to revelation. Valiant and good men for the most part, brave, humble, and dedicated, they were left without leadership while trying to hold together the church. They shine less because they are less. They were good men in an impossible situation and, along with the rest of the church, faced the future with fear. For them, loss of the apostles was an unmitigated tragedy.

Subsequent generations dubbed them the "Apostolic Fathers," and the rose-tinted glasses of time and tradition transformed them into something they were not. They were *local* authorities, not *general* authorities of the church. Faced with insurmountable problems, they fought to save the whole church. Guided by what they had learned—or what they thought they had learned—they tried to spiritually reinforce each other.

In their efforts to influence others—some beyond the limits of the local church their authority was limited to—they wrote letters and exhortations and called all to brotherly love. Zealous in their beliefs (and sometimes the source of error themselves, as Paul warned they would be), they felt forced to take stands against innovations sweeping through the church. Out of their conflicts emerged the first non-biblical Christian literature, the writings of the Apostolic Fathers. If we compare these documents with the New Testament, it is evident they fall far short of the original force, depth, and spirituality of that text.

Philip Schaff quotes one writer as saying that the comparison between this group of writings and the New Testament is like "an Eastern city in the desert, from which the traveler passes by a single step into a barren waste."[6]

The reason for that harsh judgement, of course, is obvious. New Testament authors were writing under the direct guidance of God. The Apostolic Fathers wrote without authority, quite on their own, and produced relatively inferior works.

The early church fathers present a problem. On the one hand, they are the closest to the original and one would therefore think that some of their ideas would contain the seeds of the original truth. At the same time, we recognize that tradition has transposed these men to larger-than-life caricatures. Later generations endowed them with legend and superstition and elevated them to pedestals they never occupied in life. They were not the super-saints they later became. They were, as a matter of fact, quite inferior to the men they followed. In their writings, personal, as opposed to inspired, interpretation of the gospel first acquired significance.

Are the patristic writings, then, of no value? Quite the contrary. They are extremely important for two reasons. First, the nature of their writing is evidence alone of the Apostasy, as the abrupt step from apostles to the fathers is sharp and clearly marked. Second, they give us, in spite of other errors, our only glimpse of the primitive church after the apostles are gone. In their writings are the clues to the nature of that church.

Although we can assume many errors in this new order of things, we can also make the logical assumption that these early remnants of the church still possessed more tag ends of the truth than anything later. Man changes, invents, and "improves." As more and more Christians disagreed on doctrine later on, more confusion arose. So there is justification in going back to the beginnings to get at the germ of truth. We are indeed greatly indebted to these early church fathers. They didn't record much, and what they did record was not intended as doctrinal exposition and is very prone to error, but the tiny fragments they left offer us a limited view of the original church. They contain the truth, or that which is least removed from the truth; the earliest records of a church that was already undergoing change.

Interestingly enough, both Catholics and Protestants admit this closeness of the Apostolic Fathers to the original gospel and profess it as a basis of their beliefs. They reverence these early fathers in terms of awe all out of proportion. But it is lip service only, as these churches generally contrive to ignore or otherwise evade the many uncomfortable or simply inconvenient doctrines and principles that were everyday assumptions to the early fathers. Indeed, many items of common knowledge among the fathers (revelation, baptism by immersion, the nature of God) are a grave indictment against descendant churches and their doctrines.

> It is well to keep in mind that none of the doctrines considered "orthodox" by the churches in the first quarter of the nineteenth century is found in the early fathers of the church—in the writers who, as yet, attempted only to state what they had received from those who had known the apostles.[7]

But already, early in the second century, error was creeping in. The diverse elements in the churches were forcing changes which would, over the years, bring about radical changes in doctrine.

Not a Church, But Independent Churches

The church itself, the organization, had already plunged through a drastic and radical transformation. In fact, it is a mistake to refer to "The Church," as this implies there was one single, coherent, unified group functioning as an organization. There wasn't; there were branches of the original church, each struggling for order, truth, and harmony. They were like swimmers violently heaved into the water after the shipwreck, each struggling to survive. Those branches had no foundation, no overall authority, and no revelation.

Historians commonly use the term, however, of "The Church," and how it did this or that, adopted this doctrine or that, taught one thing or another, when in reality there were many viewpoints on what Christianity was, various doctrines, as many ideas as there were bishops. The term *church*, therefore, should not be misinterpreted. There were many churches, not *a church,* and while writers (including myself) refer to the church, that is simply a term of convenience and does not mean such a unified organization actually existed.

Our own well developed love of order impels us to hope for a clear, orderly, and coherent transition through early church history. And indeed, some have tried to supply it, describing an even flowing passage of power to the Roman Church and the continuation of a unified church. That kind of history, however, is inspired by wishful thinking, and judicious rearrangement of, or omission of, many facts.

After the death of the apostles the affairs of each branch were conducted by the local officers, and an exaggerated sense of equality pervaded; no branch at first claimed any kind of supremacy over the other. Indeed, they were completely independent of each other. Each Christian branch was sort of a little state, governed only by its own laws and none else from outside interfered.[8]

> Every society formed within itself a separate and independent republic; and although the most distant of the little states maintained a mutual as well as friendly intercourse of letters and deputations, the Christian world was not yet connected by any supreme authority or legislative assembly.[9]

They were autonomous churches, then, each growing or declining in power to be sure, but none claiming jurisdiction over any other. Cyprian, a well known bishop two hundred years after the death of Christ, still taught that the bishops of his day were supreme in their own diocese. None had the right of jurisdiction over another.[10]

The leaders of the apostolic church had a single interpretation of doctrine, that given by God through revelation. Without that kind of guidance and with hundreds of separate, autonomous churches, it takes little imagination to guess what would happen.

> Diversity, lack of communication between Christians of different backgrounds and customs, disagreement on strategy, differences in liturgical practice, wide discrepancy on the attitudes Christians should

> have to the state, as well as different experiences, from toleration in some areas to repression in others, and theological disputes—these were the marks of Christianity at this time.[11]

Each church went merrily on its own way, formulating its own interpretations of the gospel; each with its own standards, separate from the other churches and their standards.

> There was at first no prescribed formula of faith binding upon all believers. Each of the leading churches framed its creed (in a sort of independent congregational way) according to its wants . . . Hence we have a variety of such rules of faith.[12]
>
> There were no set beliefs agreed on by all; nor were there any ground rules on how to determine what to say or think or do; nor was there any acknowledged authority for deciding such questions.[13]

So, each decided questions on his own. Swimming around in this confusing ocean of ideas, then, are these many independent entrepreneurs, each deciding for himself how to fight off sharks and drowning, each on his own in defining just what Christianity was. Some were stronger than others, naturally, as we shall see. Some ganged up together to do in a heretic or debate a doctrine, while others strove by various means to convince individual swimmers to join their particular lifeboat for unity's sake.

In this situation they came hard up against three very serious problems: (1) there was no force on the horizon capable of forging a strong and unified church; (2) they faced a hostile and skeptical world; and (3) they faced contentions and questions *within* the church. These three factors would force—and already had been forcing—drastic changes on "The Church." In the year AD 100 the Church of Jesus Christ no longer existed and the Catholic Church lay hundreds of years in the future. The floundering but independent branches—the embryonic new church of the future—had to find some authoritative doctrine, some kind of unity, and some way to placate the scorn and hatred of the world. The church feverishly searched for answers.

The Search for Authoritative Doctrine: "The Old Days Were the Best"

The early leaders of local Christian churches faced an impossible dilemma. Questions from new and old converts alike pounded at them daily. Somewhere, somehow, they must find some answers. There was no more revelation. How then, to get those answers? Only one source was readily available—the past. It seems only natural for them to reach back to an earlier time and dip freely into the apostolic age and doctrine. Thus, the transformation of the apostolic age into a golden age began early, as the later leaders idealized the past to provide answers for their present. They clung to the past, like drowning men to a life raft. They turned in desperation to those who had been there, those who had known those who had been there, and in the last resort to those who were local leaders (bishops) of churches founded by those who had been there! Mere proximity to the apostles and elders became a special mark of sanctity and authority.

Tradition is the word. Everything was measured by the past, and clinging to the past became the norm for the next 1900 years. "Instead of asking simply 'what is the truth?' or 'who teaches the truth?' Christians began to ask 'who preserved intact the apostolic tradition?' "[14]

Very early then, particular churches founded by the apostles were singled out as repositories of the most reliable "truth" and succession now loomed over the church as a determining factor in correct doctrine. Eusebius took great pains to detail all the successions of the bishops in the important churches up to his day. Others, such as Tertullian and Irenaeus, early church fathers, also pointed out this increasing reliance on tradition.

> It is admitted by all that the Lord confided to the apostles the preaching of his doctrine; therefore only the churches founded by them, and not heretics, can be admitted to testify to Christian truth.[16]
>
> If such is the case, then all doctrines which agree with the teachings of the apostolic churches, the source and origin of faith are to be considered true. . . . If you desire to satisfy the desire for knowledge, so make a journey through the apostolic churches.[17]

Thus, very early the new church leaped desperately into a trap of its own making. The leaders pinned everything on the apostles or bishoprics founded by the apostles, as if mere proximity meant everything. Note those early fathers writing as if the *churches* of themselves could talk and spout doctrine, and not the men who ran them; men who, as we shall see, varied greatly in morals, character, and interpretation of doctrine. We find Christian writers all through history pleading with their adherents to rely on tradition and on those who had inherited it. It is almost pitiful to witness this constant wheedling and pleading; hardly anything could so well portray the tragedy and loss of the original church and its principles.

Instead of being constantly refreshed by revelation, these churches must rely on the unreliable; the old, the stale, word of mouth, rumor, stories passed down through generations, hearsay, interpretation, and the intermingling of fact, fiction, and fantasy. Quickly, the servant became the master as tradition began to dictate its harsh and ever changing terms to succeeding generations.

No matter what churches try to tell us today, tradition as practiced by Christian churches of the past has never been stable, consistent, and reliable. Chaotic is a more descriptive term. Tradition's one constant pattern was its inconsistency, as standards and interpretations changed from one generation to another and even within generations, depending on who was in power. Men of equal learning quickly discovered that they formed different conclusions on the basis of the same doctrine! This quickly led to disarray, arguments, and even war in the early churches. Each expert would interpret a particular doctrine, saying, or writing, according to what he thought. Humans being what they are, this quickly led to all sorts of opinions and a hopeless confusion of doctrine.

It was right to think there was an original, correct way (though not a golden age), but wrong to think it could be kept intact by tradition without revelation. Had an apostle or prophet been available, perhaps he could have obtained answers from God to correct the problems racking the churches. Sadly, there was none, and with the idea of tradition firmly in hand, the churches proceeded on their way to evolving into "Christianity."

The Change in the Bishop's Role

One of the first changes in the new order was in the role of bishop. The problem with understanding the original concept of a bishop's calling is the very changed nature of a bishop in today's churches. No matter what he may be in our time, however, in the original church he was simply a leader of a local congregation—and nothing else. It was not a full-time calling just as a cleric, nor was there a salary or other means of support. He held the same priesthood as everybody else and was different only in that he was called as a local leader—with the consent and vote of the members—by the general officers of the church. "The term 'bishop' in the early period was not applied to a general superintendent, but to the pastor of a local congregation."[18]

As the reader can well imagine, this didn't last long. Without general officers to govern the church, the bishop's role was radically altered.

In desperation, early churches grabbed at whatever was available to keep their organizations intact. The bishop, the highest officer left, became the center of the church and was elevated far beyond his original status in the apostolic church. Inevitably the bishop's office expanded into the power vacuum left by the death of the apostles.

Very early, for example, Ignatius made the bishop almost equal to God and proclaimed that all decisions and activities must revolve around that officer.[19] Such ideas quickly spread.

This authority that bishops assumed in the second century, however, was not derived from apostolic doctrine.[20] Nonetheless, Christians began to rely entirely on the bishop for all spiritual decisions and interpretations. The job became one of lifetime tenure. Bishoprics and other clerical offices, instead of being part-time functions of all priesthood holders sharing the load, became full-time jobs—professions, really—and the men taking those jobs formed a new and separate class from the rest of the people, who became laymen. Now there was a whole new set of rules, and the bishops were writing them, each one as he pleased. From humble servants of the church they were swept by the tides of change into positions of authority. Many at first surely tried to maintain their offices as the apostles had intended, but the pressures against that were intense. Someone had to exercise power. Reluctant or not, all bishops found themselves in the position of decision and policy makers, with ever increasing authority, prestige, status, and income. One needs little imagination to realize what happened next.

In the original church the bishop had worked hard at tending the flock. His only reward was spiritual wealth and well-being. Now, bishops had available much more tangible rewards, and the nature of the office turned around. Men began to seek after and compete for the more down to earth rewards of bishoprics, and the bishops became ever more corrupt and arrogant in their use of power.

Clement, an early bishop in Rome (AD 95) and one of the Apostolic Fathers, had full insight into what was already beginning in his time and would get worse. He wrote that "our apostles knew also, through our Lord Jesus Christ, that there would be strife over the dignity of the bishop's office."[21]

This increasing corruption of the bishop's role is well known to history and has been recorded by many observers. The change was dramatic. Bishops zealously began their pursuit of the world, satiating themselves with arrogance, princely living, pleasure, and gain. In the process, they also managed to usurp the original rights of the congregation and center all authority in their own offices. The record of history is harsh, but clear. A couple of examples will suffice to illustrate how badly the bishops corrupted their role.

> Even many bishops, who ought to be guides and patterns to the rest, neglecting the peculiar duties of their stations, gave themselves up to secular pursuits—they deserted their places of residence and their flocks: They traveled through distant provinces in quest of pleasure and gain; gave no assistance to the needy brethren; but were insatiable in their thirst of money—They possessed estates by fraud and multiplied usury.[22]
>
> As the legislative authority of the particular churches was insensibly superseded by the use of councils, the bishops obtained by their alliance a much larger share of executive and arbitrary power; and as soon as they were connected by a sense of their common interest, they were enabled to attack, with united vigor, the original rights of their clergy and people. The prelates of the third century imperceptibly changed the language of exhortation into that of command, scattered the seeds of future usurpations, and supplied, by Scripture, allegories and declamatory rhetoric, their deficiency of force and of reason.[23]

Bishops in larger cities, naturally enough, became richer and more powerful than others, and differences of rank stained the former equality. Big-city bishops soon assumed the title of metropolitans and took upon themselves a power or presidency over bishops of more limited jurisdictions. They decided—quite opposite to Christ's and the apostles' plan—that local congregations should no longer have bishops. A bishop in a small and lonely congregation obviously detracted from the status of the big-city bishops, since all bishops were theoretically equal in authority and status.

> At an early age, the country bishops, because of inferior education, were discredited. The councils of Ancyra (314) and Antioch (341) considered the restriction of their prerogatives; and finally, the council of Sardica (344) decreed that "in order that the episcopal name and authority be not vilified, it is forbidden to establish a bishop in a small village or hamlet for which a single priest would suffice."[24]

From this point, of course, it was only a small step to grant the bishops of larger cities more and more power.

All this came about through a process of natural selection. There was no churchwide leadership. Anybody who showed much ability and talent at all rose quickly to power and dragged along other bishops who were anxious to ride the coattails of the stronger leader. Such stronger bishops became known as metropolitans. Some of them soon rose to even stronger positions of influence, particularly those in cities like Alexandria, Antioch, Jerusalem, Rome, and Ephesus. Thus, they were archbishops, or bishops of greater authority.[25]

Montanus (around AD 150), supposedly a heretic and perhaps deservedly so for many of his doctrines, nonetheless came under much of his vilification because of his very unheretical demand that the churches return to Christ's standards for bishops. He objected to the way bishops and priests established themselves as a self-perpetuating hierarchy over the church while the congregation was being ignored. Montanus got nowhere, of course; the bishops were already too fond of the status quo, and the path of change being laid out by the "orthodox" bishops was one of continued growth in power.

Early on in the church, individual bishops sought advice from other bishops. This soon grew to councils, or group meetings of bishops for policy making and doctrinal discussions. This mushroomed ever larger until general church councils began to meet. In all these proceedings, the bishops from larger cities had a corner on power and prestige. That power grew steadily stronger within the councils.[26–30]

And so, the search for legitimacy gradually molded the calling of a bishop over the years. Bishops became ever more powerful, and early in the history of the church, the nature of the original office as defined by Christ and the apostles was lost completely.

Notes

1. Schaff, Vol. II, 7.
2. Ante-Nicene Fathers, vii.
3. Nibley, *The Passing of the Primitive Church*, 142.
4. Ibid., 143.
5. G. Bardy, "La Conversion au Christianisme," in Nibley (a), 140.
6. Schaff, Vol. II, 636.
7. Barker, 662.
8. Mosheim, Cent. II, Part II, chapter 2:2.
9. Gibbon, chapter 16.
10. Lyon, 121.
11. Wilken, 38.

12. Schaff, Vol. II, 529.
13. Wilken, 165.
14. Ibid., 42.
15. Eusebius, Book I, chapter I.
16. Tertullian, in Bardenhewer, 185.
17. Irenaeus, "Against Heresies," in Barker, 644.
18. Payne, 39.
19. Schaff, Vol. II, 146–47.
20. Payne, 39.
21. Clement, in Bettenson, 63.
22. Milner, Century III, chapter 8.
23. Gibbon, chapter 16.
24. Barker, 140.
25. Lyon, 128.
26. Ibid., 127–28
27. Schaff, Vol II, 176.
28. Durant, Caesar and Christ, 616.
29. Gibbon, chapter 16.
30. Lyon, 122.

CHAPTER 5

The Christian Wars: Orthodoxy versus Heresy

Christ emphasized unity as a sign of his people and church. During the last moments of his life this concern was uppermost in his mind as he prayed in Gethsemane that the authorities of the church (the apostles) would be so unified that they would be one. The apostles in their turn carried the same message to the church in general.

Modern churchmen like to preach the same thing, of course, and even go so far as to present an idealized picture of early Christian "unity" that enabled the church to survive. Nothing could be further from the truth, and the early history of Christianity mocks the claim. For, even while Christ and the apostles knew that unity was a sign of validity for the original gospel, they knew that the descendant and substitute organizations would lack this key quality. Indeed, Christianity failed dismally at coming even close to unity.

We have already seen that serious apostasy began during the time of the apostles. After their deaths, however, the real danger violently exploded. If it was a sickness before, it now became a raging epidemic. Virtual warfare erupted over orthodoxy and heresy, so much so that dogma became more important than morality, a point of order of more magnitude than charity. Gentile and Jew, trying to embrace the same religion, mixed like oil and water:

> It will easily be imagined that unity and peace could not reign long in the church, since it was composed of Jews and gentiles, who regarded

> each other with the bitterest aversion. Besides, as the converts to Christianity could not extirpate the prejudices which had been formed in their minds by education, and confirmed by time, they brought with them into the bosom of the church more or less of the errors of their former religions. Thus the seeds of discord and controversy were easily sown and could not fail to spring up soon into animosities and dissensions, which accordingly broke out and divided the church.[1]
>
> Christians in different places did not believe the same things about Jesus and his message, about Judaism, the church, the Spirit, even during the first three decades of the church's history. Diversity of belief and practice existed from the beginning.[2]

Unity?

The one things that were unanimous in the early church were heresy, schisms, wars, and controversies. *Unity* is the last word one could think of to describe early Christianity, and serious divisions popped up everywhere into separate groups and even separate Christian churches.

"The Christians were soon embroiled in endless controversies among themselves."[3] These controversies began early, and the very first apostolic fathers, much like the apostles before them, found themselves warning the members about the doctrinal wars, then erupting more fiercely than before. They spoke of divisions, Christ betrayers, deceivers, corruption of the word, changing of the definitions of God and Jesus, envy, strife, sedetion, disorder, tumults, contentions, and so on.[4–6]

Naturally enough, with everyone trying to prove his own point, forgeries abounded and confused even further this already terribly confusing picture of early Christianity. Second century Christianity wallowed in gospels, epistles, apocalypses, and acts.[7–8]

Unity was a chimera, a product of the imagination of later writers and inventive theologians. During the third century, there were probably 1500 bishops presiding over several thousand congregations.[9] In theory, that meant the possibility of 1500 different opinions. In practice there were probably fewer, but still plenty to go around.

> Celsus . . . had sarcastically observed that Christians were "split up into ever so many factions, each individual desiring to have his own party." About 187 Irenaeus listed twenty varieties of Christianity; about 384 Epiphanius counted eighty. At every point foreign ideas were creeping into Christian belief, and Christian believers were deserting to novel sects.[10]

What were these offshoots of the church and who led them? We might easily think of heretics being automatically doomed-to-hell sinners, the scabs of the church, doing their best to ruin the "acceptable" doctrine. Indeed, that is exactly what descendant churches have taught. It was not, however, the case. In many cases the most respectable sons of the church, perhaps fed up with corruption or bad doctrine, led "heretical" fights to reform and thereby created splinter groups.[11]

The real "orthodox" were simply the ones that won the war and could then with some impunity label the others as heretics. The names and policies of the "heretics" were legion and could easily fill a book by themselves: Nestorians, Eunomians, Anomeans, Apollinarians, Macedonians, Sabellians, Novatians, Manicheists, Montanists, Gnostics, Docetists, Donatists, and Marcionists.

It is not important to understand the incredibly complex ramifications of all these offshoots of Christianity, but to realize that the church was up for grabs. Whichever group could prevail would be the "Christian" church.

Montanus, for example, saw that the church of the second century was not the same as it had been in the apostolic period. He wanted it to return to original norms, and that was part of his "heretical" doctrine. Montanism was so popular that is spread more rapidly than Christianity had originally done.[12] The Donatists kept the church in North Africa in constant turmoil.[13] Marcionism spread rapidly into all parts of the empire and became a competing church for more than two centuries.[14] Novation "split the church asunder."[15]

The success of the Gnostics was rapid and extensive, and they were a serious challenge to the other churches (in part because they counterfeited so closely the *original* gospel). They covered Asia and Egypt and established themselves firmly in the West.[16]

(The Gnostics were some of the most formidable foes of the "orthodox" groups and were so successful that the church had to quickly drum up arguments against them and ended up compromising so extensively that the church has carried a distinctly Gnostic stamp ever since. Gnostics finally did lose the war, however, and were completely suppressed. The orthodox winners did all they could to destroy all Gnostic works but didn't entirely succeed. Recent discoveries of some Gnostic documents embarrass Christian scholars by pointing out some deft rearranging of history by—and for the convenience of—the surviving churches.)

Of all these different brands of Christianity, which was right? That was part of the dilemma, of course.

Since one's own opinions were always thought to have been received through the unbroken apostolic succession and were therefore indubitably orthodox and apostolic, those who differed could only be unorthodox and unapostolic—even if their succession was as certain as anyone else's.[17]

This standard of succession was an artificial one, devised by men as a substitute for the original vision of Christ. Any bishop under this system had as much right to claim the true orthodox faith as another—and they did. Their squabbling could be heard all over the empire. Eusebius highlighted some of the results.

> But when by excessive liberty we sunk into indolence and sloth, one envying and reviling another in different ways, and we were almost, as it were, on the point of taking up arms against each other, and were assailing each other with words, as with darts and spears, prelates inveighing against prelates, and people rising against people, and hypocrisy and dissimulation had arisen to greater heights of malignity, then the divine judgment began to afflict its episcopacy And our pretended shepherds, laying aside the rule of godliness, practiced among themselves contention and division. . . . But some that appeared to be our pastors, deserting the law of piety, were inflamed against each other with mutual strifes, only accumulating quarrels and threats, rivalry, hostility, and hatred to each other, only anxious to assert the government as a kind of sovereignty for themselves.[18]

During the Arian controversy, clergy and laity divided bitterly and made the cities ring with such "tumult and disorder . . . that the Christian religion afforded a subject of profane merriment to the pagans, even in their theaters."[19]

Bishops began excommunicating each other with abandon, bishops of the East wiping out wholesale lots or individual bishops of the West. The latter reciprocated in turn. At other times councils excommunicated the leaders of opposing councils.

There were so many heretical divisions that it became impossible to determine whether one's baptism was validly "orthodox" or not—depending on which bishop made the definition.

For example, the "church" supposedly banned Montanism. Nonetheless, Tertullian, an early and major Christian philosopher who formulated many "church" doctrines, later became a Montanist.

Again, Origen was a great Christian leader and philosopher of the ancient church; "nearly every later Christian savant for centuries learned from him, and depended upon his work; and his defense of Christianity impressed pagan thinkers as no 'apology' had done before him."[20] In spite of this, Pope Anastasius condemned him in AD 400, and the Council of Constantinople pronounced him anathema in 553. Those actions were meaningless. Origen's thinking and philosophy had already influenced all Christianity, as did the thinking of many another heretic. It would be unnatural to suppose that the surviving form of Christianity was not stained by the hullabaloo of the Christian wars. It absorbed many elements of the defeated heresies.[21]

The wonder in all this is not so much that something labeled "Christianity" managed to slug its way out of that brawling cat fight and eventually consolidate the leftovers into some sort of unified whole. We could almost expect that from an institution that democratically combined Christianity, paganism, philosophy, political muscle, and human wiles and ingenuity. The surprise is that subsequent priests and scholars could convince huge portions of the world's population that early Christianity had been a time of unity and that the resulting "church" represented the original church and doctrine of Jesus. This has been one of the great whitewash applications of history and is finally today receiving the serious scholarly criticism it merits.

Meeting the World Halfway: How to Win Friends and Influence People the Early Church Way

Changes began early in the Christian churches; Christianity adapted by absorbing elements of the world it found itself in. Gibbon said in his classic history of Rome that "a melancholy duty is imposed on the historian. He must discover the inevitable mixture of error and corruption which she (the church) contracted in along residence upon earth."[22]

Bereft of revelation, relying only on man's power of reasoning, the church quickly adapted to the world. The resulting churches bear the unmistakable marks of cultures in which they were nourished. "In the process of becoming predominant, it (Christianity) absorbed so many elements of the surrounding culture that ever afterward it has been largely identified with it."[23]

The elements absorbed were many and diverse, but all tended equally to distort the doctrine originally given. "Christianity did not destroy paganism; it adopted it. The Greek mind, dying came to a transmigrated life in the theology and liturgy of the church . . . Christianity was the last great creation of the ancient pagan world."[24] "Paganism survived . . . as a religion . . . in the form of ancient rites and customs condoned, or accepted and transformed by an often indulgent church."[25] "A dozen absorbed and rival faiths, entered into the Christian synthesis."[26]

The emerging Christians freely domesticated and cleansed their old pagan practices and presented them to an obliging church for rehabilitation. And it was not all done innocently, or by mistake, or simply by falling into it. Misguided prelates often felt this was the way to make—or keep—more converts.

Montanus, regarding these and other matters, was a thorn in the side of the church. He preached that the people had grown extremely lax in moral standards.

"Maybe so," said the churchmen, "but times have changed."

They argued that the old standards of discipline had to be modified because a second and third generation of Christians had been born into the church and they desired to hold the allegiance of these people who were not actually converts. This could not be done if the standards were too strict.[29]

Thus the later church, by embracing pagan doctrines and ritual and by lowering its standards, "improved" the institutions given by Christ and the apostles. By the standards they set, it worked. It was, however, Christianity that changed and society that remained, not vice versa.[30] The standards of the church were progressively lowered and tempered to the weakness of the people.

Modern churchmen have been happy with the arrangement. Some of them even seem grateful at escaping the "primitive" moral codes that reigned in the ancient church.

The Philosopher's Christianity

We have mentioned the ways this humanly guided church strained and sundered the limits set by Christ. The gospel was slowly becoming ordinary human stuff. The final step to complete the rupture was for philosophy and reason to impose their standards on what was left. That didn't take long. There was an early tendency to get away from the simplicity of the gospel and to interpret its principles mystically, symbolically, and philosophically.[31–33]

> As time passed, the simple sayings of Jesus were orchestrated, becoming vast with organ notes never heard by the apostles. History was to deflect Christianity into its own courses. . . . When Christianity entered Greece, it was compelled to confront the whole body of Platonic and Neoplatonic doctrine and henceforward would always wear the shimmering veil woven in Greece.[34]

> The original gospel was simple and straightforward. There was almost a "total absence in the New Testament of the mystical or ecstatic expression of Christian faith. . . . There is no evidence that Paul tried to make a mystical experience out of the sacrament of the Lord's supper. On the contrary, he rebuked the Corinthian saints for turning their sacrament service into what bore a resemblance to a pagan feast. . . . Nowhere in the New Testament is mention made of shrines or places associated with Christ. No importance was given to objects that might have had intimate relationship to the apostles. There is no mention of pilgrimages to shrines or an attitude of reverence for tangible objects that were connected with Jesus, his mother, his home, or his public ministry. As far as Peter and Paul were concerned—or Luke, or Matthew, or other writers—there appears to be no evidence that they were interested in that phase of devotion that produced esoteric attitudes toward things or places."[35]

The New Testament gives not one iota of evidence that Christianity was to become the ceremonial religion it turned into.

Paul, of course, understood the nature of the gospel and warned against corrupting its simplicity.

> But I fear, lest by any means, as the serpent beguiled Eve through his subtility, so your minds should be corrupted from the simplicity that is in Christ. (2 Corinthians 11:3)

> For Christ sent me not to baptize, but to preach the gospel: not with wisdom of words, lest the cross of Christ should be made of none effect. . . . For after that in the wisdom of God the world by wisdom knew not God, it pleased God by the foolishness of preaching to save them that believe. . . . But we preach Christ crucified, unto the Jews a stumbling block, and unto the Greeks foolishness. (1 Corinthians 1:17, 21, 23)

> Let no man deceive himself. If any man among you seemeth to be wise in this world, let him become a fool, that he may be wise. For the wisdom of this world is foolishness with God. For it is written, He taketh the wise in their own craftiness. And again, the Lord knoweth the thoughts of the wise, that they are vain. (1 Corinthians 3:18–20)

Paul knew philosophers well, and what they would do to the gospel, but it was all in vain. Once the philosophers got their teeth into the gospel, the church fell headlong into the trap in spite of Paul's warnings. Once philosophers had this marvelous new toy in their hands, it didn't stand a chance of surviving as a simple, straightforward teaching of the meaning of life. Everything had to be interpreted, reinterpreted, given symbolic meanings, couched in mysteries, and in general removed from the understanding of ordinary people and made the realm of theologians and philosophers—and in the process made almost unintelligible. *And it was done deliberately.*

> No one before Origen had thought seriously of presenting Christianity as a philosophy, but this "innovation," after much opposition, came to be tolerated, accepted, and finally celebrated by Christians of every stripe. . . . *We probably owe the survival of Christianity as a religion within the Roman Empire to this interpretation of the earlier Christian beliefs.* Now Christianity could present itself as a legitimate way of life whose teachings had the power to rescue men from evil and turn them to lives of goodness and virtue.[36]

That statement by historian Robert L. Wilken perhaps best sums up, however unintentionally, the bankruptcy of philosophical management of the gospel. Presumably, Christianity could not "present itself as a legitimate way of life" before the philosophers got hold of it. By that reasoning, what Christ gave was not quite good enough and had to be improved, upgraded, and edited by the "good old boys" of philosophy. Certainly man's meddling made Christianity more palatable to the world at large.

Earlier Christian beliefs, i.e. original Christianity, did not do well, did not convert the world, and were quickly lost. The new Christianity, molded to form fit the more elastic standards of the world, was much more successful, and in fact is the Christianity that has descended, with various modifications, to modern Catholic and Protestant churches.

A New Christianity

The world in general has sat comfortably back on its collective haunches and contemplated—some with satisfaction, some with awe, and a few with skepticism—how Christ's doctrine conquered the world. But, as many historians have recognized, it was not Christ's Christianity that did the conquering at all, but a man-made Christianity that was molded, warped, traditionalized, and mixed in well with various philosophies and pagan beliefs.[37–38]

> But for Jesus, the Christian churches would not have come into existence. Yet many other forces have shaped them and there are those who declare that, compared with these, *the influence of Jesus has been relatively minor.* . . . Without Jesus it would not have been, but in it the impulse which came from Jesus is only one element and that *at times a minor one.*[39]

That is an honest and an accurate summation of the Christianity inherited by descendant Christian churches. It is a "Christianity" vastly different from that one presented by Christ.

Even relatively early in the church's history, dramatic changes were taking place, so much so that the first apostolic fathers would not have recognized the theology of Augustine. Given man's nature, the changes—without higher authority to correct them—were only natural.

> What is usually called Christianity is more than the impulse which came from Jesus. It is at once a growth and a series of accretions.[40]
>
> In the year 500 Christianity was not the same as at its inception. . . . It had been largely shaped by its environment, some of the features then acquired persisted into succeeding ages and were accorded sanctity and regarded as norms. Indeed, the vast majority of Christians in the centuries since AD 500 have been in churches whose creeds, ritual, and organization are lineal descendants of the Christianity which took form in the period which we have been describing.[41]

So, what we see in today's churches is an evolutionary product, directed by human agency. These churches by all accords are jury rigged, editions stuck together with gum and glue. Odd growths and changes were stuck on wherever and whenever convenient.

> The sect that sprang up in Palestine gave way within two hundred years to a universal religion deeply impregnated with the cultural and philosophical concepts of the Greco-Roman world. At a later date this same religion won over most of the citizens of the Roman Empire to its faith, and by the year four hundred it had become the official religion of the Roman Empire.[42]

"So molded to men's wants, the new faith spread with fluid readiness."[43] Now it will be called the Roman Catholic Church, a new church. It was not the Church of Jesus Christ that existed only briefly during the apostolic period; history seems clear on that. It was a syncretism, a molding of many regional churches—each with its own varied dogma and ceremonies—into a well nigh indigestible compromise. Only after several hundred years were most finally convinced to gag it down, and even then many refused. In spite of that, this religion was the one that conquered and from which both Catholic and Protestant churches have descended. It would yet change much more, however, before it was cast into final shape. But remember, it was not a unified religion at all until after AD 500. Before that the individual churches were still slugging it out for supremacy.

Notes

1. Mosheim, Cent. I, Part II, chapter 3:11.
2. Wilken, 163.
3. Talmage, 97.
4. Irenaeus, Trallians VI; Ante-Nicene Fathers.
5. Clement, III, Ante-Nicene Fathers.
6. *Loc. cit*
7. Durant, *Caesar and Christ,* 616.
8. Eusebius, Book IV, chapter XXIII.
9. Lyon, 118.
10. Durant, *Caesar and Christ,* 616.
11. Gibbon, chapter 16.
12. Lyon, 99.
13. Ibid., 141.
14. Ibid., 96.
15. Eusebius, Book VII, chapter VIII.
16. Gibbon, chapter 16; Lyon, 93; etc.
17. Wilken, 86–87.
18. Eusebius, Book VIII, chapter I
19. Durant, *Caesar and Christ,* 659.
20. Ibid., 615.
21. Ibid., 603.
22. Gibbon, chapter 15.
23. Latourette, Vol 1, 8.
24. Durant, *Caesar and Christ,* 595.
25. Durant, *The Age of Faith,* 75.
26. Durant, *Caesar and Christ,* 618.
27. Mosheim, Cent. II, Part II, chapter 4.
28. *Loc. cit*
29. Lyon, 101.
30. K. Lake, in Nibley, *The Passing of the Primitive Church,* 142.
31. Payne, 222.
32. Latourette, Vol 1, 308.
33. Milner, Cent. Ill, chapter 17.
34. Payne, 59.
35. Lyon, 42.
36. Wilken, 178; italics added.
37. Nibley, *The Passing of the Primitive Church,* 81.
38. Wilken, 143
39. Lautorette, Vol. 1, 240; italics added.
40. *Loc. cit*
41. Ibid., 362.
42. Wilken, 194.
43. Durant, *Caesar and Christ,* 602.

CHAPTER 6

Unity and Authority: The Politics of Power

For several hundred years after the death of Christ and the apostles, the leftover churches were in a state of extreme flux, and confusion reigned. Multitudes of ideas, theories, and dogmas bubbled up and spread their ripples through the many churches contending for power. The "church" was up for grabs. Each power group had about as much right to claim the truth as the others. In their battles over who would get the leftovers, it was not the group that was most right that would win, but the strongest.

Into the vacuum sneaks Rome. Not striding forward with the power and authority it was later to claim, but sliding in the back door when no one was looking and taking over the house room by room.

Rome at first was simply another branch of the church that produced no leaders of any stature at all during the first centuries. Its power grew slowly, not because of innate tightness or the specious claims of priority, but simply because of political developments and association with the most powerful city in the world. Eventually Rome would win this giant crap shoot for authority over the remnants of the church, but only after a long war of attrition and eventual suppression of all other groups and opinions. Later, tradition would be imposed on history to bolster Rome's claim to power. It is important to understand this Catholic claim to supremacy and how it squares with history.

Peter—Bishop or Apostle?

The key ingredient to the Roman Catholic claim to being *the* church of Jesus Christ was Peter. Supposedly Peter founded the Roman church, was its bishop, and before dying in Rome, passed on all his authority to a succeeding bishop. Aside from the fact that this claim wasn't filed until several hundred years after Peter died (any time before that it would have been quickly slapped down by the other churches), it has two major flaws.

First, Peter was an apostle, not a bishop. In order to make its proposal stick, Rome had to demote Peter to bishop or elevate the Roman bishop to apostleship. History supports neither idea. Second, while Peter was supposedly passing on all his authority to a bishop—a lesser office than an apostle—John was probably still alive and directing churches in the East. We will examine these two ideas in turn.

Bishops Are Not Apostles

Bishops, a lower office than apostles, were local officers and never had any authority over the whole church. Apostles were general officers in charge of the entire church.

> As chief of the apostles, Peter, with the other apostles, had the general oversight . . . of all the churches, and this is true whether he was in Antioch, Ephesus, Jerusalem, Rome, or elsewhere; but the very fact that he was not continuously in Rome made it necessary for the Roman community to have a group of elders . . . or a bishop . . . at its head as did other communities.[1]

Whenever the apostles spoke, acted, or wrote, it was in the name of the whole church, and never in the name of an individual city or branch of the church.

> The apostles had been chosen individually, and when they spoke or wrote, they did so by virtue of their apostolic calling and not in the name of a local community.[2]
>
> As long as the apostles lived, they exercised their authority over all the communities as a whole. . . . They who replace them have only limited powers.[3]

It strains our credulity to believe that Peter was demoted as chief of the apostles to become a bishop of a local branch of the church.

One might stretch the claim to point out that Peter had ordained the first bishop of Rome. He may well indeed have ordained a bishop there, or several. He also did the same in other cities. If the Roman claim were followed, then Antioch could have been equally the head of the church.

> Tradition gives to him the title of bishop of this city. The city of Antioch has always honored in him its first founder. . . . In reality the apostles were the bishops (overseers) of all the churches that they had founded; their authority over these churches can be called an episcopacy (overseership), but we must not imagine this episcopacy organized like that of their successors. The latter, attached to a single church and residing there, were alone the true bishops, in the meaning which we give to the word.[4]

Just as he did in Antioch, Peter also ordained bishops in Rome, Caesarea, and other cities. But that was within his apostolic calling. He called and ordained bishops, and was their superior officer in the church.

"Linus and Cletus were, no doubt, bishops in the city of Rome before Clement, but that was during Peter's lifetime; that is, they performed the episcopal duties while he filled the office of apostolate. He is known to have done the same at Caesarea, for there, although he was himself on the spot, yet he had with him Zaccaeus, whom he had ordained as bishop."[5]

In the early history of the churches there is no evidence that Rome claimed any mandate of supremacy over the church because of its connection with Peter.[6–7]

But that was not to last. After the first two centuries, the race for power among the churches intensified—and along with it a scramble for authoritative traditions. Churches built long and impressive lists of bishops, tracing their lines back to an apostle—any apostle. Soon, to bolster their claims to authority, they began including that apostle as one in the list of bishops of their city or branch.

> There soon arose a tradition that the apostles themselves had appointed bishops in several communities, and hence came the custom of drawing up episcopal lists in Asia, Rome and Lyons. But it was not before the year 220 that Apostles themselves were set down in these lists as bishops of a community.[8]

Rome had a distinct advantage in this game of line tracing, since they could go right back to the *chief* apostle, Peter. Again, however, it was all dreamed up long after the breakup of the original church. The game was clearly fraudulent. However, much the Catholic Church of today would like to make Peter its first bishop, for example; it simply won't hold.

> The claim that Peter was bishop Rome for twenty-five years is not found before the *Liberian Catalogue* in 354, and is historically inadmissible, as it cannot be reconciled with the earlier texts . . . not until 354 . . . do we find Peter definitely and positively styled the first bishop of Rome.[9]

Eusebius, a Christian bishop of the fourth century, was the first to put together a history of Christianity. In his book he takes pains to mention the succession of bishops in the major cities, including Rome, but only as local officers. There was no bishop at the head of all the church in his time, and to list one never occurred to him. The idea of any Roman supremacy, then, was built up long after the fact and rests on shaky ground.

First of all, Rome's claim implies several assumptions, none of which can be easily granted. First, that Peter directly transferred his apostolic authority upon a bishop. Of this there is not the slightest historical or ecclesiastical evidence. Indeed, it is completely contrary to the order of the original church.

Second, that it wasn't just any old bishop Peter shifted his authority onto, such as Antioch or Jerusalem, but the bishop of Rome. Again, there is no evidence at all to boost this claim.

Third, that Peter actually acted as bishop of Rome (or of any city) and appointed a successor. Not only is there a complete lack of evidence for such a demotion, the idea again clashes sharply with the order of the General Authortiy possessed by the apostles and the limited local authority of the bishops.

> Evidently, in the early church the bishops were bishops and not apostles, and considered themselves bishops. And later, in tracing their authority to the apostles and drawing up lists, they did not elevate themselves to the rank of apostles, but lowered the apostles to the rank of bishops.[11]

Who's in Charge Here?

The second major flaw in the Roman Catholic claim presents an even more tortuous contradiction, as it supposes that a bishop (in this case the bishop of Rome) outranked an apostle.

John was probably still alive as late as AD 98 or 100. "About this time, the beloved disciple of Jesus, John the apostle and evangelist, still surviving, governed the churches in Asia, after his return from exile on the island, and the death of Domitian."[12]

So, here is a real problem. John, an apostle, was whipping around ordaining bishops while another bishop (of Rome) was already supposed to have supreme authority over all the church and everybody in it!

At the time, Clement was probably the Roman bishop. If, as Catholics contend, that bishop inherited general power over the church, why didn't Clement receive the revelations about the several churches in Asia (Revelation 1–3)? It is a little silly to argue that Roman bishops had the same power as apostles while John, a living apostle, was still receiving revelation; and not just any old revelation, but direct instructions for supervision of that church which was supposedly in the hands of the Roman bishop. The difference between the Roman bishop and John is readily observable. The latter was still receiving direction from heaven, while the Roman bishop was already captive of the doctrine that the heavens were sealed.

The people involved, of course, had no problem at all, since an attempt to take over the apostle's authority didn't occur to them. Such claims could only be made much later after Rome became powerful enough to need to make its aspirations stick. But that power had to grow over the centuries because Rome was at first well isolated from the real power of the church.

For a while, it was anybody's ball game.

The Power and the Glory: Who Will Get the Brass Ring?

When Jerusalem was destroyed in AD 70, church headquarters were also lost. Christians began looking elsewhere for authority: Antioch, Alexandria, Ephesus, Corinth—and Rome.

> Instead of a united Christianity, all under the direction of a universally recognized head, the church was characterized by disunity and disorganization. Alexandria, Caesarea, Antioch, Rome, Carthage, Smyrna, Ephesus and other centers were coming to the front as leaders of churches in the surrounding geographical areas. The strength of any one city as a Christian center, and the amount of influence it exerted over other churches were determined by the personality and forcefulness of the bishop. There was no accepted rule that made the office of bishop of any particular city pre-eminent.[13]

During this time of turmoil and jockeying for position, Asia Minor and Africa were the centers of the church, not Rome.

> During the period of activity of the apostles in Jerusalem and Palestine, Jerusalem was the Christian center; later, Antioch in Syria, and still later, Ephesus, where John resided at the end of the century.[14]
>
> It was in Asia Minor that, by the beginning of the fourth century, Christianity had been adopted more widely than in any other large section of the empire.[15]

Contrary to what we're usually taught, then, there was no rapid surge of power in Rome. Quite the contrary. The exuberance and power of Christianity was exploding in Asia. There, its major leaders operated and its major doctrines evolved.

> Asia Minor was in these centuries the stronghold of Christianity; by 300 the majority of the population in Ephesus and Smyrna were Christians. The new faith fared well in North Africa: Carthage and Hippo became leading centers of Christian learning and dispute; here rose the great fathers of the Latin Church—Tertullian, Cyprian, Augustine; here the Latin text of the Mass, and the first Latin translation of the New Testament, took form.[16]
>
> On the north shore of Africa west of Egypt, and especially in and around Carthage in the present Tunis and Algeria, Christianity was very strong by the time of Constantine. Indeed, here and in Asia Minor appear to have been the two greatest numerical strongholds of the faith at the end of the third century.[17]

Even the strength of the Latin form of the church was in Africa, not in Rome. Rome, at the time, was at most simply a branch of the church, if not a minor branch at that.

> Though the Roman church is heard of before 313—especially in the time of Bishop Victor—it had little influence and most of the time apparently tried to exert none. . . . Until the last quarter of the Fourth Century, Rome played only a minor role in the history of the church at large.[18]
>
> The bishop of Rome elected like other bishops was, like them, only a local officer; and during the first two centuries, with the exception of the Easter question, took no prominent part in the affairs of the Christian communities.[19]

Here is an intriguing thought. In spite of all the post-event claims of the Roman church to build its claim to supremacy, history is clear. The church was developing and evolving in Asia with no direction of any kind—let alone from Rome. Through the first four centuries no bishop of Rome rose to any position of authority or importance. Indeed, the famous Catholic historian Duchesne conceded that "at the end of the fourth century . . . the papacy, as it was known later, was yet to be born."[20]

> The papacy grew up in silence and obscurity. The names of the earlier bishops of Rome are known only by barren lists, spurious decrees and epistles inscribed centuries later. . . . For some considerable . . . part of the

> first three centuries, the Church of Rome, and most, if not all the churches of the west, were, if we may so speak, Greek religious colonies.[21]

But Rome could not long remain in the bush leagues. In a time when foundation by an apostle meant everything, Rome claimed Peter *and* Paul. During the centuries when political and physical muscle meant even more, the Roman church was associated with the most powerful city in the world. With a double whammy like that, it was only a matter of time. Because of its metropolitan position, Rome naturally grew in importance and influence with the spread of the Christian religion in the empire.[22]

Of course, events tripping along in history helped Rome's cause considerably. Lautorette described five types of regional Christianity that controlled the Christian faith in the early stages of the churches' development (Syrian-Persian-Nestorian; Syrian-Monophysite; Egyptian-Monophysite; Greek orthodox; and Roman Catholic).

> Of the five, the first three were in regions which in the seventh century fell under Moslem Arab sway. . . . The fourth was always under the control of the state and in addition for centuries confronted Islam and finally became subject to Moslem rulers. . . . Of the five, the roman Catholic form of Christianity enjoyed the fullest opportunity for expansion.[23]

The winner! Roman Catholicism and its philosophy was imposed on the Western world. Of course, from the traditional aspect of history, this "winning" is presented as a smooth, orderly, and divinely planned transition. It was not, of course, and the war was long and costly with many victims, some strong enough to almost win themselves. Their histories are largely unknown, and for very good reason. Naturally enough, as Durant says about this early Christian war, "The records of a victor are more likely to be preserved than are those of its defeated rivals."[24]

Records of the losers were usually destroyed.

> Some of the commentaries [of Origen] have survived in Latin Translations, but purged of "heretical sentiments" and with doctrinal errors "corrected by Jerome."[25]
>
> Most of the writings of Arius were burned and what he taught is known chiefly from the accounts of his adversaries.[26]
>
> In 432, Pope Celestine, to prevent him [Nestorius] from doing any harm, requested of the emperor his exile . . . he was condemned to perpetual deportation in Arabia; besides all his works were to be given to the

> flames and the partisans of his doctrines fell under severe penalties.[27]
>
> Dioscorus and Eutyches had already been sent into exile, and the writings of the latter condemned to the fire.[28]

That was the pattern of all the Christian churches at the time. Once firmly in power, the Roman church also began a restructuring of history and tradition to bolster its claims. In the process, of course, everything had to be judged by the apostolic period and tied firmly to the toes of those innocent servants of God.

"Whatever is distinctly Christian must be found in the Apostolic age; those institutions essential to Christianity, whether the papacy, the episcopacy, apostolic succession, the Eucharist, must originate in apostolic times"[29]

Even, as it turned out, if they had to be invented.

Notes

1. Barker, 631.
2. Ibid., 640.
3. Bardy, "La Theologie de l'Eglise de Saint Clement de Rome a Saint Irenee," in Barker, 137.
4. Mourret, "Historie Generate de l'Eglise," in Barker, 630.
5. Ruflnus, "Praefatio ad Recognitions," in Shotwell and Loomis, 162.
6. Foakes-Jackson and Kirsopp Lake, Vol. 1, 339.
7. Barker, 598.
8. A. Harnack, in Schaff-Herzog Encyclopedia . . . , 226.
9. Shotwell and Loomis, 60–61.
10. Schaff, Vol II, 155.
11. Barker, 632.
12. Eusebius, Book III, chapter XXIII.
13. Lyon, 119.
14. Barker, 117.
15. Latourette, Vol. I, 87.
16. Durant, *Caesar and Christ*, 602–03.
17. Latourette, Vol. 1, 91.
18. Barker, 558.
19. *Ibid.*, 648.
20. Duchesne, "Histoire Ancienne de l'Eglise," in Barker, 566.
21. Historians History of the World, Vol. VIII, 591.
22. Schaff, Vol, II, 157.
23. Latourette, Vol. I, 360.
24. *Ibid.*, 69.
25. Barker, 34.
26. *Ibid.*, 240.
27. Jacquin, "Histoire de P'Eglise," Vol. 1, 555, in Barker, 355.
28. *Ibid.*, Vol. 1, 580, in Barker, 382.
29. Wilken, 21.

CHAPTER 7

After 300 Years: Where Do We Go from Here?

After about three centuries, the original church and doctrine of Christ disappeared and were replaced by a brawling, contentious, amorphous hodge-podge of churches, each anxiously carving out as much authority and independence as possible and concerned mostly with dogma and personal aggrandizement, not morality.

This new "Christian" church is the spiritual progenitor of all descendant Catholic and Protestant churches. No matter what they claim for themselves today, they are a product of this organization and must ask themselves hard questions. Such questions seem necessary in light of what we know about this Christian church that gave birth to so many future offspring.

Even official Catholic historians have admitted the growing depravity of the early church and recorded that toward the end of the third century, Pentecostal outpourings of the Holy Spirit had become exhausted, and that there remained little proof of any close relationship between Christ and the Church.

> Outward peace and secular advantages completed the corruption. Ecclesiastical discipline, which had been too strict, was now relaxed exceedingly; bishops and people were in a state of malice. Endless quarrels were fomented among contending parties, and ambition and covetousness had in general gained the ascendancy in the Christian church.[1]

Historians have also pointed out the ambitious spirit of many in aspiring to the offices of the church, the ill-judged and unlawful ordinations, the quarrels and the contentions.

> The corruption of manners and principles so forcibly lamented by Eusebius may be considered not only as a consequence, but as a proof, of the liberty that the Christians enjoyed and abused under the reign of Diocletian. Prosperity had relaxed the nerves of discipline. Fraud, envy, and malice prevailed in every congregation. The presbyters aspired to the episcopal office, which every day became an object more worthy of their ambition. The bishops who contended with each other for ecclesiastical preeminence. appeared by their conduct to claim secular and tyrannical power in the church.[2]

Money and power, twin evils, became the goals of Christian leaders. The corruption of the church was widespread.

> In the interval between the Decian and Diocletian persecution the Church had become the richest religious organization in the Empire, and had moderated its attacks upon wealth. Cyprian complained that his parishoners were mad about money . . . that bishops held lucrative offices of state, made fortunes, lent money at usurious interest, and denied their faith at the first sign of danger. Eusebius mourned that priests quarried violently in their competition for ecclesiastical preferment.[3]

In such a state the church seemed ready for Constantine—like a well used and anything but virgin bride seeking legitimacy through marriage to a strong but equally tainted husband. It is a common error to assume the church began her decay from that time. Constantine did not start the corruption of the church. He simply accelerated and completed it. Before his time no bishop had authority over the whole church; there was no central authority of any kind. Groups of bishops had tried to rule—unsuccessfully—via councils and dictatorial opinions on dogma. Constantine assumed, entirely on his own initiative, the authority that no bishop claimed or possessed and became the head of the church as well as the state. That completed the transition from the church of Christ, through the scattered confusion of leaderless branches, to the philosophers' restructuring efforts (although these would still continue), to councils of world bishops, to Constantine—the pagan, immoral, murderous Constantine—the new head of the church. What should we now call this church led by such a man? Reason stares at the incongruity of trying to reconcile him at the head of a church supposedly representing the moral character of Christ. Constantine did not receive control of the church by revelation; he seized it by power of the state and used it for political purposes.

Just what kind of man was he, and what exactly was his influence on the churches?

There is much to be said, of course, for Constantine the statesman, the general, and the ruler. He was a wise and far-seeing man and, by the standards of his time, a reasonably benevolent prince. But his qualification as a man of God—supposedly the savior of the church—were slim; indeed, if present at all, they were mostly on the negative side of the ledger. He was harsh, unforgiving, terrible in his wrath, and goaded by worldly pride. He was the hero who degenerated "into a cruel and dissolute monarch, corrupted by his fortune,"[4] whose heart was sufficiently hard to order the execution of his wife and son. The difficulties of reconciling such a man with the virtues taught by the biblical Christ make the mind whirl with admiration for the dazzling dexterity of churchmen who fashion God-like qualities from this very earthy clay.

The churches had been illegitimate orphans for two hundred years, floundering about in search for an identity. Constantine gave them legitimacy, and in grasping gratitude for the boon, the churches were willing to overlook any amount of reality necessary and make Constantine equal to the very apostles.

The story of Constantine's "conversion" is well known. Supposedly he received a vision of the cross inscribed with the words "by this conquer." As the story goes, this rather amazing occurrence astonished even the whole army and converted Constantine on the spot. Christ later supposedly appeared to him and told him to use the cross as a standard and thus vanquish his enemies.

In view of his unscrupulous life, his reluctant deathbed baptism twenty-five years later, and his lifelong support of both pagans and Christians, it is unlikely that Constantine was ever "converted" to Christianity. Gibbon thoroughly debunks the whole vision story as a fabrication concocted after the event. Eusebius, who prostituted history in his blatant and unashamed paean of praise for Constantine, simply accepted without question the emperor's vision. Thus, just two men, Euscbius, interested in promoting Constantine regardless of facts or truth, and Constantine himself, who used the church for his own purposes, combined to convince the world of the legend. The Catholic Church, following in their footsteps in preference for legend, bought the whole package.

All this, however, is relatively minor. That Constantine would attempt to invent a story to make himself look better is not unusual—quite the contrary. Much more telling is the whole life or a man supposedly converted by this dramatic event. You or I, upon receipt of such a heavenly manifestation, would rush quickly to the nearest stream to be baptized into the kingdom. Not Constantine. In spite of being "converted," he remained a pagan all his life and baptized a Christian only at the very last minute. Strange behavior indeed for such a favored convert.

The truth is, that although Constantine paid some lip service to Christianity, gave it legal status, and even made it an official state religion, "he was never completely reconciled to the Christian faith."[5] He simply tolerated it as he did pagan religions.[6] He celebrated pagan festivals, minted coins in honor of pagan gods, erected pagan statues, and donated large sums of money to further pagan worship.[7] This was certainly not one of your most dedicated converts!

The likelihood that Christ or God would choose such a man to give legitimacy to what Christ had originally taught seems farfetched. The truth is simpler—and certainly much more satisfying—than the legends and inventions that Eusebius created and the church perpetrated. The context of history shows the events and the man clearly. The intelligent Constantine clearly saw the political advantages of favoring Christianity, then becoming more popular than ever. He did favor it, while at the same time currying the favor of his other constituents, the pagans. He was a politician who dispassionately used Christianity for his own purpose, nothing more, nothing less. But he was never a Christian at heart and became one in name only when the fear of death had a stranglehold on his throat.

Is Constantine to be condemned for such cold-blooded use of the church? Not really, if we remember what the church had become—a disorganized, warring group of clerics who themselves were already corrupted and highly politicized. That a man like Constantine had to rescue the church points out in stark outlines the nature of a church needing such a savior.

How did Christians at the time receive the rescue operation of Constantine? With open arms.

> He was the divinity whose light was so blinding that men averted their eyes; he walked in solemn radiance, and his divine intelligence sent the shadows of perplexity hurrying away . . . the preeminent possessor of all the virtues that true religion can confer. . . . After his death he became *isapostolos,* equal to the apostles.[8]

As we have already seen, after the Apostasy the churches had bobbed erratically through history without any recognized head or central authority. Rome would eventually take that role upon itself, but in the interval the vacancy was filled by the state—in the form of Constantine.

> The papacy, such as the West knew it later, was yet to be born. In the place which it did not yet occupy, the State installed itself without hesitation. The Christian religion became the religion of the emperor, not only in the sense that it was professed by him, but in the sense that it was directed by him. Such is not the law, such is not the theory, but such is the fact.[9]

That conclusion by the prominent Catholic scholar Duchesne, unwelcome at it may be to the church, is clear from history. Constantine had no ecclesiastical authority and claimed none. He assumed leadership of the church as a political move and used it as such. The clue to Constantine's outlook on Christianity is contained in his letter sent to Alexander and Arius—those two cantankerous priests whose arguments over the nature of God turned the world upside down.

> I feel strongly that if I could induce men to unite on that subject, the conduct of public affairs would be considerably eased . . . there was no need to make these questions public.[10]

Constantine wasn't interested in who was right or wrong (if either was). He just didn't want the empire upset by squabbling prelates. That desire was never to know satisfaction, as this particular argument would hound him till his death—and others for long after.

The Nicene Council

The problem with Alexander, Athanasius, and Arius just wouldn't go away. These Christian "brothers," as well as their supporters, squared off against each other in a bitter and vindictive battle that would rip the empire apart for years to come. The history of this incredibly complex affair will be condensed into some kind of order—if that is possible—in chapter 14. Now we want to note the role of Constantine in the council and its importance in Christian history.

Regardless of whatever personal beliefs Constantine may or may not have had, he wanted a *state* religion. He coolly elected Christianity to that role and manipulated it without hesitation for his purposes. But even Constantine had his limits. Try as he might, he couldn't contain the fighting among Christian prelates.

The worst squabbling of all was that between Athanasius and Arius. To settle it (as well as other troublesome points—the Christian churches weren't even sure about when to celebrate Easter), Constantine called for a council of all Christian bishops at Nicea. It was to become the most famous of all councils.

To understand it, and its results, we must picture the Christian condition. The churches—all Christian in name—had been fighting each other for two hundred years, over almost everything. To top it off, they were by now not even sure what kind of God had founded their churches and what kind of God they all claimed to worship. Athanasius and Arius were stirring the bitter waters of natural antagonism with their sophistic and esoteric arguments over Christ.

Who stepped in to solve the war? Does the voice of a righteous man pierce the anger of prelates with heavenly revelation? Do we hear the roar of a prophet of God sent to set the world straight? No, only the firm tread of a pagan and immoral foot on the neck of bickering churches trying to redefine the biblical Christ with philosophy. It was Constantine that dictated to the church that they should have a council and who would preside over it. Not a bishop, not a priest, certainly not the yet non-existent pope, but the emperor.

One has to pause in wonder at what kind of church this was. Constantine called the council of Christian bishops, directed their activities, preached sermons to them, and used his absolute authority to force down their throats a compromise decision that almost nobody liked (and since it was a compromise, no real solution was reached; the battle continued for decades). Yet, he was not even a baptized member of the church, let alone any kind of authorized clergyman. Civil authority at this and subsequent councils forced the final decisions about God and Christ upon the church.

At no time did the bishop of Rome (or any other patriarchs) assume any role of leadership. Rome was a minority group at Nicea—the power of the church expressed here was that of the Eastern churches. The bishop who was supposedly at the head of a unified organization—for some church historians would like us to believe—did not even attend the most important council in all of Christian history. His representatives, going along with the doctrines decided on, had no say in their conception or formulation. Rome was certainly not in charge of the council or the churches. Constantine was, and he made sure the final decision, however unpalatable to almost everyone, was unanimous.

By taking sides in this religious entanglement, Constantine fell headlong into a pernicious trap—and took the state and the church along with him. Now, for a good long while, the state would have to decide which Christian faction was the correct one, support it, and suppress the rest. This led, naturally, to an orthodoxy of the state. And also, of course, prelates learned to compromise extensively in order to gain favor with the might of ruling powers. Now "Christianity" would be run by the whims of emperors as they vacillated violently between support of warring and opposite factions.

What was the gift that the state gave to Christianity? Christian officials viewed the new order as an unparalleled blessing. In reality the marriage between church and state produced an illegitimate daughter that nobody wanted on their conscience. Whatever leftovers of genuine Christianity may have overwintered the terrible storms of apostasy were now buried completely in the abuses that followed the church's elevation to state religion.

Constantine, for example, exempted the clergy from the onerous duties and details of government obligations as well as from taxes and contributions that weighed so heavily on everyone else. Bishops were granted richly rewarding jobs, and Constantine showered money and gifts on individual prelates and the church in general.

Not surprisingly, there was an immediate and overwhelming clamor for priestly roles and offices. "There was great competition for church preferment. The office of bishop came to be more highly esteemed than the rank of general."[11]

So much for a humble, contrite, and righteous clergy desiring only to serve God. What about the everyday citizen? Constantine had something for them also.

Take one item, the Sabbath day. Although for two hundred years it had been a day of Christian worship, it had not been a day of rest—simply another work day for the masses. In 321 Constantine granted to

Christians in cities a day of rest on Sunday. Historians—and you and I along with them—think this had tremendous effects on the popularity of Christianity. Pagans found it an easy conversion to Christianity and a day off. But there was more.

In 324 Constantine issued an official invitation to all his subjects to investigate Christianity and accept it without delay.[12]

Now, put yourself in the shoes of an ordinary citizen number in AD 324, trying to make a living and get ahead. The most powerful ruler in the world issues a scarcely veiled threat to accept Christianity in a government that already favors this particular brand of religion, and couples it with the promise of a day off (and in some cases a new white robe and twenty pieces of gold[13]). What would most people do? Especially those who had always belonged to a formalized state religion anyway?

After this, of course, it required little or no sacrifice to become a Christian. Quite the contrary. Once the government fell on the side of Christianity, self-interest demanded conversion to the new order for the ambitious, and the world followed in well worn treads of popularity. What lowliest official wanted to offend his superiors—and jeopardize his career—by clinging to the dying forms of paganism? Why not take the money, the day off, the approbation of the world, and a few drops of water on the head? Why not indeed.

> To appear touched by the truth of Christianity . . . to be particularly accessible to the arguments of the emperor . . . was . . . for every good courtier, the known manner of gaining favor. Then, there was no limit to the confidence of Constantine, and the converts he made enjoyed a favor almost without control. Honors and even money rained on their heads.[14]

Christianity became a popularity contest, as anxious converts outdid each other in the race to the baptismal waters. But it wasn't only the positive inducements of self-interest, social pressure, and official power that turned the river of converts into a flood. Negative forces made the alternatives even more unpleasant.

The church, once seated firmly in the saddle of official approval, showed no mercy to its former opponents or would be reformers. Before, tolerance had been Christianity's plea, but once in power tolerance disappeared and vengeance took its place. The church harshly persecuted—and exterminated in many cases—any rival groups no matter what they preached. Liberty and freedom of thought and belief touched no nerve of mercy in the new and harsh mistress of the state.

Julian, who later attempted to restore paganism as the official state religion while he was emperor, saw pious Christian statesmen murder his father, brother, and many more. Little wonder he concluded that "there were no beasts more ferocious than Christians."[15] Julian deserves more than he got. Downgraded and dragged through the mud of moral condemnation by a vengeful church, he nonetheless saw the absolute inconsistency of a degraded and immoral church piously pretending to live the principles taught by Christ. He preferred the less perfect but more honest ways of paganism.

The Donation of Constantine

In Christianity's view at the time, Constantine's intervention in favor of the churches was an unconditional blessing. It was, in fact, anything but. Constantine's assistance accelerated corruption in the clergy; participated in the church's arrogant use of power to crush dissent; and pushed, pulled, bribed, or threatened hundreds of thousands of uninterested, hard-hearted, ambitious, weak willed—and unconverted—non-Christians into a politically attractive state religion for personal gain.

The last donation Constantine supposedly granted to the church was control and leadership in the form of the Roman bishop.

The emperor, so the story goes, visited Rome just before his death, suffering from leprosy. The bishop of Rome healed him, and in gratitude Constantine recognized his supreme religious jurisdiction over the entire world (as well as temporal sovereignty over Italy and the West).

This story first appeared in the eighth century, when the Catholic Church was doing all it could to bolster its claim to a supreme leadership that had never existed in the past. From then through the fifteenth century the "donation of Constantine" was used as a basis for papal claims to power. Nonetheless, it was completely false. The whole thing was blatant fabrication from the beginning, a complete forgery.[16]

Be that as it may, the Roman church was not to be deterred by anything as simple as historical truth; they used the documents anyway, to help them consolidate their power over the church in general.

The important point here, of course, is that regardless of the falsity of the donation, the Roman church used it. One pauses again, of course, to wonder at the need of false documents to help the church that should be representing Christ. Does any means justify the advancement of the church?

> From the eighth to the fifteenth centuries when the "Donation of Constantine" and the other forged decretals were accepted as genuine, they were a powerful force in strengthening papal claims . . . the forged decretals gave an apparent sanction to papal claims for temporal power.[17]

So, a major plank in the Roman platform of supremacy was based on wishful thinking and legend. But beyond this lies a point of even greater significance. Even had the "donation" been genuine, the political authority of a pagan and immoral emperor to name the head of the Christian church grinds out a vivid statement.

In fact, however, the donation was not genuine, and competition for the head position of Christianity continued unabated. Constantine had unwittingly fomented a great part of the competition by establishing his capital at Constantinople, giving ever greater status to the metropolitan bishop of that city. (There was no central head of the Christian church and extreme rivalry eventually developed between five metropolitan bishops—Constantinople, Rome, Alexandria, Antioch, and Jerusalem. We hear little of the others today for good reason. They were eliminated from the contest by the Moslem conquest. That eventually left two, Constantinople and Rome, and friction between them was almost continuous from the beginning—now heating up and then cooling off).

It was almost inevitable. There was no head of the church, and Rome was frenziedly trying to push her claim to that title. At the same time, Constantinople remained powerful and independent, and certainly not subservient to Rome.

The separation was widened further by the slow but irreversible competition between the Byzantine Empire and the West. In 800, the quarrel heated up dramatically when Pope Leo II crowned Charlemagne as emperor.

Finally, in 1054, Cardinal Humbert (representing Rome) and the Eastern patriarch challenged each other in a bitter and vindictive personal fight and the cardinal, entirely on his own, decided to excommunicate the patriarch and all his associates. The charges were misinformed, trivial, and baseless, and the excommunication has never been confirmed or repudiated by any subsequent pope.[18] From then on, however, the separation was inexorable. As a result, there finally arose two distinct churches, each professing to be the sole legitimate representative of Christ.

Something important emerges here. Up until 1054, both accepted each other as belonging to the "one true church." There were differences over doctrine, but that had existed for hundreds of years between all the leaders and even bishops and theologians. Then, because of a purely personal quarrel between two proud and stubborn prelates, one of them, without any authorization from his leader, excommunicated the other; suddenly they were each flatly stating the other was apostate.

And there we will leave it. The reader will have to decide on the validity of two political entities each calling the other false because of a personality clash and subsequent shoot-out. The separation stuck, however, until our time, when both groups are now talking about getting back together!

Notes

1. Milner, *Church History,* Century III, chapter 17.
2. Gibbon, chapter 16.
3. Durant, *Caesar and Christ*, 657.
4. Gibbon, chapter 18.
5. Payne, 100.
6. Ibid., 104.
7. Gibbon, chapter 20, Lyon, 139–40.
8. Payne, 101.
9. Duchesne, "Historie ancienne de l'Eglise," Vol. ii, 659–61, in Barker, 565.
10. Eusebius, "Life of Constantine," II, 63–70, in Lyon, 147.
11. Talmage, 76.
12. Schaff, Vol. Ill, 1–37.
13. Gibbon, chapter 20.
14. De Broglie, "L'Eglise et l'Empire Romain," in Barker, 272–73.
15. Durant, The Age of Faith, 11.
16. Foakes-Jackson, *History of the Christian Church*, 322.
17. Lyon, 159.
18. Zaehner, 96.

CHAPTER 8

The Tradition Trap

Zeno, emperor of the Roman Empire (474–91), was on the spot. Trying to unify the warring churches in his kingdom, he had invoiced the highest authority he could think of to gain a consensus among fighting bishops—the doctrine hammered out at Nicea. The action was necessary. Ever since Nicea, prelates had fought and squabbled over the supposedly "inspired" doctrines decided on in that council. Their wars rocked the empire and civil powers. To gain peace, Zeno had to prove his orthodoxy.

> The emperor Zeno Caesar, pious, victorious, supreme, ever worshipful Augustus to the very reverend bishops and clergy, and the monks and people throughout Alexandria, Egypt, Libya and Pentapolis. We are convinced that the source and stay of our sovereignty, its strength and impregnable safeguard, is that only genuine and true faith which, by the inspiration of God, was published by the 318 Holy Fathers assembled at Nicaea. . . . Therefore we were eager that you should be informed that we and the churches throughout the world neither have held nor do we hold nor shall we hold, nor do we know of any that hold, any other symbol of the 318 Holy Fathers . . . and if any hold such, we count him alien. For we are assured that this symbol alone is the safeguard of our sovereignty.[1]

No appeal to God, an apostle, a prophet, not even Christ himself as a source of unity and a proclamation of faith, but an invocation to the hallowed name of tradition itself was established at Nicea.

The early church that wasn't really a church faced some enormous difficulties. The original doctrine had already been lost or altered. The rumblings within the leftover churches were signs of the seething mass of doubts, questions, and perplexities that faced bishops, theologians, and everyday members alike, and threatened momentarily to burst out into the open and sink the struggling churches. The old authority was gone, revelation dried up, and without inspired teachers to prime it again, the doctrine was hopelessly confused. Where would they turn?

In retrospect the answer seems obvious, the thought not any more comforting for that. Irenaeus was the first to come up with the answer. Casting about for some guide to Christian orthodoxy, he turned to the past. Of course, all leaders had always relied on the apostles and Christ himself. Now, however, it was stretched even further than before—quite past the breaking point. All reason was cast aside, and the past, enthroned on a holy altar, supplied the answer to every single question. What's more, the past was not to be questioned or doubted.

> But what if some novel contagion try to infect the whole church, and not merely a tiny part of it? Then he will take care to cleave to antiquity, which cannot now be led astray by any deceit of novelty.[2]

Antiquity, an easy escape. Now the search narrowed down not to what was right, but what was closest to tradition.

> Seeing therefore, that we have such testimony, we do not need to seek elsewhere the truth which it is easy to find in the Church. . . . For this reason we ought to . . . love the things of the Church with utmost diligence and lay hold of the tradition of the truth. What more? Suppose that a disagreement on some important question arises among us, *must we not then have recourse to the most ancient churches, with whom the apostles lived, and ascertain from them what is positive and clear in regard to the question in dispute,* . . . If then we would discover the extra-biblical tradition we should have recourse to those churches where it is possible to trace an unbroken line of succession in the bishopric back to the apostles.[3]

Such an easy answer; the oldest churches must have the best answer. No matter that individuals spanning the gamut of doctrinal differences dominated those churches and gave voice to the opinions Irenaeus leaned on so heavily. Furthermore, those very oldest churches that Irenaeus wanted to turn to were at war with each other, all espousing different doctrines and interpretations.

So, very early, the last ship that can save the "orthodox" doctrine sets forth from harbor with a generous supply of holes and leaks—into very deep water.

But with the original church gone, there is nothing else left, so the churches cling to the past desperately, entrusting their whole cargo to this very unstable and dangerously leaking boat.

During this time, Christian writers began to cite long lists from the "holy fathers" as support for their particular arguments. This authority from the past became second only to the authority of the apostles. Every group and church were desperately squeezing any holy father available, hoping to force out a few drops that would support their chosen contention and bolster their particular viewpoint. Now they were in the age when "orthodoxy," or conformism to evolved status quo, was everything. It didn't matter that no single orthodoxy existed—other than very generalized ideas. Every Christian under the jurisdiction of a particular bishop, church, or scholar had to conform to that group's image of orthodoxy. The bishop or scholar and his supporters would then scan the historical record and pounce upon any morsel of doctrine of some holy father that supported their thesis, and reject all the rest. The morality, spirituality, and ethics of the holy father in question were completely irrelevant, and any other holy father that disagreed with theirs was a heretic.

> Arnold showed that some of the revered fathers of the church who were doctrinally pure in their theological works were scoundrels as persons and as churchmen, and that some of the most pious, devout and faithful Christians were not doctrinally sound. Even heretics often lived more God-pleasing lives than the church fathers. . . . Many orthodox bishops had no genuine spirituality, and many of the heretics who were condemned by these same bishops showed greater love for their fellows and more fervent devotion to God than the proud judges who sat in councils or issued decrees.[4]

Orthodoxy—as defined by any particular group clawing its way to the top of the pile—became more important than righteousness, a point of order of more magnitude than morality. Orthodoxy was the only qualification for acceptance—provided it met *your* standard of orthodoxy. The orthodoxy of others was, of course, heresy. Christian priests, scholars, and bishops now spent much of their time in endless and bitter arguments over who had the "true" doctrine.

> The age of Constantine was a time when Christian leaders lusted for power, and instead of thanking God for their new freedom, they spent their time fighting over points of dogma.[5]

Philosophic reason and force blossomed into the twin powers that determined "Christian" doctrine and behavior. The old standards established by Christ and his apostles were jettisoned in favor of chaos.

> True and active faith no longer had a place, and religion consisted of certain concepts and terms invented by reason, as well as of outward oral confessions and other works performed without faith. Whoever could adapt himself properly to the established authority and power of the bishops, was called orthodox; he might or might not have been an upright Christian.[6]
>
> While men quarreled over minute points of doctrine, wrote learned tomes on the chief articles of faith, and worshipped before the altar of the apostolic faith, the churches were in disarray. . . . Men had abandoned the life of faith and devotion.[7]

Righteousness and spirituality became expendable qualities in the mad rush to establish oneself as orthodox. Almost any behavior could be excused under such innovative standards.[8]

> There are many wicked popes plunged in hell [quite an astounding admission by itself], but all their lawful acts on earth are accepted and confirmed by God, and all priests who are not heretics administer true sacraments, *no matter how depraved they maybe.*[9]

Thus, political savvy in knowing which doctrine was in the ascendancy and adroit sidestepping of controversial issues were the *only* qualifications of any value for Christian ministers. Heretics who may have lived the most saintly and spiritual lives of all times were ruthlessly exterminated or hounded in the name of Christ. Using the same name of Christ, the "orthodox" could, with enough money, buy absolution for the vilest of crimes and sins.

Athanasius, for example, who fomented one of the most foolish and bitter arguments between the developing churches, was hailed by the eventual winners in Christ's name as the very epitome of orthodoxy and stalwartness in the *true* faith. He was also a ruthless and vindictive church politician.[10]

"St." Jerome was another outstanding example of that kind of standard. The appellation of Saint can apply only to an ascetic life devoted to the church—and little else. Jerome was unscrupulous, abusive, coarse, and vindictive. "He was hardly a saint in character or speech. It is sad to find in so great a man so many violent outbursts of hatred, misrepresentation, and controversial ferocity."[11]

Cyril of Alexander has been described as the "most illustrious doctor of this time, (and) a remarkable theologian."[12] At the same time, his character was admittedly indefensible. He was violent and unscrupulous.[13]

One is hard put to reconcile conniving, scheming, unprincipled, and immoral politicians as acceptable representatives of the New Testament Christ just because they were theologically correct according to prevailing standards.

Nonetheless, doctrine and orthodoxy were the standards of the new Christian church and morality was indeed irrelevant. In their frenzied search for orthodox support, Christians in the evolving churches overlooked any possible sin as long as the holy fathers backed up their particular concept of orthodoxy. So much so that even legends and fables were eagerly pounced upon and put into church service to prop up the creaking edifice. This was carried even further, to the acceptance of outright lies; under the curious doctrine that "it was an act of virtue to deceive and lie, when by that means the interests of the church might be promoted."[14] From the time of Constantine on (at least), tradition became preferred over truth.

At the first Vatican Council of 1896–70, where papal infallibility was laid down as official doctrine, many bishops pointed out the obvious; that is, that popes were not infallible at all. If anything, quite the opposite, and history was a shouting witness to it all. Such nonsense was quickly struck down by the majority of bishops on the theory that the traditions of the church and memories of the collective bishops were so much more real and valuable than any collections of historical fact. "The Big Lie" was better than objective truth, since it led where the majority wanted to go.

As the reader will have surmised, however, tradition was not very reliable at all, which led to the many definitions of orthodoxy in the first place. When the scriptures disagreed, Christianity turned to the apostles. When it couldn't agree on what the apostles had said, it grasped at the apostles' self-appointed successors, the bishops. Alas, in vain; they also disagreed and one could, with a diligent search and imaginative interpretation, find evidence for almost any stand. The same authorities could be used by opposing teams to "prove" their particular truth! Naturally enough, authorities that disagreed were simply ignored.

Such a simple matter of when to celebrate the death and resurrection of Christianity's founder—surely one of the more important dates in history—became a heated surface of controversy in early church history. The churches even argued over *what* was to be celebrated: the death or the resurrection. The churches diverged, some choosing one date and stressing one event and others picking another date and commemorating the opposite. The question became acute, and ludicrous, around AD 180, when some of the Roman congregations were feasting while others were fasting in celebrating the same event![15]

It was no wonder. The early Christian effort to build on the left-over remains of previous opinions was doomed from the start. Peter Abelard, in his famous book, *Sic et Non* (Yes and No), written in the twelfth century, catalogued the reasons reference to authority was doomed, and confirmed the teachings of the fathers as very human—not inspired enterprises. He gathered together a long list of citations of the holy fathers on 150 questions. Placed side by side, the fathers not only diverged sharply, but in many places they diametrically opposed each other. Very simply, some fathers said yes on gravely important matters, while others said no. Abelard further showed that the general picture was really worse than that. He pointed out that some contradictions were caused by later retractions of the particular father; and worse yet, that standards changed from generation to generation, now approving, now rejecting, identical doctrines.[16]

Not a reassuring picture to be sure. If standards were changing in each generation, if "fathers" vacillated in sacred opinions, and if the conglomerate fathers—supposedly the very bulwark of the church and the founders of unerring and infallible tradition—disagreed, where do we turn?

One attempt to squirm out of this disquieting and melancholy train of contradictions surfaced in the Vincentian Cannon. We might call it the lowest common denominator theory. The idea sprouted early in the churches as they desperately tried to stitch together some degree of common ground between the many competing forms of Christianity. Agreement on important dogmas seemed impossible, but union desirable, as the evolving mainline church wanted all in one flock. Power and position were dominant factors in the bludgeoning politics of the church, and more bodies meant more power and influence. Therefore, in order to encompass the maximum number of adherents, the church decided to accept as catholic (universal) doctrine only that which was believed *everywhere by everyone.* Since controversy and argument were running rampant, that meant adoption of only those very most vague and generalized items that wouldn't offend anybody, the lowest common denominator. The Vincentian Cannon, promulgated in AD 434, officially enthroned this particular standard as doctrine. Recognizing the babble and cacophony of all groups clamoring to be heard as the truth, the cannon declared:

> Now in the Catholic church itself we take the greatest care to hold THAT WHICH HAS BEEN BELIEVED EVERYWHERE, ALWAYS, AND BY ALL.[17]

But even within those very vague and generalized guidelines—and they took in a wide range of opinion and doctrines only faintly related to Christ and the original church—there were still large areas of disagreement. The act of enshrining the past and elevating tradition to unassailable and infallible dogmas led to a hardening of division.

The logic was simple. There could be only *one* authorized version of truth and tradition (this in spite of the glaring inconsistencies of the fathers). Therefore, all divergent views opposed the "true faith." This soon turned into an endless merry-go-round of confusion, however, as the disagreeing groups could all justify their version of the truth by using the same Bible and body of tradition as their opponents.[18] They all possessed the truth, but not together. The end result, as we have already seen, was a knock-down-and-dragout affair until only one group survived and could impose its interpretations of history and tradition on all.

All this, of course, makes a sham of some official doctrines and professions of faith hinged on the unanimity of tradition. The "Tridentine Profession of Faith" of 1564 stated that "nor will I ever receive and interpret the Scripture except according to the unanimous consent of the Fathers."[19] The "unanimous consent of the Fathers" was, of course, illusion. This put any adherents to such a creed in an uncomfortable position if they knew the truth.

A little reflection on all this will yield some very valuable conclusions. Disagreements, arguments, vacillation, name-calling, and labelling of opponents are all clearly the signs of human enterprise—most often characteristic of politics. These would all be tolerable, perhaps, for a normal human organization of those times. Indeed, it is one that of necessity we must accept and expect. However, such all too human maneuvering in the church of Jesus Christ (which theoretically established unvarying and unequivocal standards) is somewhat less than reassuring.

Absolute standards were characteristic of the New Testament Jesus, and wavering and hazy rules of conduct are in complete antipathy to the body of doctrine established in both the Old and the New Testaments. So much we would know on our own, without having to read much of the Bible, but we will shortly see just how far astray the churches had gone from the original ideas.

Notes

1. "The Henotikon of Zeno," 482, in Bettenson, 89.
2. "Vincent of Lerins, Commonitorium, 434, in Bettenson, 84–85.
3. Bainton, 38; italics added.
4. Wilken, 126.
5. Ibid., 127.
6. *Loc. cit*
7. Ibid., 125.
8. Schaff, Vol. III. 739–40.
9. Lea, *A History of the Inquisition*, 641; italics added.
10. Wilkin, 126.
11. Durant, *The Age of Faith*, 54.
12. Jacquin, "Histoire de l'Eglise," Vol. 1, 557, in Barker, 357.
13. Clark, 66–67.
14. Mosheim, Cent. IV, Part II, chapter 3:16.
15. Bainton, 41.
16. Wilken, 101.
17. The Vincentian Canon, in Bettenson, 83–84.
18. Wilken, 102.
19. *The Tridentine Profession of Faith*, in Bettenson, 266–67.

CHAPTER 9

Councils and Their Roles in Christian Dogma

Where did the traditions that became the body of Christian beliefs come from? We saw earlier that the founders of the original church asked for (and received) revelation to solve the knotty problems that swelled and burst periodically. Once the original church was destroyed, however, revelation ceased.

After that, Christians relied on opinions of their bishops and occasional Christian philosophers. But this wild cacophony of diverse theories threatened to engulf the remaining churches in a mad sea of contradictions. Soon, bishops began to gather together to hammer out compromises and to excoriate others disagreeing with them. At first these gatherings were strictly local, but the idea took hold until finally huge councils were held supposedly representing the whole church.[1] In theory, these councils could establish general truths and dogmas for all. They were later hailed by the churches as authorized foundations of traditions where holy fathers unanimously proclaimed sound doctrine.

Nothing could be further from the truth.

The first crack in this fragile lie of unanimous and holy prelates convening under inspiration appeared early. As mentioned above, local councils were the first to appear and were generally convened by a local bishop. The churches saw the wisdom of *general* councils, but—surprise—no one had the authority to call one! There was no presiding authority in "the church." The Catholic Church promulgates the wishful thinking that the popes called all the councils and as supreme heads of the church directed their efforts. That simply was not so. Aside from the fact that the office of pope did not even exist yet (more on this later), no bishop had any *universal* authority of any kind. "This theory [of papal approval] was imagined long after the events. The efforts to justify it historically are a pure waste."[2]

Who, then, called the first ecumenical council? The state. Who called most of the subsequent councils that laid the foundation of Christian dogma and tradition? Again, the state. Furthermore, the state, in the form of emperors, often dictated doctrine and theological decisions to the councils. Such decisions were then imposed by civil force (and banishment where necessary). Most participants were glad to align themselves with the prevailing notion of truth in order to avoid discomfort. At the next change in civil authority—and therefore possibly of doctrine too—most prelates felt no hesitancy in switching their opinions.

> During this whole period, the emperors claimed the right of convocation. They supported their pretensions on the principle that it belonged to them to assure order and tranquility in the empire and, in consequence, to put an end to the controversies that troubled this order. . . . The external policing of the council is likewise made by the emperor or by his delegates.[3]
>
> There is no doubt that until the ninth century, the emperors thought to convoke the general councils by virtue of a right, proper and inherent in their offices. Of this, one has superabundant proof in their letters of convocation. . . . None of these letters contains anything which recognized a delegation, or even a consent, expressed or implied of the pope; on the contrary, the convocation is presented as an act of the imperial authority.[4]

So, in this supposed church of Christ, we have official councils called—not by the authority of the church—but by the power of civil government. Perhaps even more telling is why the government stepped in at all. First, there was an obvious power vacuum. With no overall leader, a man like Constantine would not hesitate long. But more important, the reason he intervened at all was to end the squabbling and arguing of hundreds of bishops over what doctrine might be most acceptable and "true."

Council Standards versus Christian Morals

> The council in Ephesus in 449 . . . was a riotous and boisterous affair, at which the bishops debated with their fists instead of with arguments. Business took place amidst great tumult.[5]

One would think, and descendant churches would like us to believe, that the general ecumenical councils convened to decide on the most holy and important of Christian doctrines would be models of Christian thought and virtue. The churches do proclaim the sanctity of the holy fathers (thus their name) and the inspiration of their decisions, but that is an exercise in wishful thinking. The men themselves were as often immoral as moral. The decisions they reached were political compromises, often pleasing no one and ground out through the most bitter and vindictive arguments and tradeoffs to gain some slight advantage in the political in-fighting that characterized the early councils. Truth was often the least important goal as prelates struggled to maintain political position and power. Principle was quite easily laid upon the altar of convenience and self-interest.

> The quarrels and conciliar struggles that developed these doctrines were not the result of seeking for the truth in the spirit of forgetfulness of self. They were in the nature of contests of individual against individual, of school against school, of bishop against bishop, of patriarch against patriarch, of East against West. And they came about as the outcome of speculation, debate, quarreling, compromise, the intervention of the state and the use of force.[6]
>
> Nowhere is Christianity less attractive . . . than in the councils of the church. It is in general fierce collision of rival factions, neither of which will yield, each of which is solemnly pledged against conviction. Intrigue, injustice, violence, decisions on authority alone, and that the authority of a turbulent majority, decision by wild acclamation rather than after sober inquiry, detract from the reverence, and impugn the judgments. . . . The close is almost invariably a terrible anathema, in which it is impossible not to discern the tones of human hatred, or arrogant triumph, of rejoicing at the damnation imprecated against the humiliated adversary.[7]

The Council of Ephesus in 449 was called the Robber Council by Pope Leo, not because of the violence of its conduct, but because he was the doctrinal loser—Pope Leo and his supporters used the same methods as their opponents. Behavior of prelates in councils or elsewhere was not even a matter of concern. All that mattered was winning political support at councils. Indeed, the picture of the Christian churches and their bitter wars of the time presents a most discouraging ideal.

> The experience of Ammianus had convinced him that the enmity of the Christians towards each other surpassed the fury of savage beasts

> against man; and Gregory Nazianzen most pathetically laments that the kingdom of heaven was converted by discord into the image of chaos, of a nocturnal tempest, and of hell itself.[8]

Church councils degenerated into an ugly mixture of intrigues, bribery, imperial pressure, scandal, lying, and cheating—but all any of the prelates concerned worried about was doctrinal orthodoxy, the holy grail for the times.

> Now followed a succession of mutual criminations, invectives, arts of Church diplomacy and politics, intrigues, and violence, which give the saddest picture of the uncharitable and unspiritual Christianity of that time.[9]

Since all the important decisions of such councils were made in the midst of such strife, it follows that many would not voluntarily accept them. Therefore, force was necessary to make any decisions stick. The government, convener of the councils, enforced resulting doctrines. The first example was Athanasius's doctrine, which was imposed on the church and the empire by Constantine and some of his successors. Succeeding councils appealed to their emperor for enforcement, as freedom to believe what one wanted—if it disagreed with the majority—was not to be allowed, and the councils lacked the moral or physical authority to impose their decisions on others.

It seems appropriate to compare the tactics of the councils to the moral and ethical principles left by Christ and the apostles. What did they feel were the accepted methods? Here are a few samples.

> Brethren, if a man be overtaken in a fault, we which are spiritual, restore such a one in the spirit of meekness, considering thyself, lest thou also be tempted. (Galatians 16:1)

> Let nothing be done through strife of vainglory; but in lowliness of mind, let each esteem other better than themselves. (Philippians 2:3)

> He is proud, knowing nothing, but doting about questions and strifes of words, whereof cometh envy, strife, railing evil surmisings, perverse disputings of men of corrupt minds, and destitute of the truth. (1 Timothy 6:4–5)

> To speak evil of no man, to be no brawlers, but gentle, showing all meekness unto all men. (Titus 3:2)

> Now the works of the flesh are manifest, which are these . . . wrath, strife, seditions, heresies, envyings. . . . They which do such things shall not inherit the kingdom of God. (Galatians 5:19–21)

> For where enying and strife is, there is confusion and every evil work. (James 3:16)

> By this shall men know that ye are my disciples, if ye have love one to another. (John 13:35)

The Changing Standards of Councils

So far our view of councils is not particularly encouraging. We must now add one final weakness to the system. Churches today paint a picture of councils establishing immutable concepts impervious to change; decrees to rely on because of their inspiration and consistency. Again, truth must shred the myth. The long train of councils presents an amazing record of flip-flops of doctrine, as succeeding councils waffled on issues according to the strong wind of power—and who controlled its hot breath.

As one example, in 449, at the council held at Constantinople, the assembled bishops had condemned Eutyches for various and sundry reasons—mostly because he was on the wrong side of the political fence at a particular time. One year later Emperor Theodosius II called a council at Ephesus and made it clear that Eutyches's case should be reexamined. The bishops hopped to it with alacrity. Many of the very bishops who had one year before been "inspired" to see the error of Eutyches's ways now saw inspiration in a different light, made an about face, and acclaimed Eutyches and his doctrine.

And so it went, through council after council; shifting, changing, ever alert to the prevailing political wind, the force of the emperor's decrees, and the brutal in-fighting for political dominance over their brothers. Sometimes a council split into two enemy councils. At other times a council would reverse the decrees of a preceding council. Bishops of some councils excommunicated other bishops, who would then reciprocate, in the "Bang! You're dead!" theory of the children's shooting game. After this particular cry, the argument erupts: "I shot you!" "No, you didn't. You missed. I shot you first!"

Children demand some very real reactions to pretend. So did bishops. Both those of Rome and other places pretended to have all authority, but they didn't. Individuals and councils would mutually excommunicate each other and both continue on as before, nothing having been accomplished unless one side had imperial muscle to enforce its decrees. Of course, this was a dangerous game, as the politically acceptable doctrine today might be anathema tomorrow. Political leaders could—and did—come and go rapidly, and banished bishops could be brought back and it would be their former enemies' turn—unless they waffled enough to reverse their previous beliefs.

> "It is a thing," says Hilary, "Equally deplorable and dangerous, that there are as many creeds as opinions among men, as many doctrines as inclinations, and as many sources of blasphemy as there are faults among us; because we make creeds arbitrarily, and explain them as arbitrarily. The *Homoousion* is rejected, and received, and explained away by successive synods. . . . Every year, nay, every moon, we make new creeds to describe invisible mysteries. We repent of what we have done, we defend those who repent, we anathematise those whom we have defended. We condemn either the doctrine of others in ourselves, or our own in that of others; and reciprocally tearing one another to pieces, we have been the cause of each other's ruin.[10]

The most holy and revered of all the councils, the original set of "holy fathers" at the Council of Nicea is one of the best examples of the qualities Hilary described—qualities that are the very antithesis of the real Christian ethic.

Constantine, in AD 325, assembled all the bishops of the church together to strive for peace among them all. These holy fathers, tearing at each other's throats, threatened to blow apart the kingdom with their battles over God. Constantine's aim may have been laudable, but naive and unobtainable.

> This motly crowd of bishops represented all the varying traditions of Christianity. Among them were sharp-featured intellectuals, men of abstruse book learning who were capable of splitting hairs by the yard, but there were also old hermits who spent their days clothed in goatskins and living on roots and berries. . . . There were also cantankerous men riddled with heresy, and others who rode to Nicaea only in the hope of preferment from the hands of the emperor. Some came peacefully, intending only to observe and then report to their flock, and others came determined to wage war on the Council itself. . . . In theory they came to the Council to put an end to the heresies which were splitting the Christian Church apart; in fact, the warring factions were at each other's throats. . . .

> . . . And he extinguished the hope of peace and toleration, from the moment that he assembled three hundred bishops within the walls of the same place.[12]

The squabbling never did really end, and finally Constantine the pagan emperor had to force the bishops into a decision. That decision, the Nicene Creed, was a compromise that pleased few, if any. Many bishops signed it simply from fear of banishment.

Constantine celebrated the conclusion of the council with a royal dinner for the bishops and sent them on their way with a wish that they would not tear each other to pieces.[13] He was deluded if he truly felt the controversy was over. It was not, and Constantine himself would stir the cauldron to overflowing by later changing his own mind on the matter.

It was by virtue of the tradition trap that this hotly debated compromise was later elevated to an untouchable status as holy doctrine.

> During the first fifty years after the council of Nicaea, the decisions of the council were widely contested within Christendom. By the end of the fourth century and the beginning of the fifth century, i.e., approximately one hundred years after the council, its decisions were thought to be identical with the apostolic faith. Anyone who questioned Nicaea was thought to be heretical.[14]

Which all makes later claims to enshrine it a bit flimsy—something based on wishful thinking for something that was never really there. Catholics and Protestants alike would later fashion these creeds into unanimous holy opinions, "clearly deduced out of the scriptures."[15]

Somehow, in the passage of time and in the desperate effort to find solid anchor in the shifting shadows of the past, that unholy congregation of self seeking and power hungry opponents at Nicea was transformed in the holy orthodox standards for all time. This, in spite of the fact that it wavered like a mirage during the first years of its existence and was accepted reluctantly, if at all, by those closest to it in time who realized what it was and was not.

During the first fifty years of its existence, wars, argument, and bitter enmity raged throughout the empire over the correct interpretation of the Nicene Creed. Only long after the event were the final winners able to nail it down to their own viewpoint and enforce it. They then began obliterating all traces they could find of any ideas contrary to their particular philosophy. In the process they also began to enshrine the past and transform the Nicene participants from ordinary men into holy relics.

None of this had anything to do with innate righteousness or truth but was simply the survival of one political party (within a church) over another. Church historians are generally agreed that the Nicene Creed cannot be expressed in quotations from scriptures, nor does it agree with any of the very early church fathers. Therefore, some of the most basic beliefs of descendant churches cannot be traced past the Nicene Council of AD 325.

As a matter fact, the battles over this particular creed, supposedly both holy and unanimous, were the very basis for further councils—called to iron out the conflicts and differing interpretations. These in their turn led to further councils, as opinions shifted according to who was in power.

It is not our purpose here to follow all of the incredibly complex politics of the various councils that convened from the times of constantine on; that would be a book by itself. But at least we can appreciate the crudity of the system that supposedly was derived from Christ: self-promotion, invective, politics, civil enforcement power, bitter and hateful fights, and confused, uninformed, and strangely ignorant participants.

Notes

1. Barker, 150.
2. Funk, "Historie de l"Eglise," Vol. II, 273, in Barker, 327.
3. Boulenger, "Historia de la Iglesia," 170, in Barker, 324.
4. Hefele, "Histoire des Conciles . . . ," Vol. 1, Part 1, 10, in Barker, 325.
5. Wilken, 79.
6. Barker, 660–61.
7. Milman, "Latin Christianity," Vol. 1, 227, in Barker, 420.
8. Gibbon, chapter 21.
9. Jacquin, "Histoire de T'Eglise," Vol. 1, 551, in Barker, 352.
10. Gibbon, chapter 21.
11. Payne, 106.
12. Gibbon, chapter 21.
13. Durant, Caesar and Christ, 660.
14. Wilken, 99.
15. John Cosin, in Bettenson, 305.

CHAPTER 10

The Change in Doctrine

Christ gave his disciples a straightforward admonition to teach. Certainly the disciples never questioned it, as they strove to inculcate the doctrine he gave them. Moreover, a number of New Testament passages indicate that there was a set pattern of belief. So that we find references to "the faith which was once for all delivered unto the saints" (Jude 1:3) and to "the pattern of sound words" (2 Timothy 1:1–13). The Thessalonians were told to "hold the traditions which ye were taught" (2 Thessalonians 2:15), and the Romans were reminded that they "became obedient from the heart to that form of teaching whereunto ye were delivered" (Romans 6:17). There were no "creeds" in the later sense of hammered out compromises of various factions trying to find a common ground of belief, but rather an organized body of belief common to all.

In the churches of the second century, however, (and from then on) serious problems arose as different doctrines sprung up like spring weeds. Just which particular one was to be taught? There were plenty of choices.

Once the falling away began and serious strife between various Christian groups broke out, the doctrine left by Christ and his followers suffered; this was only to be expected. If the very nature of the church was changing, so also would the doctrine. This would be particularly true in a world of private interpretation, bitter fights of councils, and reliance on tradition. We should therefore expect numerous adaptations, additions, subtractions, and new interpretations of those basic doctrinal ideas left by

Christ and his immediate followers. We have already exposed this process in relation to the office of bishop, revelation, councils, and tradition. Now we shall see the changes creep stealthily over the fundamental beliefs of the early church—so much so that the new beliefs replaced the old.

Many forces contributed to the changes. One of the most important was the urge to meld Christianity with various odds and ends of paganism and philosophy, improving it and allowing a maximum number of converts who otherwise would have resisted giving up their old beliefs. In sum, accommodation of principles to the people rather than the reverse procedure that Christ taught.

Pope Gregory the Great was a proponent of this idea. Indeed, he formalized it to the degree that it was used as official operation procedure of the church. When he asked Augustine the missionary to go to Britain and build up the church with new converts, he advised him thusly:

> My advice to you is that you should . . . make a careful selection of anything you have found either in the Roman Church or that of the Gauls, or any other church, which may be more acceptable to Almighty God, and diligently teach the Church of the English, which is at yet is new in the faith, whatsoever you can gather from the several churches. . . . Choose, therefore, from each Church those things that are precious, religious, and seemly, and when you have . . . incorporated them, let the minds of the English be accustomed thereto.[1]

To missionaries ready to preach to the Saxons, Gregory repeated similar advice. "Remember not to interfere with any traditional belief or religious observance that can be harmonized with Christianity."[2] What could be harmonized, of course, had a wide interpretation both then, and earlier. In the early unformed and unorganized churches, where this doctrine had always been present (although not perhaps as official doctrine) each church decided what could or could not profitably be included. This mixed bag of adaptations was later bundled together as official church practices and beliefs. The churches, lacking fixed anchors of beliefs, simply collected odds and ends here and there as they evolved into "Christianity."

The end result was "an organization that acquired many practices foreign to the Christianity of apostolic times. The church was a changing church and ceased to bear resemblance to the original Christian norm."[3]

Gregory simply accelerated such changes. The process of corrupting and adapting the church to prevailing standards began long before that.

> The church liturgy began to form and evolve and change very early. By the third century, the patriarchates of Rome, of Antioch, and of Alexandria, had well-defined liturgies of their own, different from one another and also from the more simple ritual of the primitive church.[4]
>
> In the third century, the usages of Rome, of Antioch, and of Alexandria, must have been already quite different from the primitive unified usage.[5]

Later on, more changes boiled up and spilled their stains on the church. The Roman church, for example, under the prodding of the Frankish Kings Pepin, Charlemagne, and Louis the Pious was forced to adopt new ideas instigated by these civil rulers.

> To the original Roman rite, which was severely simple, the Franks added several ceremonial and symbolic features—for example, the use of ashes and palms, together with many details of the Holy Week services.[6]

In 1014, "another liturgical usage adopted by Rome about this time was the Gallican custom of swinging incense before persons and images."[7]

The changes in doctrine took place in all the competing Christian churches. However, the ones best known survived in the Roman Catholic group and its competitor, the Greek Orthodox. These many changes carried with them the seeds of yet further changes, future apostasy, and reformation, as later parties thought they could somehow return to the pattern of the original church. The Protestant groups, for example, later tried to reform many of the corrupted standards but made just as many mistakes on their own.

Following, then (chapters 11–13), are just a few of the items that suffered drastic changes from the original doctrines given by Christ.

Notes

1. Gregory Epistles, XI, 64, in Lyon, 217.
2. F. Legge, "Forerunners and Rivals of Christianity", in Lyon, 218.
3. Lyon, 220.
4. McSorley, 57.
5. Duchesne, "les Origens du Culte Chretien," 56, in Barker, 533.
6. McSorley, 237–38.
7. Ibid., 310.

CHAPTER 11

Celibacy: The Spiritual Eunuchs

Perhaps the most uncomfortable and depressing change of all concerned celibacy, as the new church strove to alter the very nature of man. Celibacy is a well-known doctrine today, of course (and still opposed by the clergy), and perhaps considered by many to be part of the original gospel. It was not.

> In the first three centuries of Christianity, celibacy was not required of a priest.[1]
>
> The Apostolical Constitutions nowhere prescribe clerical celibacy, but assume the single marriage of bishop, priest, and deacon as perfectly legitimate.[2]

Clearly in the early church, marriage of those officiating in priesthood ordinances was the *norm* (indeed, this follows logically, as there was no separate clergy, but members themselves all participated in priesthood functions). Even past the time of Nicea, there was no interference with married priests. "Many bishops," wrote the famed Athanasius, "have not contracted matrimony, while, on the other hand, monks have become fathers. Again, we see bishops who have children, and monks who take no thought of having posterity."[3] The whole message there is that some were *voluntarily* celibate (wisely or not). Even at that late date, there was no church ruling. Further testimony on this is abundant.[4]

The scriptures themselves, containing the utterances of Christ and his followers, are clear on the nature of man and marriage. Christ was emphatically specific.

> And he answered and said unto them, Have ye not read, that he which made them at the beginning made them male and female, And said, for this cause shall a man leave father and mother, and shall cleave to his wife: and they twain shall be one flesh? Wherefore they are no more twain, but one flesh. What therefore God hath joined together, let not man put asunder. (Matthew 19:4–6)

Peter, the chief apostle and married himself, repeated the admonition: "Likewise, ye husbands, dwell with them according to knowledge, giving honor to the wife, as unto the weaker vessel, and as being heirs together of the grace of life; that your prayers be not hindered" (1 Peter 3:7; italics added).

Not only did Peter endorse marriage, but he also implied that the fulness of grace of life can only fall on husband and wife as a team; if they aren't united, even their prayers will be hindered.

Paul was no less emphatic in spite of the fact that he is often used as an authority for celibacy!

> Nevertheless neither is the man without the woman, neither the woman without the man, in the Lord. For as the woman is of the man, even so is the man also by the woman, but all things of God. (1 Corinthians 11:11–12; italics added)
>
> Husbands, love your wives, even as Christ also loved the church, and gave himself for it. . . . Nevertheless let everyone of you in particular so love his even as himself; and the wife see that she reverence her husband. (Ephesians 5:25, 33)
>
> Marriage is honorable in all, and the bed undefiled: but whoremongers and adulterers God will judge. (Hebrews 13:4)

Paul carried it further and gave specific instructions that priesthood officiators—bishops and deacons—were required to be married as part of their office (which makes it curious indeed for some to use Paul as their authority for celibacy for the priesthood).

> A bishop then must be blameless, the husband of one wife, vigilant, sober, of good behavior, given to hospitality, apt to teach. . . . One that rules well his own house, having his children in subjection with all gravity; For if a man know not how to rule his own house, how shall he take care or the church of God. . . . Let the deacons be the husbands of

> one wife, ruling their children and their own houses well. (1 Timothy 3:2, 4–5, 12)

The same advice was repeated in the first letter to Titus (1:5–8), which presents a certain mystery. If Paul is so definite on the need of marriage for priesthood officiators, how can he also preach celibacy?

There were a couple of occasions when Paul seemed to be against marriage. Proponents of this kind of doctrine have fastened onto these in desperate and unseemingly haste (while ignoring all the overwhelming statements to the contrary). For example, in writing to the Corinthians (1 Corinthians 7:25–26), Paul states: "Now concerning virgins I have no commandment of the Lord: yet I give my judgement, as one that hath obtained mercy of the Lord to be faithful. I suppose therefore that this is good for the present distress, I say, that it is good for a man so to be."

Again, Paul wrote, "But I speak this by permission, and not of commandment. For I would that all men were even as I myself" (1 Corinthians 7:6–7). But to fasten an unnatural dogma from such diffident statements is stretching things indeed, especially in view of Paul's many other positive statements on marriage. For one thing, Paul admits openly that his advice to the Corinthian saints is personal, not from God, and that it is temporary, some kind of impermanent distress is afflicting the saints in Corinth. Furthermore, we can by no means assume Paul himself was not married (although he might have been widowed). He nowhere states that he was single. As a man who practiced all facets of Jewish law very strictly, before his conversion he would have probably have followed the tradition of marriage as well.

Throughout the Bible marriage is represented as the right and proper status of men and women.

> The Bible represents marriage as the first institution of God dating from the state of man's innocency, and puts the highest dignity upon it in the Old and New Covenants. Any reflection on the honor and purity of the married state and the marriage bed reflects on the patriarchs, Moses, the prophets, and the apostle.[5]

Undisputedly, at least Peter and several other apostles were married[6] (and as followers of Jewish law, they probably all were). If marriage did not detract from the dignity, authority, and spirituality of an apostle, could it so detract from a bishop, deacon, or priest, admittedly lesser offices? The emerging Roman-dominated church certainly believed it could (and still does). In spite of the many biblical examples of married men of God (who in the new classification would always be less holy than any celibate monk afterward), the later Roman church could conceive no real holiness without celibacy—and all scriptures and early church standards be damned. That marriage was a Godly approved institution is clear. Equally clear was Paul's specifically pointed comment that a corning prohibition of marriage was to be part of the apostasy we have been discussing.

> Now the Spirit speaketh expressly, that in the latter times some shall depart from the faith, giving heed to seducing spirits, and doctrines of devils; speaking lies in hypocrisy; having their conscience scared with a hot iron: Forbidding to marry, and commanding to abstain from meats, which God hath created to be received with thanksgiving of them which believe and know the truth. (1 Timothy 4:1–3)

The process of making the change was gradual. There was no sudden shift in which the later church abruptly decided to change what had been installed in the early church. During the first ages of the Christian churches, some individuals apparently opted for celibacy on a personal basis, believing it would make them more spiritual. Such an act had particular impact as a counterpoint to the extreme sexual license of pagan morals, perhaps a case of leaning over backwards so far from the abhorrent morals of contemporary society that the leaners fell over. Christian enthusiasts soon concluded from the cautious and limited warnings of Paul that any commerce between the sexes was sinful. The provincial council of Gengra (362) denounced such beliefs as heretical—but to no avail. As well try and bailout the Mediterranean with a bucket. The movement was too powerful.[7]

By the fifth century, St. Patrick freely applied the parable of the sower to celibacy—with a strict and narrowly prejudicial scorecard. Recall that the parable classified the seed as bringing forth one-hundred-, sixty-, and thirty-fold in production, depending on how good the soil was that it fell in. Good St. Patrick rated bishops, doctors of the church, monks, and virgins at one hundred; widows got only a sixty; general members of the church, being married, got the low end of the judgement.[8]

> Jerome's contempt for marriage was so strong that he felt justified in retroactively rearranging the standings of the apostles on his own. No matter that Christ had chosen Peter as the chief apostle. Jerome demoted him, deciding that Peter was clearly inferior to John, as the former had been married and John, he supposed, was not.[9]

St. Martin of Tours just barely admitted that marriage was pardonable, virginity glorious. Others in his time, in less generous terms, equated marriage to lechery. A treatise on chastity under the name of Pope Sixtus III only "barely admits that married people can earn eternal life."[10]

Pope Gregory the Great asserted that married pleasures could not possibly be free from sin, and that the only possible salvation for mankind was chastity. Even more extreme opinions began to form, as some bishops proclaimed that married people could not be saved at all and were to be treated with contempt.[11]

Somehow, a condition instituted and blessed by God himself and reaffirmed by Jesus and the apostles (and every prophet through the ages) had changed over the hundreds of years of Christian evolution and mushroomed into a dangerous poison; if not actually evil, it was at least a degraded and pitiable condition for the weaker portions of mankind. Had the positions of those days been upheld, all humans would have been forced into chastity, thereby ending the human race. The church actually did destroy many families by so openly encouraging celibacy.

> Too many Christians of these early centuries thought that they could serve God best—or rather, most easily escape hell—by abandoning their parents, mates, or children, and fleeing from the responsibilities of life in the frightened pursuit of a selfishly individual salvation.[12]

How could church officials so blatantly, albeit gradually, change the doctrines of the original church, reversing them entirely? No satisfactory or logical answer exists. They simply did it. When the Reformation finally forced later leaders to take a hard look at what had been done, they felt compelled to back up their predecessor's changes (to do otherwise would be to admit the church had indeed erred and changed, and thus endanger their claim to direct descendancy from the original). To do so they frenziedly searched through scripture and tradition, seeking to prove celibacy's early existence and blessings from the fathers.

Before the hot breath of the Reformation rattled the shaky foundation of the then dominant descendant church, however, Catholics had freely admitted the absence of celibacy in the early church.[13] (Only the honest pressure of the reform movement backed the church into a corner, thus forcing it to justify its previous practices in order to defend its present).

> The fact is that prior to the sixteenth century the Fathers of the Church had no scruple in admitting that in primitive times the canon had no existence and the custom was not observed.[14]

Jerome, for example, whose attempts to impose celibacy outshone all others, admitted that no such requirement existed in the early church. To justify it in his time he argued that infants—the early church with its apostles, holy fathers, prophets, and other toddlers in gospel maturity—must be nourished with milk and not solid food.[15] Strange, indeed, to find this bitter, vindictive man judging the apostolic generation and the early church in general as morally inferior to his own qualifications and generation (because they believed in marriage), but he did so, and made it stick.

Any rational mind finds it incredible that any of the church doctors could argue for such a doctrine, knowing it had no justification. Yet, argue for it they did.

> There were in the twelfth and thirteenth centuries few more learned men than Giraldus Cambrensis, whose orthodoxy was unquestioned, and who, as Archdeacon of St. David's, vigorously sought to enforce the rule of continence upon his recalcitrant clergy. Yet in a strenuous exhortation to them to mend the error of their ways in this respect, he admits that clerical celibacy had no spiritual or apostolic warrant.[16]

Some went to extremes to justify it:

> A priest named Taillard . . . in 1842 . . . reasons that if celibacy was not enforced in the primitive Church, it ought to have been—"if the celibacy of the priesthood be not from the beginning of Christianity, it ought to have been there, for as our holy religion comes from God, it should contain in itself all the means possible to elevate the nations to the highest point of liberty and happiness."[17]

Aside from the dubious arguments for the blissful state of celibates over those who are married, there are some serious accusations here. If God hadn't established celibacy in the first place, he had simply made a mistake, and a serious one at that! Thus appears again and again through history this strange contradiction.

The church pretended to be the guardian of tradition and even boasted of its slavish reliance on the past. Yet neither Christ, the apostles, nor the early church fathers had anything to do with celibacy. Quite the contrary, we find them condemning it.[18] "No matter," says the later church. "We've decided it should be this way, and even if the early church didn't preach it, they should have." So, having claimed the glories of tradition, the church proceeded to ignore it in favor of innovation. Regardless of historical fact, the "inspired" church decided what was tradition.

This they did, in a slow, gradual change, beginning about the middle of the second century.[19] Until then, marriage of priests and bishops was still the norm, and the first step was to prohibit a second marriage, based on Paul's injunction concerning the bishop being "the husband of one wife" (1 Timothy 3). The next step, taken ever so gradually, was to prohibit marriage after ordination. Until the fourth century, however, all such injunctions were optional and voluntary, there being no authority for imposing sanctions on married clergy. Finally, however, the last step was taken. Sacerdotal marriage was first prohibited by Pope Siricius in 385, and then by a long line of Popes and councils, each in succession trying to make it stick —mostly in vain.[20]

So, the law had been decreed, hundreds of years after the disappearance of the original church. One would think, especially if accepting the claims of the Catholic Church today, that such a decree would have been accepted and incorporated into the bosom of the church immediately. It was not, and the church fought a protracted battle with its recalcitrant priests for the next 1300 years or so trying to enforce this particular unnatural, nonbiblical, and unsupported standard.

The signs of the church during this long battle were flagrant and vicious immorality, sensuality, hypocrisy, shameless license, and crimes (including infanticide, open cohabitation, and common-law marriages of the clergy).[21] The church threatened, exhorted, begged, perpetually legislated, and resorted to ingenious devices in its efforts to enforce this particular crown of thorns on a resistant and rebellious clergy. All to little avail, as differing groups fought and resisted the change at least through the mid-1800s (and renewed today as priests and nuns flee the church or protest within the church because of this restriction).

The long list of abuses recorded by history (and excellently detailed by Henry Lea in his *History of Celibacy*) affords ample proof of the failure. The very flagrant and cynical flaunting of any kind of moral standards eventually led to the reformation, as people could adjust to only so much immorality.

But why drag this out any further? If the reader wants detail, he should consult Lea's exhaustive and detailed catalogue of the fruits of celibacy. The truth is that the descendant church for various reasons—none of which was at all related to the man from Galilee who had laid down quite different standards—attempted to impose an unusual standard on its officiators. The attempt has been a rather miserable failure, and its fruits have been immorality, hypocrisy, and moral degradation.

Notes

1. Durant, *The Age of Faith*, 45.
2. Schaff, Vol. II, 408.
3. Lea, *The History of Sacerdotal Celibacy*, 37.
4. *Loc. cit*
5. Schaff, Vol. II, 406.
6. Ibid., 405.
7. Durant, *op. cit.,* 45.
8. Lea, *op. cit.,* 26.
9. Durant, *op. cit.,* 53.
10. Lea, *op. cit.,* 27.
11. Ibid., 41.
12. Durant, *op. cit.,* 76.
13. Lea, *op. cit.,* 10.
14. *Loc. cit*
15. *Loc. cit*
16. *Loc. cit*
17. *Ibid.,* 12.
18. *Ibid.,* 14, 15, 28, etc.
19. Schaff, Vol. II, 397.
20. Ibid., 412.
21. Lea, *op. cit.* 37–43.

CHAPTER 12

Saints, Martyrs, and Other Passersby

The past, as we have seen, held a golden halo of promise for later Christianity. To it, Christianity turned for its doctrines, ideas, and finally its heroes. Anyone attached to the early church shot right up the pedestal of worship, propelled by the heavy hammer and collective muscle of tradition worshipers. After all, those ancients were "saints."

But what was a saint? Not what we think today, which is the end product of nineteen hundred years of hoopla and tradition imposed on us by descendant churches. *Saint* as used in the New Testament was apparently just another word for *member.* Indeed, all members were saints, much as you and I might call each other brother, neighbor, or friend. Being a saint was no clarion call for obeisance and worship but simply a nomenclatural designation. "The New Testament knows no spiritual aristocracy or nobility, but calls all believers 'saints.' "[1]

New Testament letters sent from one community to another were addressed to the saints or the brethren—in sum, to all the members. Only later, again by the God of tradition, were saints lifted up out of their humble category of ordinary participants struggling to live the principles preached by Christ and the apostles (and often failing in the struggle). The "saint" of today's churches has been seriously altered into an artificial entity bearing little resemblance to the original meaning.

Becoming a saint according to the Roman definition, for example, may require hundreds of years in a long, drawn out process. Yet, in his letters, Paul addressed all the members as saints in the same generation they were baptized (indeed, for some of them, within a short time after being baptized). This leads to the only logical conclusion: the Roman Church either invented the new procedures on their own, or changed the definition of the word. Both are accurate descriptions of what happened, but either way comes up wrong; and the world today is stuck with the image of thousands of individuals—some nonexistent, some scoundrels—who must be worshipped because they lived in the past.

Unfortunately, it is not only the person we must worship, but his or her picture, statue, or some grisly remains dredged from the graveyard by church authorized grave diggers. Again, we repeat a sad succession of facts. Image worship of any kind was repugnant to the apostles, Christ, and the early church. The rituals and decorations of that church were simple, as proven by Roman raids on Christian sanctuaries, raids that uncovered severely plain chapels lacking statuary, paintings, altars, or ceremonial equipment.[2]

The Bible is replete with deity's loathing of image worship. Again, however, we have to understand a certain haughtiness in later churches, whose leaders, although claiming to reverence the past, actually regarded their spiritual predecessors as some kind of poor country cousins. Later, and today, churches like to portray these early groups as simplistic, not yet sophisticated in church worship, not evolved very far, mere beginners as it were. Only through evolution, apparently, could the "true" worship emerge. The truth seems to be the opposite.

The early church, we might logically assume, practiced simple devotion because such had been instituted by its master, Jesus Christ, and his agents, the apostles. Only after this early order disappeared did change start. Gradually, down through the ages, the churches began to "improve" their rites and liturgies. Slowly, they began to venerate the early members in a worshipful (and as we've seen, contradictory) way, imagining them to be more holy simply because of the glowing halo that tradition imposed on the past.

> After the ruin of Paganism they [the bishops] were no longer restrained. . . . The first introduction of a symbolic worship was in the veneration of the cross and relics. The saints and martyrs, whose intercession was implored, were seated on the right hand of God.[3]

A healthy respect for previous martyrs and leaders, of course, was only a short step from the beginnings of worship. In the second century, some members actually sought martyrdom as an end in itself, rather than suffer it as a price paid by a few for the faith. Ignatius, the third bishop of Antioch, started the ball rolling with his own example.

> The epistles which Ignatius composed as he was carried in chains through the cities of Asia breathe sentiments the most repugnant to the ordinary feelings of human nature. He earnestly beseeches the Romans that, when he should be exposed in the amphitheater, they would not, by their kind but unseasonable intercession, deprive him of the crown of glory; and he declares his resolution to provoke and irritate the wild beasts which might be employed as the instruments of his death.[4]

The end of this was not righteous living to help the cause of truth, but actually *seeking* death, as an insurance clause for personal glorification. Ignatius' pleas for matrydom were fanatical.

> I write to you in the midst of life, yet *lusting after* death. You will not be showing love, but envy and hatred against me, should you procure the saving of my life.[5]

Justin Martyr added further to this misguided and unfortunate corruption of the original idea of faith and its defense—and seemed to revel in potential tortures.

> Let there come upon me fire and cross, struggles with wild beasts, cutting and tearing asunder, rackings of bones, mangling of limbs, crushing of my whole body, and cruel tortures of the devil, if so I may attain to Jesus Christ.[6]

Jesus, of course, emphasized a positive life, not a lust for death, as the way to heavenly rewards.

With this kind of example, however, was it any wonder that the ordinary members of the churches should also "lust after death" in equal fanaticism and misguided dedication?

> Thus Tertullian tells of a company of Christians in Ephesus, who begged martyrdom from the heathen governor, but after a few had been executed, the rest were sent away by him with the words: "Miserable creatures, if you really wish to die, you have precipices and halters enough."[7]

Of course, it seems unreasonable to us. It was "contrary to the instruction and example of Christ and the apostles, and to the spirit of true martyrdom."[8]

These new Christians wanted to die—commit suicide, really, and the "pagan" governor recognized it—for personal glory and the ensuing rewards rather than live and practice the life of virtue required by the doctrine of Christ.

> They inculcated with becoming diligence that the fire of martyrdom supplied every defect and expiated every sin; that, while the souls of ordinary Christians were obliged to pass through a slow, and painful purification, the triumphant sufferers entered into the immediate fruition of eternal bliss, where, in the society of the patriarchs, the apostles, and the prophets, they reigned with Christ, and acted as his assessors in the universal judgment of mankind. . . . The annual commemoration of their virtues and sufferings was observed as a sacred ceremony, and at length terminated in religious worship.[9]
>
> The bishops were obliged to check and to censure the forward zeal of the Christians, who voluntarily threw themselves into the hands of the magistrates. Some of these were persons oppressed by poverty and debts, who blindly sought to terminate a miserable existence by a glorious death. Others were allured by the hope that a short confinement would expiate the sins of a whole life; and others again were actuated by the less honourable motive of deriving a plentiful subsistence, and perhaps a considerable profit, from the alms which the charity of the faithful bestowed on the prisoners. After the church had triumphed over all her enemies, the interest as well as vanity of the captives prompted them to magnify the merit of their respective suffering.[10]

Of course, the rewards might be earthly as well as heavenly. Those who had nothing to lose could well afford to gamble by becoming confessors—open acknowledgement of their Christian profession to the presiding civil authorities. The survivors of such games—no matter how wretched their past—became overnight heroes for the church and were venerated beyond reason. Their word and advice often counted more than a bishop's, their humblest desire almost a command to be fulfilled by the faithful. Members vied with each other to do them honor.[11]

Yet, they had often changed in nothing; if they were selfish backsliders before, they often remained so. Indeed, this unfortunate veneration caused great harm as the confessors abused and confused the church and its members.[12]

That, then, was the first step in corrupting the original idea. Next, the church began a yearly observance of the martyr day of those killed in the name of Jesus (albeit all too often for their own glory). This soon led to actual religious worship. The churches began an enthusiastic quest for saints, martyrs, and their remains. Andrew, Luke, and Timothy had lain quietly and obscurely in their graves for three hundred years. Their death and tranquil burial held no safety from the new zeal for holy souvenirs; they were exhumed and transferred with great pomp and circumstance to new and more elaborate churches, and there worshipped.[13] Not content with a relatively few genuine martyrs, the multiplying churches began inventing new ones. Nothing could withstand this onslaught of superstition. And if past saints, why not even their bones, skin, or leftover laundry? Why not indeed?

> The satisfactory experience that the relics of saints were more valuable than gold or precious stones stimulated the clergy to multiply the treasures of the church. Without much regard for truth or probability, they invented names for skeletons, and actions for names. . . . To the invincible band of genuine and primitive martyrs they added myriads of imaginary heroes, who had never existed, except in the fancy of crafty or credulous legendaries . . . and there is reason to suspect that Tours might not be the only diocese in which the bones of a malefactor were adored instead of those of a saint. A superstitious practice, which tended to increase the temptations of fraud and credulity, insensibly extinguished the light of history and of reason in the Christian world.[14]

Not only did saints not have to be real, they didn't even have to be righteous. The story of Thekla was admittedly falsified, a con job from the beginning. In spite of that, the imaginary and legendary Thekla blossomed into one of the outstanding saints, ranked nearly as high as the virgin herself; Thekla was worshiped through almost all the Middle Ages.[15]

The Empress Irene, in the eighth century, had her son, Constantius VI, imprisoned, blinded, and apparently killed in her greedy race to the throne. However, she was doctrinally "pure" and defended the worship of relics when it was being challenged, and so the church happily canonized her as a saint.[16] What was a little murder or torture in the face of orthodox thinking?

George of Cappadocia, Bishop of Alexandria (AD 362), was a cruel, avaricious tyrant who trod mercilessly on the people. When finally his subjects could stomach his vices no more, he was executed by mob violence and his body thrown into the sea. He died not for Jesus, but as a price for his own numerous assaults on human rights and dignity. No matter; George became a saint. "The meritorious death of the archbishop obliterated the memory of his life. . . . The odious stranger, disguising every circumstance of time and place, assumed the mask of a martyr, a saint, and a Christian hero."[17]

An so on down through the ages. Myths, legends, some absolute wretches, ordinary rank, and file Christians of the past who simply happened to live at a particular time were all transformed into "saints" by the new definition. So many bishops were canonizing anything and everything even close to Christianity that the church finally removed their authority to do so and left the power only in the hands of the pope. New, involved rules were established and long delays required. The meaning of "Paul, to all the saints in" (whichever city Paul happened to be writing to) was long lost in the past.

The New Idolatry

The teachings of the New Testament make it clear that the only permissible worship was that of God and Jesus. The new Christian churches forgot that injunction early, eagerly lining up the martyrs of the past as a new series of Gods.

To the original church, pictures, statues, and the like were unequivocally condemned. The same attitude prevailed for many years in the early churches. The Nicene Synod, in its 36th Canon, prohibited sacred pictures on the walls of church buildings.[18] That wasn't to last. The pressures of change would even burst the walls of this apparently solid and unassailable prohibition against image worship.

> As the number of worshipped saints multiplied, a need arose for identifying and remembering them; pictures of them and of Mary were produced in great number; and in the case of Christ not only his imagined form but His cross became objects of reverence. . . . The natural freedom of fancy among the people turned the holy relics, pictures, and statues into objects of adoration; people prostrated themselves before them, kissed them, burned candles and incense before them, crowned them with flowers, and sought miracles from their occult influence.[19]
>
> At first the experiment was made with caution and scruple; and the venerable pictures were discreetly allowed to instruct the ignorant, to awaken the cold, and to gratify the prejudices of the heathen proselytes.

> By a slow though inevitable progression the honours of the original were transferred to the copy: the devout Christian prayed before the image of a saint; and the Pagan rites of genuflexion, luminaries, and incense again stole into the Catholic church.[20]

By the end of the sixth century, that which was prohibited in the past had become an integral part of the new church worship. Christians throughout the kingdom prostrated themselves before a plethora of statues, portraits, and icons, and worshiped them as freely as any pagan of old before his material objects of deity. If here and there a voice tried to penetrate this gloom of superstition to differentiate between worship and honor, it was hopeless. The church had freely opened the doors to this particular pit in its anxiety to please its followers and was as much swallowed up as the lowliest sinner worshipping at the feet of a statue.

One powerful man tried to halt this slide into idolatry—and failed.

Leo III became emperor in AD 717 and was offended by the excesses of this return to paganism. He "felt keenly the satire directed by Moslems, Jews, and Christian sects against the superstitions of the orthodox multitude."[21] The "orthodox," in defiance of the order established by Old and New Testaments and the earlier church fathers, insisted on new standards defined by themselves and on regressing back to the heathen religions conquered (but never vanquished) and amalgamated into the church. They would worship statues.

Leo called a council in 726 in Constantinople, and after six months of debate the assembled 338 bishops reached the "unanimous" decision (again, the desires of the prince became the doctrines of the church) "that all visible symbols of Christ, except in the Eucharist, were either blasphemous or heretical: that image-worship was a corruption of Christianity and a renewal of Paganism."[22]

That seemed clear enough. An officially assembled council of the church, supposedly with the inspiration and wisdom to know and promulgate the truth, had spoken. Images were blasphemous. How did the church accept this ruling? They revolted! In Italy, the stronghold of image worship, imperial officers were driven out of the cities. The bishop of Rome, Gregory II, hastily summoned a local council and hotly defended the bones, pictures, statues, and other objects anathematizing the iconoclastics. Writing to Leo, Gregory betrayed a most un-Christianlike belligerency and ignorance in defending what the scriptures had condemned.

> "During ten pure and fortunate years," says Gregory to the emperor, "we have tasted the annual confort of your royal letters subscribed in purple ink with your own hand, the sacred pledges of your attachment to the orthodox creed of our fathers. How deplorable is the change! How tremendous the scandal! You now accuse the Catholics of idolatry; and, by the accusation, you betray your own impiety and ignorance. To this ignorance we are compelled to adapt the grossness of our style and arguments."[23]

Gregory tried two arguments on Leo, one false, the other shaky. First he assumed enormous historical ignorance on the part of the emperor by trying to claim "the perpetual use of images from the apostolic age, and their venerable presence in the six synods of the catholic church."[24]

Second, he argued that "the harmony of the Christian world supersedes the demand of a general council; and that such assemblies can only be useful under the reign of an orthodox prince."[25]

Curious arguments indeed. No consideration of tightness or wrongness. For the sake of tranquility, image worship ought to be retained—politics and smooth sailing above all else—even the truth! And no protesting against imperial meddling per se, only imperial meddling when it doesn't agree with Roman interpretations.

And so it went. By dint of civil war and simply ignoring the edict, the image-cherishers outlasted Leo, who died in 741. His son Constantine V and his grandson Leo IV did not succeed either. Finally, the Empress Irene ruled and called her own council at Nice. As Leo II before her, she left no doubt as to the decision she wanted from the 350 bishops, and it wasn't long in coming. The council turned about face and reversed the decisions of the earlier council.

> They unanimously pronounced that the worship of images is agreeable to scripture and reason, to the fathers and councils of the church; . . . of this second Nicene council the acts are still extant; a curious monument of superstition and ignorance, of falsehood and folly.[26]

No matter how false or silly, the church rushed to embrace the decision. Emperor Leo II had convinced one council to rule his way, and Empress Irene convinced another council to go for hers. Such was the danger of civil authority dictating to the church. Which of the political decrees does an honest Christian of today choose? His church rules that he accept the last decision, which has been in effect ever since that time.

A Rag 'o Bone and a Hank 'o Hair

There now remained but one final step in this fascinating perversion of original Christian principles of worship. First, honor and venerate the people—the saints and martyrs. Then, *worship* them. What next but to worship their picture or statue? A final and grisly step remained to close the circle. Go back and find the body, bones, the umbrella—or any other personal object—of the saint and then fall down before that.

> In the earlier periods of the church, the worship of Christians was confined to the one Supreme God, and his Son Jesus Christ; but the Christians of this century multiplied the objects of their devotion, and paid homage to the remains of the true cross, the images of the saints, and to bones, whose real owners were extremely dubious.[27]

From God, then, we have stooped to worshipping a few hairs, a vial of blood, or a moldy bone. Such items became more valuable than familiar objects of material worth.

> So we later took up his [Polycarp's] bones, being of more value than precious stones and more esteemed than gold, and laid them apart in a convenient place.[28]

This emphasis soon degraded the churches even further. After the seventh council in 787, bishops were denied permission to consecrate new churches that possessed no relics. Apparently one could worship only in a building with a "certified" bone in it. Naturally, this led to wholesale abuse. Entire graveyards, containing a mixture of saints, sinners, plebians, and pagans, were hastily endowed with martyr status and mass excavations of these gruesome remains became the pastime of Christians all over the empire. (Where facts were insufficient, legend saved the day, as when 10,000 Christian soldiers were supposedly crucified in one day by the emperor, thus providing an open hunting license in that particular graveyard for "legitimate" relics).

> Princes rivaled each other in collecting the relics of saints. . . . In the time of Luther, Frederick the Wise . . . had accumulated no less than five thousand of the sacred objects. In a catalogue of them, we find the rod of Moses, a bit of the burning bush, thread spun by the virgin, etc. The elector of Mayence possessed even a larger collection, which included forty-two whole bodies of saints and some of the earth from a field near damascus out of which God . . . created man.[29]

Before long the combined Christian churches had enough slivers from the original cross to create an entire forest.

A Case in Point—Mother Seton's Bones, or Holy Grave Digging!

The search for and honor of such relics was by no means only an aberration of the church of a thousand years ago. It continues in the Catholic Church—the literal descendant of the early Christian competitors—in much the same fashion today. The important religious communities maintain officials in Rome with only one duty—to push particular candidates for sainthood. Mother Seton of Maryland is a recent example. She was canonized in 1975 after ninety-three years of being touted as "extra-human," a saint. Some estimate that the sisters of Mother Seton's order spent millions of dollars on this cause; the church will officially admit only about two hundred thousand dollars. No matter that Seton was widely recognized as a genuinely good person who used her life to help others. She must be officially recognized as a "saint," an important status symbol and financial windfall for modern Catholic orders. Naturally, no one talks very openly about the considerable prestige thus generated.

Mother Seton was finally recognized. This meant her relics (excavated earlier) could now be officially venerated. So, poor Mother Seton, who had worked for the love of God and her fellow humans, had her parts rather unceremoniously hauled from the grave by officially approved grave diggers to be exposed to public worship. The mechanics of this operation afford a fascinating view of this innovative practice that originated in the Christian church of the third century.

> The doctors immediately picked out two long bones placing them on the cloth on the bier; these were the two femurs. Then two humeri bones, all well preserved, two iliac bones, one patella, a good many pieces of ribs, the skull almost complete though in two pieces, one heel bone, mandible, metacarpal bones, tibia, several teeth, sections of the vertebra, and all these were recorded by Father Gossman, the notary. . . . Two beads from a rosary, a corpus from a crucifix, some pieces of the wood of the first casket, as well as a good quantity of the "ex copore," ("from the body") completed the findings.[30]
>
> On the occasion of the Seton beatification, the backers of her cause presented Pope John XXIII with a gold-plated silver statue of Mother Seton standing on a gem-studded base cut in the outline of the United States. In a little glass container set into the base was a bone from one of Mother Seton's fingers. The pope's relic, the ones owned by the Cardinal

Cicognani, the slivers now available in Emmitsburg for donations of $5.00 or $2.50 . . . all came from the bones obtained in 1962.[31]

So the process worked. The ethical and moral principles established and emphasized by Christ were not enough; changes were made, and the worship of a heel bone, a tooth, an elbow, or some other leftover was added onto—and in many respects substituted for—the saner principles. In Mother Seton's case the relics were genuinely hers, but throughout the middle ages countless Christians groveled before the remains of someone just like themselves from an earlier age, or in many cases simply fraudulent and manufactured relics.

Salvation by Tourism—Holy Jogging

Perhaps even more meaningless than bone worship was a later practice that promised remission of sins simply by *visiting* certain churches—not performing any righteous acts, just being physically present at a particular building. Presumably one could have ruthlessly trod down or clambered over numberless innocent necks to get there:

> For the first time in its history [13th century] the Church, speaking through the mouth of boniface, announced a plenary indulgence for the remission of punishment due to sin. The faithful were promised full remission of Purgatory if they visited the seven basilicas. Those who could not undertake the pilgrimage were promised the same heavenly reward on payment to the church of the traveling expenses they would have incurred if they had gone on pilgrimage.[32]

Pope Boniface stated something entirely new here not only by announcing a doctrine never known in the original church or by the early church fathers, but also by publicly announcing that the rich could *buy* their way out of the sufferings of purgatory. All this was very convenient for those living near the basilicas and the rich, but hard on everyone else, and all were foreign to the original gospel.

> By way of contrast to all the foregoing, there was almost a total absence of any mystical expression of faith in the early church, or any faith connected to things, or money. . . . Nowhere in the New Testament is mention made of shrines or places associated with Christ. No importance was given to objects which might have had intimate relationship to the apostles. There is no mention of pilgrimages to shrines or an attitude of reverence for tangible objects which were connected with Jesus, His mother, His home, or His public ministry.[33]

> The apologists frequently assert, that their brethren had neither temples nor altars (in the pagan sense of these words), and that their worship was spiritual and independent of place and ritual. . . . Clement of Alexandria refutes the superstition, that religion is bound to any building.[34]

But, of course, that was in the old—the "primitive"—church. This new, and supposedly more sophisticated church had its own way of worshipping.

Notes

1. Schaff, Vol. II, 124.
2. Gibbon, chapter 49.
3. Ibid., chapter 49.
4. Ibid., chapter 49.
5. Payne, 55; italics added.
6. Durant, *Caesar and Christ*, 611.
7. Schaff, Vol. II, 77.
8. Ibid., 77.
9. Gibbon, chapter 16.
10. Ibid., chapter 16.
11. Schaff, Vol. II, 84.
12. Gibbon, chapter 16.
13. Ibid., chapter 28.
14. Ibid., chapter 28.
15. Wegener, 138.
16. Durant, *The Age of Faith*, 427.
17. Gibbon, chapter 23.
18. Schaff, Vol. II, 180.
19. Durant, *The Age of Faith*, 426.
20. Gibbon, chapter 49.
21. Durant, *The Age of Faith*, 426.
22. Gibbon, chapter 49.
23. Ibid., chapter 49.
24. Ibid., chapter 49.
25. Ibid., chapter 49.
26. Ibid., chapter 49.
27. Mosheim, VII, part II, chapter 3:1, 25.
28. Payne, 96.
29. Robinson, Vol. I, 390.
30. MacKaye, *Potomac Magazine, Washington Post*, Sept. 14, 1975.
31. Ibid.
32. Payne, 382.
33. Lyon, 42.
34. Schaff, Vol. II, 199.

CHAPTER 13

The Great Mother

The transformation of Mary, the mother of Jesus, into a goddess affords yet another example of the vast and sweeping changes tacked onto original Christianity by later churches.

This whole troublesome point was itself generated by yet an earlier change in doctrine—that of original sin. This last concept is far removed from any theology ever taught by Jesus or his apostles and was not part of the original gospel at all, but a personal theory and largely an invention of Augustine—and at that on very dubious grounds even for that church doctor. However, once the churches swallowed Augustine's novel theory—which they didn't do easily—their mutual stomachs churned and roared with a delicate and seemingly indigestible concept. If Christ was perfect, how could he have been born of an imperfect mother, that is, one born in original sin herself? Of course, these questions never bothered the church during the first two hundred years or so because no one had yet dreamed up original sin.

With the birth of that concept in the fourth century, however, the argument and debates erupted—and continued through hundreds of years as generations of prelates and doctors squirmed in the spotlight of contradictions of Mary and perfection. Up through the twelfth century, it was not even questioned that the virgin was conceived and born "in sin," i.e., just like everybody else (by that time of course, original sin was a sadly lamented state for everyone). Pope Innocent III emphatically endorsed that plain fact.[1] But the pressure for worshipping a new deity was building up too high to allow any accepted truth of history stand in its way. Mary must be removed from that sin and enthroned.

> "The Virgin," says Peter of Blois, "is the sole mediator between men and Christ. We were sinners and feared to appeal to the father, for he is terrible, but we have the Virgin, in whom there is nothing terrible, for in her is the plentitude of grace and the purity of human life:" and he goes on to virtually prove her divinity by showing that if the Son is consubstantial with the Father, the Virgin is consubstantial with the Son. In fact, he exclaims, "if Mary were taken from heaven there would be to mankind nothing but the blackness of darkness." God, says St. Bonaventura, could have made a greater earth and a greater heaven, but he exhausted his power in creating Mary.[2]

Silly as it may sound, the church and the people bought it. Mary slowly took on all the attributes of God—many preferring to pray to her rather than anyone else. That fact that Jesus and the apostles had made clear that prayers were to be directed only to God, and that nowhere in the Bible is Mary mentioned as anything other than what she was—a mother—was unimportant. As with idols and relics, the church multiplied its many gods into a pantheon. Whereas the early churches abhorred any charge of polytheism (and had created a new definition of God to avoid it) the new church welcomed the trait—if not the name—with open arms.

Finally, in 1849, Pope Pius IX brought things to a head, and consulted all the bishops. Those of Italy, Spain, and Portugal were almost unanimously in favor. Many in the other churches either hesitated or vociferously opposed it. Pius accepted the vote that supported what he wanted and ignored the rest. In 1854 he declared Mary free from all sin (which considering the negative opinion of the earlier Innocent III, puts a serious hole in infallibility). So, by popular demand, Mary was elected a goddess.

Strangely, it took eighteen hundred years to discover the overwhelmingly dramatic presence of this new deity. A Catholic apologist argues that in 1854 the Pope was not inventing a new doctrine, but merely declaring what the Catholic Church always believed.[3] It had not been believed earlier, however. It was not, moreover, what the original church believed or even the early churches through the first several hundred years of Christianity; or even the later churches through the first ten or eleven centuries. It was a new invention.

Curious, indeed, is this situation. In one way the early church did believe that Mary, and everyone else, were born innocent. The doctrine of original sin had not even appeared as a gleam of some bright soul's imagination yet. After the doctrine came the dilemma of Mary being born in sin—an impossible situation. So they had to invent a new doctrine to excuse Mary, but nobody else, from this curse that nobody had previously believed in anyway!

But surely confusion calls enough. Let's leave it there. The various inventions of the churches led to endless circles of problems and counter inventions. Mary is only one example.

And Various Other Changes

It is impossible, of course, to trace in this short book all the changes in Christianity as it evolved through the centuries. We have touched in some detail on a few, and perhaps two more vignettes of very basic contradictions will suffice.

The original church held individuals responsible for their rewards in heaven. God's grace is essential for salvation, but people have to earn their rewards by virtuous and rightful living (Romans 2:6–8; 2 Peter 3:15–16; James 2:14–24; Revelation 20:12). Many have tried to argue that Paul himself preached that all rewards were by grace alone, but his letters thunder with the need of individual, and positive, action. Paul did indeed inveigh against relying on "works of the law," but usually in context of the old law of Moses and its massive and mindless ritualization that had grown over the years.

For three hundred years, then, the church was secure in the knowledge that the kingdom of heaven was based soundly on a merit system. Heaven could only be won, not dispensed haphazardly on the heads of passersby here and there. Until Augustine, that is. Combining philosophy, reasoning, and careful selection of a few scriptures that seemed to agree with what he wanted (and ignoring those that didn't), Augustine developed a *new,* and *personal* religious philosophy, including original sin and predestination.[4]

Catholic and Protestant churches have adapted Augustine's philosophy, with minor adjustments, into church doctrine. Theologians ever since have been hard put to extricate themselves from the quagmire thus created. How, for example, can prelates argue for good works from their flocks when they accept Augustine's thesis of predestination? One is damned or blessed regardless of any act on earth. Original sin, as we have already seen, presented the Catholics with an almost insurmountable problem with Mary that took fifteen hundred years to solve.

Baptism, the very key to the entrance to the kingdom, according to Jesus (John 3:5), also suffered rapid and drastic changes. At first, of course, the doctrine was clear. The very meaning of the word, its very translation, is "to immerse, to be immersed." How else could Paul refer to baptism as a burial (Romans 6)? In the early churches, immersion was the only method used to baptize.[5] Of much more significance, however, were the absolute conditions of repentance and faith—qualities expressed in adults or, at the very least, older children. Certainly not in babies.

Who changed all this? History provides no exact answer (although again, Augustine helped)—only that it was changed. Gradually, sprinkling was substituted for immersion (until much later when some Protestant groups returned to immersion) and one no longer had to repent and have faith (scriptural demands to the contrary), but was baptized as a babe. The Catholic Church generated the new idea that tiny unbaptized babies were condemned to hell (or a place very much like it) with no chance of obtaining heaven.[6] That this condemned literally millions of babies to an everlasting torment of some kind doesn't seem to bother authorities in the church.

Again, this doctrine was freely coined by the philosophers of the day and swallowed whole. This all seems strange in view of Jesus' assertion of the moral purity of children (Luke 18:16–17; Matthew 18:3–6). Indeed, his warning thundered out; we should all have to be like them to enter heaven! Nonetheless, baptizing (and condemning) children began in the third century, thanks to the hardworking Augustine and others.

Change, change, and more change. The Eucharist, from a simple commemoration of Christ, was changed almost virtually into a literal eating of Christ's body as partakers were asked to believe the wine and bread were "not only a sacrament but also the true body and blood of our Lord Jesus Christ and that these are sensibly handled and broken by the hands of priests and crushed by the teeth of the faithful, not only sacramentally, but in reality."[7]

In other words, it was Christ' literal flesh and blood; it only looked like bread and wine.

And so on and on. Use of the cross, rosaries, crucifixes, incense, ceremonial altars, masses, archbishops, cardinals, and popes were all additions and changes to the original church and doctrine. Combine this with the corruption that penetrated the Catholic Church, and it was little wonder that a reformation burst upon the world. Indeed, the invention of new doctrines was the necessary seed for reform, as later churches would do their own thing in trying to correct an abuse or change. But they too had their problems and succeeded no better than the Catholic Church in reforming itself, as we shall see.

Notes

1. Lea, *A History of the Inquisition*, Vol. III, 596.
2. Ibid., 597.
3. Zaehner, 161.
4. Barker, 458.
5. Talmage, 125.
6. Durant, *The Age of Faith*, 77.
7. *Aquinas on the Eucharist*, in Bettenson, 147.

CHAPTER 14

The "Nature of God" Controversies

The year was AD 325. Constantine held the Roman Empire firmly in his mighty grip, but he was troubled. The infant church he was backing as a new state religion was proving a liability. Indeed, if problems continued, it would become an acute embarrassment. Already the Christian churches were the laughingstock of the world as their prelates were hopelessly mired down in bitter and acrimonious warfare, bickering and backbiting over the nature of their god. Splitting theological hairs down to the infinitesimal, they trudged back and forth over the same points. Was Christ God, man, or both? Was he more one than the other? A perfect blend of the two? Was there one God or three? One nature or three? How many wills did they have? Human and divine, or both? Nothing so well shows what Christianity had become as the some six hundred years of insane and deadly warfare and argument over who, or what, Jesus and God were.

The arguments over Christ's nature tumbled out fairly early (around the second quarter of the third century). Just where were they going to put him? In the human camp, or the divine? In the second century, philosophers had gone to work on the problem (which interestingly had not been a problem to the early church at all). They saw complications in the fact that Christ was both human and divine. This posed a metaphysical conundrum no true philosopher could resist, and once broached, this discussion reaped bitter arguments, heresy, division, and confusion.

If Christ were God, then Christians were polytheistic, as they would have two gods to worship, the Father and the Son. Polytheism, of course, smacked of paganism—an abhorrent thought to these newly minted Christians who were fighting tooth and claw against the detested pagans. Again, we need to emphasize the artificial creation of the problem to begin with. The early church had no difficulty at all that we can detect understanding Jesus' nature. As with Jewish monotheism, which they had been taught by the Jewish Christ, they recognized only one supreme being. Christ, God's son, had existed with God before, and as his son was therefore important but still subordinate to the Father. Later generations, however, saw problems where none existed for the first church members. Christ was also God (the Son), and therefore the pagans could indeed accuse Christians of having more than one god. Add the Holy Ghost and the problems multiplied.

To avoid any such charges (from both Jews and pagans) Christians went through complicated arguments, over the relationships among God, Christ, the Holy Ghost, and humanity. Philosophers trying to reconcile three Christian gods into monotheistic unity stimulated an almost endless mass of literature and fierce advocates for every variety of interpretation. The battle raged for years before the Nicean Council. The years just prior to that event, however, were particularly frantic; thus Constantine's decision to box his squabbling prelates together and force them into some semblance of unanimity. The subject matter of this council (and the ones that followed) is vast. Historians and theologians have produced hundreds of volumes on the topic. The purpose of these forbidding tomes and impressive councils, however, was simply to try and find out who Christ and God were—something that had been lost—and to drum out of the church any who didn't abide by majority opinion. Councils were largely a means to power, to do in an opponent, or to manipulate the church or government.

We will not delve into the many devious and philosophical arguments of the councils—that is subject matter enough for many books and the reader may refer to any number of the volumes available on the subject. We will mention here only the main issues and summarize the results.

The first skirmishes in the battles erupted seriously in the third century. The first major battle was Nicea; the main protagonists, Anus and Athanasius.

Arius was head of one of the Alexandrian churches. The "heresy" he preached narrowly missed becoming the "orthodox" doctrine of the church, as his and Athanasius's doctrines raged back and forth over decades; first one in the ascendancy and then the other.

Unfortunately, most of Arius's writings were burned by his triumphant enemies, so what he taught is known mainly from whatever part of his ideas his adversaries chose to print in their counter arguments. In essence, however, he apparently argued simply that Christ did not exist from all eternity. He was at one time created by the Father and was of a relative or secondary divinity to the Father. Therefore, he was not *of the* divine substance of the Father. This last was a most crucial point.

Bishop Alexander of Alexandria and his deacon Athanasius were opposed to the teachings of Arius. Alexander allowed Athanasius to be the spear carrier for the fight. These two believed in an absolute divinity of Christ; he was entirely God and not subordinated to the Father—they *were* of the same substance.

The storm generated by the two local camps soon turned into a full-fledged hurricane of words, arguments and bitter enmity. A letter from Constantine to Alexander expressed the former's curiously insensitive feeling of right or wrong, the silliness of the arguments, and his gut instinct for disastrous politics.

> I had proposed to lead back to a single form the ideas which all people conceive of the Deity; for I feel strongly that if I could induce men to unite on that subject, the conduct of public affairs would be considerably eased. But alas! I hear there are more disputes among you than recently in Africa. The cause seems to be quite trifling and unworthy of such fierce contests. You, Alexander, wished to know what your priests were thinking on a point of the law, even on a portion only of a question in itself entirely devoid of importance; and you Arius, if you had such thoughts, should have kept silence . . . there was no need to make these questions public . . . these are silly actions worthy of inexperienced children, and not of priests or reasonable men.

In vain did Constantine state plain facts. The letter did no good, and the arguments intensified. Constantine was trying to take candy from very spoiled children. It was all finally brought to a head at Nicea by the emperor, interested not so much in truth, as in public tranquility. The council was assembled in Nicea in 325, all travel expenses provided by the emperor. In spite of that, most western bishops ignored the whole affair (estimates of their numbers range from 6 to 18). Silvester I, bishop of Rome, was content to be represented by some priests.

The Theological Problem at Nicea

There were actually three contending parties at Nicea, the Athanasian (or Alexandrian), the Arian, and the moderate Arians. They attempted to deduce the nature of Christ by speculative reasoning, argument, debates, and compromise. "From the outset the controversy between both parties took place upon the common basis of the neoplatonic concept of substance, which was foreign to the New Testament itself."[2]

The Arians saw no problem in the Son being less than the Father—that seemed to be natural. The Athanasians would have none of it—the Son must be somehow *equal* to the Father in spite of numerous scriptural references to their real Father-Son relationship. The debates were so bitter that the opposing parties would go to any lengths to discredit the other—even to creating new ideas with no basis in scripture.[3] The final vote favored the Athanasians and read as follows:

> We believe in one God, The Father Almighty, maker of all things visible and invisible.
>
> And in one Lord Jesus Christ, the Son of God, begotten of the father, only-begotten, that is, from the substance of the Father, God from God, Light from Light, very God from very God, begotten not made, from the same substance as the Father, through whom all things were made, both things in Heaven and things on earth; who for us men, and for our salvation, came down and was made flesh, was made man, suffered and rose again the third day, ascended into Heaven, and shall come to judge the quick and the dead.
>
> And in the Holy Ghost.
>
> Who pretend that the Son of God is "of other hypostasis or substance" or created or "alterable" or "Mutable" the Catholic church anathematizes.

The council had backed itself into a corner. The Son was numerically distinct from the father (this agreeing with the scriptures); at the same time, however, they were of the same substance, that is, the same person. Somehow three personages had become one but were still three. How to explain it? They couldn't.

> He conceded the difficulty of picturing three distinct persons in one God, but argued that reason must bow to the mystery of the Trinity.[4]

So, rather than have the hated Arians win anything at all, the Athanasians cut off their noses to spite their faces. They adopted a theology that no one—not even they—could understand; and since they couldn't explain it, it was conveniently labeled an "incomprehensible mystery." Churches yet today are still trying to explain it.

> The difficulty presented by the doctrine of the trinity is how we can conceive of God to be both three and one at the same time . . . but there are other unities than mathematical ones, unities which are multiple and in particular organic unities . . . the higher the organism the more complex its unity, so that the unity of the human body is far more complex than the unity of the amoeba. The godhead may be understood from this point of view—its unity or oneness is that of a living organism and comprises three constituent elements.[5]

There, perfectly clear. God is some sort of giant and complex organism, a universal protoplasm of some sort who appears in three different forms, yet is one. The analogy to ourselves as complex beings must be interpreted as saying the legs, arms, hands, head, and so forth are separate beings but all in one. As they say, however, "the doctrine of the Trinity, *though strictly rational,* surpasses our full comprehension".[6] It certainly does, and the justification sounds suspiciously like whistling in the dark.

> Such was the Nicene Creed as approved by the emperor in council, a weapon forged on abstractions, possessing little merit except the merit of keeping the Arians at bay.[7]

After looking at all this, it may pay to examine what Jesus and the apostles taught on the same subject. During the council, Athanasius made frequent use of the following scriptures: "I and my Father are one" (John 10:30). "The Father is in me and I in him" (John 10:38). "He that hath seen me hath seen the Father" (John 14:9). Their use in such a cause is endowed with some risk. In John 18:11, 21–24, Jesus prayed:

> And now I am no more in the world, but these are in the world, and I come to thee. Holy Father, keep through thine own name those whom thou hast given me, that they may be one, as we are. . . . That they all may be one; as thou, Father, are in me, and I in thee, that they also may be one in us: that the world may believe that thou hast sent me. And the glory which thou gavest me I have given them, that they may be one, even as we are one: I in them, and thou in me, that they may be made perfect in one; and that the world may know that thou hast sent me, and hast loved them; as thou hast loved me.

A strictly logical look at that casts some doubt on Athanasius' interpretation. Did Christ intend for the Twelve Apostles to become a "mystery" twelve in one composite? Did Paul, when he said, "For we being many are one bread, and one body: for we are all partakers of that one bread," (1 Corinthians 10:17) intend the whole church to achieve this mysterious status? Were these men somehow preaching Eastern mysticism and a union of all beings with God to form one great being? To a reasonable mind the first interpretation is to accept what the authors are saying. That is, unity is desirable just as God and Jesus appear unified in purpose (so much so that they are virtually alike), but with bodily merging a remote possibility at best.

References to Christ as a very distinct and quite separate person and less than equal to God the Father abound, as for example:

> For my Father is greater than I. (John 14:28)
>
> But he [Stephen] being full of the Holy Ghost, looked up steadfastly into heaven, and saw the glory of God, and Jesus standing on the right hand of God, and said, Behold, I see the heavens opened, and the Son of man standing on the right hand of God. (Acts 7:55–56)

But Stephen, seeing the resurrected Christ on the right hand of the Father and Christ himself stating that he was less than the Father, were ignored—or at least overruled by the Nicene polemicists.

> Thus church historians generally agree that the Nicene Creed cannot be expressed in quotations from scripture—the very terms used in the creed had to be coined for the purpose—and the creed is not in harmony with the early church Fathers, neither as to the nature of the Father nor as to the relationship of the Son to the Father. In consequence the most fundamental beliefs of the historical churches cannot be traced farther back than the Council of Nicea (AD 325).[8]

Some later prelates were alarmed when they made that discovery on their own and tried to prove that the early church fathers really taught Nicene doctrine. Hefele, the Catholic Historian of Councils, admits their search was in vain, as no trace of any such doctrines can be found in the teachings of the early church leaders, those closest to the original church and doctrine.[9]

Unfortunately, the Nicene Creed was no unanimous decision, even for those present at the council, but a compromise with which few theologians were satisfied. The "unanimous" decision of the holy fathers lauded by history was coerced by the emperor in the name of unity. Out of self-interest, everyone eventually signed the document in public and then spit out their disgust and arguments in private.

Coercion and threats, however, do not end strife even for emperors. Arguments continued. Constantine himself aided and abetted the confusion. Having made his choice for the Athanasians, he shortly began to vacillate. Each tiny tremor of change in the emperor sent violent spasms of reaction through the church and empire. As the persuasions of various interest groups alternately changed Constantine's loyalties from one to another doctrine, lesser lights scurried to stay safely in the sunshine of official favor. This required a great deal of double talk and careful side-stepping or backstepping. During Constantine's life, Arius was forgiven and Athanasius banished. Finally, both Arius and Constantine died, the latter in 337. Then the struggle really began.

The Heirs of Constantine

After Constantine's death, his three sons divided the kingdom among themselves. The two Western emperors, Constans and Constantine II, were Athanasians. The Eastern emperor, Constantius, was Arian. They first agreed to recall Athanasius and his supporting bishops from exile. That forgiving attitude lit the fire of controversy all over again. When the Athanasian bishops had been exiled, their churches had been given to Arians. Now the returnees demanded back their sees, the competing bishops excommunicated each other, and conflicts burst out that frequently ended in bloodshed and death.

For example, Athanasius in particular wanted back his episcopal seat in Alexandria, one of the three most important sees in the church. It was restored to him by imperial edict but the Arian bishop there simply refused to relinquish it. Athanasius therefore called a council (at Alexandria, in 337), which violently attacked the decisions of the Council at Tyre (held in 335 and at which Athanasius had originally been deposed). Both groups now tried to get Rome lined up on their team. Rome was not the head of the church at the time, but as the most powerful church in the West, it had great influence and independence.

Meanwhile, with the support of Constantius, a new (Arian) bishop, Gregory, was installed in Alexandria. With imperial troops behind him, Gregory trampled over the bodies and blood of supporters of Athanasius to take his seat of power. Bishop Julius of Rome, meanwhile, had decided in favor of Athanasius. Not only that, he took it upon himself to reprimand the Eastern bishops and their "wrong" judgment, threatening them, and warning them to cease their innovations. The Eastern bishops spared no pains to inform the bishop of Rome that no matter how much they all honored the Roman church, they were not about to take orders from it. They would have been glad to receive support, but when Rome didn't agree with them, they lost no time in criticizing the "pope" and his meddling.

> For they acknowledge . . . that the Roman church was honored by everyone. . . . But they did not propose on that account to take second place. . . . And they brought charges against Julius for communing with the party of Athanasius and were indignant with him for disdaining their synod and annulling their verdict. And they denounced his action as unjust and as contrary to ecclesiastical law. Then after upbraiding him in such style and declaring that he had done them grave injury, they offered Julius peace and communion if he would recognize the deposition of those whom they had expelled and the ordination of those whom they had elected instead, and they threatened him with the contrary, if he overrode their decisions.[10]

Rome was only one of the churches and did not then (or even till much later) control anything but a local area. "The importance of a city adds nothing to the prerogatives of its bishop who has only the same honors of all; the pope Julius has no preeminence over them."[11]

Julius did write again to inform the Eastern bishops that "no sentence could be pronounced against the bishop of Alexandria without the assent of the bishop of Rome."[12] That injunction was ignored by the Eastern bishops. Despite his protestations to the contrary, Julius had no authority in Alexandria (unless the emperor happened to support him with imperial armed might). Gregory remained as bishop of Alexandria and Athanasius stuck tight to this new supporter in Rome.

But then the political picture changed again. In 340 Constantine II had been defeated and killed by his brother Constans. The latter, Athanasian, now controlled two-thirds of the entire empire. His very considerable power as sole master of the West made his opinions count heavily. Arians chewed their fingernails closely and worried, as Constans soon began to threaten and intimidate the weaker Constantius. This was unfortunate for the Eastern bishops, who had just been prepared to call a council of their own to create a new Arian creed to supersede the Nicene Creed. The shift in power quickly changed their minds for them, and they caviled delicately before the new reality and simply and plainly compromised their profession of faith at their council. But, of course, the arguments went on, even among the Arians themselves (who were seriously divided).

Finally, Constans, desperately trying to impose peace in a kingdom where the "followers of Christ" kept things in constant turmoil with their endless arguments and warfare, called a council of his own. It took place in 343, and the 160 bishops were about evenly divided between East and West. Almost before the council could begin, however, Constan's purposes were ripped to shreds by the arrogant, proud, and argumentative bishops. No sooner had the council debates begun, when the Eastern bishops, offended, withdrew to hold their own, and separate, council at Philippopolis. They then proceeded to again condemn Athanasius and all who received him and topped it off by excommunicating Julius, bishop of Rome. They also drew up a new creed which made no reference to the *omoousias* (one substance).

The Western bishops in their turn proceeded to excommunicate the Eastern bishops (both teams were enthusiastically playing "Bang! You're dead!"). They also carried ever further the buildup of Rome which would culminate eventually in her taking over the church many centuries in the future. The end result of the council was not peace, then, but war—continued war.

> The mutual excommunications served only to envenom the relations already bad; the project of a symbol was rejected; the canons proved impracticable. Finally, the most evident effect of the assembly, intended to bring peace in the church, was to cause the schism to break out, which for several years had been latent, between the two halves of the Christian world.[13]

The tide for the moment, however, favored the Athanasians. In 344 the powerful Constans put pressure on his brother to recall all banished Athanasian bishops. Constantius yielded and even restored Athanasius himself to this Alexandrian bishopric after the death of Gregory. With civil power at their backs, the Athanasians were on the verge of winning the bitter, political battle for supremacy in the "Christian" church. But then they suffered a near lethal blow, as political winds again shifted, and most Christian churches easily adjusted their sails of belief to curry favor with the new situation.

In the West, Magnentius overthrew Constans and was crowned emperor. Three years later Constantius conquered Magnentius and became the sole emperor of all the empire—and he was Arian. The merry-go-round began again. Constantius convened a council of three hundred bishops at Milan. Presiding over the council in person, much like his father at Nicea, he asked for, and received, a condemnation of Athanasius. Any not signing would be banished. Only three bishops (of the many who had been firm Athanasians) stuck by the suddenly unpopular bishop of Alexandria. They were indeed banished, but the number is surprisingly small, considering the four hundred bishops who had shortly before committed themselves to the "correct" doctrine of Athanasius.

Many bishops simply shifted with the political tides, but Constantius, not content with that, sent his agents from city to city, forcing the bishops to accept the deposition of Athanasius—or else. Liberius, bishop of Rome, would not sign and was banished—for the moment.

Now, Arianism had triumphed, and he became the reigning doctrine of the churches and empire. Success, however, disclosed the weakness in the winning party. There had actually long existed two Arian parties—the hard core Arians and the "semi-Arians." So divided, the Arians began to weaken themselves with internecine warfare after winning the battle—repeating, in effect, previous Christian history. Each obtained the support of the emperor in a succession of councils. Bishops who had formerly been Athanasian now embraced one or the other of the prevailing Arian doctrines.

Meanwhile, Bishop Liberius of Rome, unable to stand banishment, found himself seeing the light. It was more convenient to change his beliefs and return to his bishopric. Naturally, this required some significant waffling and adjustment of past statements, and in his letter asking to return, Liberius did both easily.

> I did not defend Athanasius but, because my predecessor, Bishop Julius of honorable memory, had received him, I was afraid that I might be considered a traitor of some sort. But when, by God's will, I realized that you had been right in condemning him, I straightway gave my assent to your judgment. . . . So now that Athanasius has been excluded from communion with all of us and his official letters are no longer to be accepted by me, I assert that I am in peace and harmony with you everyone. . . . Moreover, you may be sure that I am professing the true faith in this letter. . . . I confidently believe that I may entreat your holiness [Emperor Constantius] now that you behold me in hearty agreement with you, to put forth your efforts graciously in common council and zeal that I may be released from banishment.[14]

In a similar letter to the Arian leaders, Liberius wrote:

> Whereas I know you are sons of peace and love the concord and harmony of the Catholic church therefore, under no compulsion whatever—as I call God to witness—but for the sake of blessing of peace and concord, which is preferable to martyrdom, I approach you with this letter . . . to go graciously to our most clement emperor, Constantius, and ask him for the blessing of peace and concord, in which his reverence always finds delight, that he may order me to return to the church divinely committed to me. . . . By this letter you are to understand fairly and honestly, dearest brothers, that I am at peace with all you bishops of the Catholic church.[15]

No old fashioned stick-to-your-principles-come-matrydom-or-banishment for Liberius! How much nicer the comforts of home and adjustment of belief.

Liberius denied the Athanasian doctrine and quite specifically accepted Arian teachings. (His return, however, was complicated by the presence of his replacement, Felix, appointed in his absence. Until Felix died a short time after, Rome was treated—with much indignation by the populace—to two bishops ruling separately).

In the meantime, however, the struggle still continued over an exact definition of the Godhead. Finally, at the fourth council of Sirmium, Constantius once more forced the bishops to accept a supposedly final Arian formula. All bishops not at the council were also forced to sign. None objected this time, perhaps instructed by the banishment of those who chose principle at the previous council.

Plainly, the church was controlled by the emperor. Whichever party had his support was *the* Christian church. Doctrines had become politically controlled and installed. Had an Arian emperor stayed in power, that would have been the doctrine of today. The bishops certainly had no compunctions about sacrificing principle for political expediency. They all adjusted their beliefs to curry political favor. None were willing to defend what had before been the orthodox "truth."

Naturally, this didn't do much for the Catholic position. Not only have Popes always been infallible, but the church itself has been "indefectible." Nonetheless, Felix, bishop of Rome, was Arian. Liberius signed an Arian statement of belief in order to regain his throne. All the bishops, in fact, had signed what is for the Roman church today, a "heretical" doctrine.

The reason Arianism is heretical is that Athanasianism was about to triumph for the final time and would become the orthodox doctrine of the church. Once more, the bishops would shift their Jell-O-like stance and opt for the imperial-backed majority.

The Final Triumph

Constantius, the Arian defender, passed on to whatever reward he earned in AD 361. The battles then broke out again as overeager bishops saw a chance to reinstate the "correct" doctrine that they had been denying while Constantius was alive. For eighteen years the fortunes of the various parties waxed and waned as the support of various emperors draped itself arbitrarily here and there over different groups. Liberius, bishop of Rome, had now seen the light again and had switched back to Athanasianism—which he had only recently condemned. In 378 the last imperial defender of Ariansim, Valens, fell at the battle of Adrianopel. Theodosius and Gratian then ruled the empire and both were Athnana-sian. The tide shifted for the last time in this sad history of Christian warfare.

Athanasian bishops were installed almost everywhere, backed by the naked power of imperial forces. In 381 Emperor Theodosius—not the Roman bishop or any other bishop—called a council in Constantinople to cap off fifty years of violent argument, vindictive warfare, and incredible chicanery. The Nicene Creed was officially reaffirmed.

So, in 325 one council convoked by an emperor had adopted a political compromise on the nature of God and Christ. After a quarter of a century of conflict, maneuvering, and shifting, the Arian belief was forced onto Christianity by imperial forces as true doctrine. After another quarter of a century, Athanasianism triumphed by political power and became the belief of the Christian world.

The gullible might argue that right had triumphed over all opposition of wrong—and so trumpeted the winners at the time, and so maintains the Catholic Church today. We may be forgiven, however, if we, after studying the events, might want to conclude something different. Not much of righteousness and Christian ethics or morals was involved here. For one thing, these political opponents took too much glee in crushing, humiliating, and even physically harming their enemies—fellow Christians. For another, the doctrines argued and fought over were foreign to the scriptures and to the early church—as even the protagonists admitted. Moreover, attachment to one or the other of these doctrines was not done for faith, but for power and position. All in all, a sad travesty of "Christian" virtues.

Notes

1. Eusebius, "Life of Constantine," 63, in Lyon, 147.
2. *Encyclopedia Britannica,* Macropedia, Vol. 4. 485.
3. Foakes-Jackson, 312.
4. Durant, *Caesar and Christ,* 660.
5. Zaehner, 72.
6. *Loc cit;* italics added.
7. Payne, 110.
8. Barker, 266–67.
9. Hefele, "Histoire des conciles . . . " Vol. 1,449, 52, in Barker, 267.
10. Hefele, *op cit,* Vol I, Part 2, 698, in Barker, 286–87.
11. Hefele, *op cit,* Vol. I, Part 2, 689, in Barker, 287.
12. Foakes-Jackson, 335.
13. Barker, 295.
14. Shotwell & Loomis, 583–84.
15. Ibid., 584.

CHAPTER 15

The "Nature of God" Controversies (Continued)

One would think that fifty years of argument over the relationship between God and Christ would be enough, but it wasn't. The churches now embarked on an even longer and, if anything, more bitter war. For the next three hundred years they fought over the nature of Christ. Fighting was a natural result of what the churches had become. Whereas the original church had been guided by revelation directly from heaven, the later groups attempted to define God by speculative reasoning, at the same time trying to reconcile the scriptures with philosophy. The result, as we shall see, was near chaos.

The trouble began, naturally, with the Nicene definition of Christ and God, now officially accepted. The end result of the Nicene Council was an abrupt break with the original theological concepts of the first church and the early churches. The new definition of God was one outside of time and space. Reconciling the mortal Jesus with this new immaterial and unfeeling God caused some serious problems. Theologians wrestled with the heavy question of whether Christ had two natures—divine and human—or only one. The fight began.

One group, the Docetists, argued he had only a divine nature—in effect, it only appeared that he had a human body. Others argued he was not divine, but only a man. Yet others argued for two natures, but only one will; while yet others plugged for two natures and two wills. In other words, just how were the human and divine united in Christ? Where the scriptures were simple and said relatively little, the theologians were willing to toss out buckets full of opinions and philosophies. The questions were debated in a spirit of combat through a long series of councils and arguments. It is almost impossible to understand the various and complicated obsessions of all the contending philosophies—nor shall we here try. The reader is again referred to any number of books that try to explain the unexplainable.

The whole story of this three-hundred-year fight over Christ and political dominance is almost beyond belief. If not for the actual facts, we might think it some wild, surrealistic dream of a mad genius of chaos or confusion. The facts, however, are real. We cannot, in this short space, follow all the details of the confusion, but we will trace at least the main lines of the story.

First, some terms are necessary. The different parties coined particular words to describe their beliefs. Monophysitism, one nature in Christ, the divine; Dyophysitism, two natures, human and divine; Monotheletism, two natures but only one will; and the solution that finally triumphed as orthodox, two natures and two wills.

Most of the problems stemmed from the philosophers. The nature of man had nothing to do with the nature of God; hence, the logos, Christ, was unrelated to the spirit of man. But, Christ had become a man. Or had he?

After a few preliminary skirmishes between a certain Apollinarus and his opponents, the battle heated up. Enter then, the first two primary antagonists, Nestorius, patriarch of Constantinople, and Cyril, patriarch of Alexandria; and one new factor of the argument, Mary. Some theologians had been calling her "the mother of God," *theotokos.* Naturally, as the veneration of Mary grew, the arguments over this term greatly affected the popular passions. Theodore of Mopsuestia opposed any such term, as he argued that "Mary gave birth to Jesus, but not to the *logos.* . . . It is not God, but indeed the temple in which God lives, who was born of Mary."[1]

Nestorius and Cyril brought these festering arguments to a head. Nestorius, a disciple of Theodore, objected to the term "Mother of God" and insisted on two distinct natures in Christ. Cyril was a monophysite and believed in the *theotokos.*

Here then, are Cyril's beliefs:

> Sets forward as the view of the Catholic Church that the *Logos* took human nature to Himself in the womb of the virgin Mary, and that therefore the title of *Theotokos* properly belongs to her. By so

> doing, he maintained that Godhood and Manhood were united in the Incarnate *Logos* in one person. Before the Incarnation there were Two Natures, but being united these can only be distinguished "in theory." The godhead is not, of course, able to suffer, but as the *Logos* was united to the flesh, we may say that His flesh tasted death. Thus we have the doctrine . . . that here on earth our Lord was one Person, but he underwent different experiences in virtue of his two different Natures.[2]

Complicating the theological argument was an intense political rivalry between the two contenders, Constantinople and Alexandria.

The battle lines were set. Jerusalem was by now no longer an important patriarchate. The four remaining powers squared off against each other; Alexandria (Cyril) and Rome against Constantinople (Nestorius) and Antioch. Both groups appealed to the two reigning emperors, Theodosius II and Valentinus III to call a council. The emperors agreed and the council met at Ephesus in 431. It was almost predetermined that no agreement would be reached between the two warring groups.

> Neither party understood, nor cared to understand the position of the other. Each sadly misrepresented the other, and by stating his own views and those of his opponents in the extremist form made the breach as wide as possible. Apart from dogmatical considerations, he [Cyril] was probably glad of the opportunity to humiliate the patriarchates of Constantinople and Antioch, and to this end he did not scruple to employ the ready instrumentality of court intrigue.[3]

The council turned into a shambles. Cyril ramrodded his way to the presidency and called the council to order before Nestorius's main support party, John of Antioch, and other friends even arrived. The few Nestorians withdrew, but the council slugged away without them. Quickly—and predictably, with the resulting stacked deck—they condemned Nestorius and his supporters. John of Antioch, on his arrival, held his own mini-council and deposed Cyril. Cyril's crew returned the favor.

> Now followed a succession of mutual criminations, invectives, arts of Church diplomacy and politics, intrigues, and violence, which give the saddest picture of the uncharitable and unspiritual Christianity of that time.[4]
>
> This is the third of the ecumenical councils, and is held therefore by all churches, in high regard. But in moral character this council stands far beneath that of Nicea or of the first council of Constantinople. An uncharitable, violent, and passionate spirit ruled the transactions. The

> doctrinal result, also was mainly only negative; that is to say condemnation of Nestorian.[5]

All this was meaningless as far as actual effect is concerned. None of the opposing groups' condemnations, depositions, and assorted slurs had any practical effect without the backing of imperial force. No church, and certainly not Rome, had any power over the others without state help.

Cyril quickly determined to end the stalemate. The emperor had refused to back either party in the controversy, but by bribes and popular pressure, Cyril wormed his way into imperial favor. Nestorius was finally deposed.

In the meantime, however, John of Antioch continued to lash out at Cyril, and the battle continued as bitterly as before. Finally, in 432, Theodosius had enough. He determined to use force, if necessary, to effect a reconciliation between John and Cyril. It didn't take much of that kind of pressure for the two warriors to see the light. They quickly struck a bargain, compromised beliefs, and signed a joint doctrine, one forced by imperial power.[6] As at Nicea, however, it didn't work. Arguments broke out as fresh and vindictive as ever. Finally Nestorius, forced out of the cloister to which he had been permitted to retire, was banished to Arabia. The violent, unscrupulous Cyril had pushed his doctrine to the top of the heap—he had won.[7]

Within ten years, however, all those involved in these bitter battles over the *Theotokoshad* died. Then it became someone else's turn to argue, and over something new.

The new period of turbulence began with a monk named Eutyches, who maintained firmly that in Christ were not two natures, only one. His opponent was Flavian, a new patriarch of Constantinople, who called a local synod and condemned Eutyches and his monophysite heresy. Dioscorus, who had succeeded Cyril as patriarch of Alexandria, talked the emperor Theodosius into calling another council at Ephesus in 449. There, "religion was subordinate to politics; the Alexandrian see continued its war upon the see of Constantinople."[8] Pope Leo of Rome didn't bother to attend the council but had sent some letters (Leo's Tome), but to no avail. The council ignored the bishop of Rome and exonerated Eutyches.[9]

The council further issued anathema against all who dared to believe Christ had two natures. This included Leo, bishop of Rome, and that worthy promptly labeled the council a *Latrocinium* (a gathering of robbers, or "The

Robber Synod"), which was only natural, since he was the loser. The label he applied to the council was a political one, not one of moral tightness; the council had dared oppose the bishop of Rome, whose power was now becoming significant—not significant enough to control the church yet, but enough to wield great influence.

However, Leo was not through yet, because shortly after these events, Theodosius II, emperor of the East, died. In him, monophysitism lost its last imperial supporter. With dyophysite emperors in the East and West, all the bishops who had previously supported "false" doctrine now saw the light.

In 451, Marcian, emperor of the West, called a council that finally convened in Chalcedon in October. That council, in light of the new political realities, fully accepted Leo's *Tome.* Christ, then, officially had two natures after the incarnation, but in one person. Nobody had consulted Christ or sought revelation. The decision was arrived at by debate, battle, and philosophical reasoning. Again, as usual, the end result was actually a "compromise, and as such, it could not entirely satisfy anybody."[10] The bishops then bowed before the imperial power that determined all this and properly gave him the credit.

> The symbol was solemnly ratified at the sixth session (Oct. 25), in the presence of the emperor and the empress. The emperor thanked Christ for the restoration of the unity of faith, and threatened all with heavy punishment, who would thereafter stir up new controversies; whereupon the synod exclaimed: "Thou art both priest and king, victor in war, and teacher of faith."[11]

Rome, of course, accepted—and accepts—the council of Chalcedon and its decisions as doctrine. One item of that council not too well advertised was that in spite of growing Roman power, its bishop still didn't outrank everybody. The twenty-eighth canon recognized equal authority for the bishop of Constantinople. Leo rejected *that* canon (while accepting the rest as inspired) and continued his fight for supremacy.[12] It is interesting, however, how the Roman Church selectively chose which decisions of this orthodox council (and others as well) were "inspired" and which weren't. *Uninspired* items were those the Roman bishop didn't like.

The decision of Chalcedon, imposed by imperial force, was supposed to bring peace. Like the previous compromises and political sidestepping before it, however, it did not.

> The Chalcedonian definition was a Roman formula forced on the Oriental church by imperial authority. As such it could not be universally acceptable, the fact being that the East was at heart unanimous in favor of the doctrine of St. Cyril. . . . So great a controversy was not to be silenced by a single council; and it continued in various forms for at least two centuries.[13]
>
> From the Council of Chalcedon started those violent and complicated monophysite controversies which convulsed the Oriental church, from patriarchs and emperors down to monks and peasants, for more than a hundred years, and which left their mark even to our day. They present a gloomy picture of the corruption of the church.[14]
>
> The Council of chalcedon had drawn up a formula, but it had unified neither the minds nor the hearts. . . . The majority of the Fathers of the council did not wish the new formula: it is that, at bottom, they wished to hold to the anathematism of Cyril. . . . It was very much against their will that they rallied to the Roman formula. . . . One should not then be astonished . . . that the decisions . . . met with lively resistance . . . an uninterrupted struggle for the conquest of the bishoprics, and especially of the four patriarchal seats, a struggle in which first one and then the other will triumph according to the religious policy of the princess.[15]

The struggle was by no means one merely of words. At one point the Egyptian clergy, who refused to accept this particular and imperial religious doctrine, revolted. Monks fought physically against those who accepted the council's decrees, and imperial forces had to intervene, occupying cities and suppressing the population through force. Thousands died.[16]

Ups and downs in the controversies over Christ continued until the first quarter of the sixth century, when East and West temporarily accepted a common doctrine. Egypt, Asia Minor, and Syria were not brought into this fold and continued in their own ideas. But even this minor agreement was short-lived. The Emperor Justinian, famed as one of the greatest emperors, meddled, and the arguments heated up again.

This period is noted in particular for the very pronounced waffling of the Roman bishop, Vigilius, who showed about as much principle and backbone as a weeping willow. Four times he switched sides to jump on the prevailing political bandwagon. As Schaff dryly understates it, "His fourfold change of opinion does poor service to the claim of papal infallibility."[17]

Another council at Constantinople (called by Justinian in 553) did little more than the preceding, and wearying, succession of political sidestepping had done. Nonetheless, the Christological controversies were showing signs of finally dying out. After five hundred years of arguments, bloodshed, and maneuvering, the Christian world decided that Christ had two natures (in one) before and after the incarnation, and that he and God were different—but the same.

Not quite enough hairs had yet been split, however; there was still one argument left that the other councils hadn't chevied down to its last particle of subdivision. Did Christ have one will (human) as the monotheitists argued, or two (human and divine)? The mind almost stops working to think of the endless arguments back and forth over what kind of hammer would be used to nail shut the lid on the personality of Jesus.

This last controversy erupted on a by-now-familiar note. The Emperor Heraclius, needing the support of the monophystte East for his wars, thought he could compromise. Accept the two natures of Chalcedon, he and Sergius (bishop of Constantinople) reasoned, but throw the bone of a single will to the monophysites to get them back into the fold; not a fold of righteousness, particularly, but of political peace. Sergius then convinced Bishop Honorius of Rome of the same thing and this later went happily along with the proposal—not realizing he was going to his own hanging. Honorius died not too long afterward, and his replacements at Rome repudiated his stand. Under Bishop Agatho (678–81) monotheism was condemned for the last time.

The controversy created quite a problem for papal infallibility, of course. At the third council of Constantinople in AD 680, Honorius was anathematized in no uncertain terms.

> And we are agreed to reject with them from the Holy Church of God and to anathematize also Honorius, who was pope of ancient Rome, because we have discovered in the letters addressed by him to Sergius, that he followed the latter (Sergius) in everything and confirmed his impious dogma.[18]
>
> The council decided to anathematize by name those who had been condemned. And so it was done: the name of Honorius appears in the series, without in any way being distinguished from the others.[19]

Yes, a pope had been condemned as a heretic by another pope (Agatho) and a council. Ever since, Catholic theologians have squirmed uncomfortably with the fact, and have invented ingenious rationalizations. None is quite successful, and all are rather obvious attempts to reinterpret hard fact in light of dogmatically imposed tradition.

> The condemnation of the unfortunate Honorius was inserted in the confession which every newly elected pope had to sign down to the eleventh century, and which is embodied in *Liber Diurnus*, i.e., the official book of formulas of the Roman church for the use of the papal curia.[20]
>
> The condemnation of a departed pope as a heretic by an ecumenical council is so inconsistent with the claims of papal infallibility, that Roman historians have tried their utmost to dispute the fact, or to weaken its force by sophistical pleading.[21]

And so, with the third council of Constantinople, in AD 680, the controversy over Christ ended. The "orthodox" doctrine would be official from now on, two natures and two wills in one person; but not really a single person, but one person who is really three. After the crucifixion, after the primitive church, after the passing of the witnesses, it took five and one-half centuries of philosophy, speculation, strife, politics, and vehement rhetoric and arguments to arrive at this new definition of Christ and what he was—or wasn't.

As gleaned from the scriptural record available, one primary mission of Jesus was to reveal God to man. He even seemed to make that knowledge a necessary part of religion when he said, "And this is life eternal, that they might know thee, the only true God, and Jesus Christ, whom thou hast sent" (John 17:3). We have to suspect that in the original church that knowledge was available, as no evidence indicates controversy over God's nature. The long, involved disputes on this subject are entirely a product of later centuries. Whatever had been given on God's nature was apparently lost—or ignored—quite early.

After the loss of Christ and the apostles, the scattered Christian churches were thrown into immediate competition with paganism. There, the later Christians had a problem, or rather three problems, because they had three gods. To avoid criticism, the Christians leaned over backwards to avoid charges of polytheism—and fell over. They did have two gods; God the Father and the superior, and his also godlike son, Jesus. Rather than accept this simple and straightforward idea of a main god and a subordinate one, they created a new creature altogether to dodge the hated polytheistic opprobrium. The new god fashioned from philosophy and reasoning was so complex and mysterious that no one—including most of the philosophers themselves—could understand it; which then put them in another spot.

After all, the definers of a god's nature ought to be able to explain him. Since their definitions were so complex as to defy any rational explanation, however, they loudly proclaimed it a mystery and praised that sidestepping as a noble revelation. Such claims, however, are at strange variance with Jesus' unequivocal statement about the requirement of knowing God.

As we have seen, the man-made formulas pleased no one, as they were in every sense of the word, compromises; arrived at trying to please the most people rather than stating a flat truth whether or not it would please. And so a long line of special councils and a never ending stream of contention evolved to try to fight through the confusion to some halfway clear idea of the nature of God. For nearly six centuries and through eight major councils (and an almost infinite number of individual and group discussions) Christian priests fought, cursed, kicked, and fussed over the god of peace and love.

> The subject was one which none but men trained in dialectic subtleties could possible comprehend . . . yet the result was to set house against house and family against family, to fill cities with confusion and the whole empire with disorder, to arouse the most furious passions and to make men at enmity with one another on questions which not one in a thousand could understand.[22]

The next to last council, the one that would finally define this god, fared no better than all the rest.

> Chalcedon, called to heal wounds in the church and to settle theological differences, led to even greater division, disharmony, and misunderstanding. The council of Chalcedon was the beginning, not the termination, of the controversy over the meaning of the person of Christ. Even today, fifteen centuries after the council, theologians are still pondering the meaning of its dogmatic statement and are trying to find a more satisfactory way to express the relation between the divine and human in Christ.[23]

These rather endless arguments and fights over the nature of Christ do little for Christian pretensions and indicate the type of church Christianity had mushroomed into. The churches had ceased to be primarily concerned with practicing the morality and ethics of Jesus. Prelates were more concerned with how Jesus could be a god and still be Jesus the man, and how to reconcile those natures, than with morality. Doctrine was the end of Christianity.

The result was a man-made and politically fashioned creed that became doctrine by enforcement of civil authorities. Constantius had made all the Christian world Arian. Had his successors also been Arian, so would the world be today—rather than Athanasian. The "robber" council of the Emperor Theodosius II enforced one set of doctrinal ideas. Had political power then shifted and called the Chalcedonian council two years later, "orthodox" doctrine would wear a different face today.

Ironically enough, in light of these hundreds of years of esoteric and intellectualized arguments over the nature of God, most modern lay Christians ignore it all. The majority seem to accept the straightforward statement in Genesis (that man was created in God's image) and envision God as a person—rather than some amorphous heavenly conglomerate of personalities.

Notes

1. Hefele, "Histoire des concils . . . " Vol. II, Part 1, 232, in Barker,345.
2. Foakes-Jackson, 459–60.
3. Newman, Vol. I, 338, 340.
4. Schaff, Vol. III, 725.
5. Ibid., 722–23.
6. Newman, Vol. I, 342.
7. Clarke, 66–67.
8. Durant, *The Age of Faith*, 49.
9. Foakes-Jackson, 472.
10. Bardy, et al., in Barker, 377.
11. Schaff, Vol. III, 746.
12. Durant, op cit, 49.
13. Foakes-Jackson, 474.
14. Schaff, Vol. III, 764.
15. Boulenger, in Barker, 382–83.
16. Barker, 385.
17. Schaff, Vol. III, 771.
18. Jacquin, "Histoire de T'Eglise," Vol. II, 291, in Barker, 407.
19. Ibid., in Barker, 408.
20. Schaff, Vol. IV., 505.
21. Schaff, Vol. III, 352.
22. Foakes-Jackson, 297.
23. Wilken, 83.

CHAPTER 16

Popes, Priests, and Politics

In 1870 the Catholic hierarchy faced a serious problem. Two years before, Pope Pius IX had called a Vatican council. It was no surprise to anyone, since preparations had been going on for years. But rumor of a particular doctrine to be discussed rumbled ominously through the church. Many feared and expected that Pius, consolidating his previous moves in the direction, would declare himself—and all other popes past and future—infallible. It was an arrogant presumption, but it fit the personality of Pius, "one of the most arrogant of popes."[1] It was not to be easily rammed down the cardinals' throats, however. Pius assumed an infallibility that quite a few were unwilling to concede him.

The opposition's arguments were simple and direct. The historical record flatly contradicted what Pius was saying. Moreover, Pius and his supporters were relying on forgeries, falsehood, and fraud.[2] The opposition maintained that the doctrine was false, "never having been confessed by any of the great names in theology, in no century," and those who worked on the proclamation "have all, without exception, worked on retouched documents."[3]

Strong words indeed. Loyal Catholic cardinals and historians established that infallibility was, in short, a fraud. They were, of course, outvoted, and popes thereby became what they had never been before. The implications of that decision loom enormously large in Christian history. The Catholic Church officially decided, solemnly declared, and widely promulgated that tradition and reconstructed history are more important than, and to be preferred over, historical fact and truth.

Such adept stretching of the fabric of tradition to cover the reality of the past has always been part and form of Roman Catholicism. It is, perhaps, only natural, as justification of present practice must always be found in the past—even if that past must be invented. The doctrine of infallibility was simply the culmination of 1800 years of changes, additions, and revisions of the original church—by now lost and purposely forgotten in the dim past.

Today, Catholic theologians accept as an article of faith that Christ arranged for Peter to transfer his power to the bishops of Rome. These latter apparently judged it better not to exercise that power at first, but used it later to maintain the sacred deposit of faith and morals.

Historical truth is completely the opposite. As we shall see, the first bishops of Rome did not exercise such power because they simply didn't have it. It took centuries for Roman bishops to see they might become *popes,* and it took the intervention of politics, war, and civil power to decide the issue, not moral or heavenly authority. The papacy is a creation of man, formed little by little over hundreds of years by historical accident and evolution. In the beginning, there were only bishops, not *a* bishop, and all were equal.

The Beginning of Evolution

As we have seen, the original church consisted of *general* officers, apostles, with church-wide responsibilities, and *local* congregational officers, the bishops. The whole system was formed from the top downwards and not vice-versa. Before long, however, the apostles were eliminated and their office (including church-wide responsibility, revelation, and so forth) lost. Once they were gone, the individual branches of the church floundered about desperately without the leadership they had provided. Only over the course of the next several hundred years were the local officers elevated to positions of more generalized authority. But even then, none of them had church-wide responsibility. Their authority was still local. Simply put, in the absence of central authority represented by the apostles, a reorganization convulsed the church through the subsequent centuries as it was rearranged from the bottom up.

The bishops became ever more important as the only surviving and continuing authority left. Originally no one could claim the apostleship had been transferred to him, as the fraud would easily have been detected and challenged. The office of bishop, however, required none of the distinct qualities of apostleship and so could easily be transferred to any good (or bad for that matter) man in the local area. This then gave the leftover Christian churches continuity. That was the first step. The second thumped down as naturally. The bishop increased in stature to fill the vacuum of leadership—but still, in the beginning, as a local officer.

> The peculiarity in this Ignatian view is that the bishop appears in it as the head and centre of a *single congregation,* and not as equally the representatives of the whole church . . . and finally, that there are no distinctions of order among the bishops, no trace of a primacy; all are fully *coordinate* vicars of Christ. . . . The Ignatian episcopacy, in short, is congregational, not diocesan; a new and growing institution, not a settled policy of apostolic origin.[4]

It was only natural for this office to expand. Obviously, the bishops couldn't become apostles, so apostles became bishops.

Why the demand at all? Primarily because the battles for Christian dominance were so fierce, and heresies of all sort so rampant, that those trying to toe the "correct" line—what they thought to be the original gospel—were in need of something, some claim to authority to combat the "heresies." So, they attached their anchors, and their hopes, to the leftover offices of the original church, the bishops, deacons, and other offices of the priesthood. No matter that they distorted them and made them something alien to the original pattern; they needed that appeal to authority to refute heresies.

At first the motives for expanding the bishop's office may have been pure. Without the general officers of the church and their authority, the church had already disintegrated, just as predicted. Arguments, heresy, and apostasy seethed and bubbled in the remnant Christian churches like some evil stew. Those who remained became desperate—and in their desperation attached more and more authority and power to their bishops. This naturally led to eventual abuse.

> As the professional clergy arose, and the bishops became supervisory officers, their prestige increased. Their income was great and they came to be, in the common mind, a group with a social status similar to that of the nobility. The residences of the bishops became lavish mansions, in keeping with the social status they were enjoying. Soon the bishop's mansions were being referred to as palaces, just as the residences of kings and princes. The position became one that was sought

> after by many, not essentially as an opportunity for service, but because of the material wealth and position that accompanied it.[5]
>
> Origen complains that there are, especially in the larger cities, overseers of the people of God, who seek to outdo the pomp of heathen potentates, would surround themselves, like the emperors, with a bodyguard, and make themselves terrible and inaccessible to the poor.[6]

When John Chrysostom (born around 345) became bishop of Constantinople, he "scolded his clergy for their lazy and luxurious lives, and their suspicious use of women to minister to them in their rectories; he deposed thirteen of the bishops under his jurisdiction for licentiousness or simony."[7]

Was it any wonder, then, that men fought, schemed, plotted for, and even offered to buy, what at one time had been a humble office of service? Ambrose and many like him so distorted the calling that it comes as no surprise that so many would clamor for the privilege of "serving" as bishop.

> The honour and sublimity of bishops, brethren, is beyond all comparison. . . . If one should compare them to resplendent kings and diademed princes it would be far less worthy than if one compared the base metal lead to gleaming gold. . . . Ye should know, brethren, that we have mentioned all this to show that nothing can be found in this world more lofty than priests or more sublime than bishops.[8]

Pretty high comment indeed, for what was supposed to be a humble servant of God and the people. Christian bishops voluntarily and easily blinded themselves with their own arrogance and regal trappings, but the outside world of the pagans easily penetrated the sham and pinpointed its roots—power and money.

> These rivalries of the catholics, this struggle to obtain the supreme power in the church shocked the pagans and provoked criticisms of the kind echoed by Aminus Marcellinus: "In truth, when I consider the luxury that surrounds this dignity of Rome, I am not astonished that those who seek it, make the most violent efforts to obtain it. For, once they have obtained it, they live in the most extreme pleasure, with presents from the ladies heaped upon them, borne in pomp on chariots, dressed with magnificence, and served with such profusion, that their feasts surpass those of the tables of kings."[9]
>
> But the episcopal chair was solicited, especially in the great and opulent cities of the empire, as a temporal rather than as a spiritual dignity. The interested views, the selfish corruption, the open and even

> bloody violence which had formerly disgraced the freedom of election in the commonwealths of Greece and Rome, too often influenced the choice of the successors of the apostles. While one of the candidates boasted the honours of his family, a second allured his judges by the delicacies of a plentiful table, and a third, more guilty than his rivals, offered to share the plunder of the church among the accomplices of his sacrilegious hopes.[10]

The Rise of the Episcopacy

The rise of the episcopacy from their humble status as servants of a local congregation to rich and power hungry arrogance was a gradual process; "the episcopate reached its complete form only step by step."[11] At first the bishops were proposed by the apostles to a local congregation who could accept or reject. Although seldom actually rejecting anyone, local congregations did indeed have the right and authority to do so.[12]

Such suffrage was not to last. As the clergy gained more power, it was less inclined to submit itself to any kind of control by its congregations.

> The inclination shown here and there by certain bishops to nominate their successors was condemned by several councils, which insisted that the custom of consulting the wishes of the Church and of the bishops of the province should be maintained. In the East, however, it was not long before the rights of the people were curtailed.[13]
>
> With the exaltation of the clergy appeared the tendency to separate them from secular business, and even from social relations—from marriage, for example—and to represent them, even outwardly, as a caste independent of the people, and devoted exclusively to the service of the sanctuary.[14]

The clergy soon became a class apart, separate from the people they controlled. And as they did, their hunger for the attractions of worldly power grew also. In this atmosphere, naturally, ambitious men rose to the opportunity. Soon, also, some bishoprics became more important, powerful, and desirable, than others.

> Instead of a united Christianity, all under the direction of a universally recognized head, the church was characterized by disunity and disorganization. Alexandria, Caesarea, Antioch, Rome, Carthage, Smyrna, Ephesus and other centers were coming to the front as leaders of churches in the surrounding geographical areas. The strength of any one city as a Christian center, and the amount of influence it exerted

> over other churches were determined by the personality and forcefulness of the bishop. There was no accepted rule that made the office of bishop of any particular city preeminent.

As one bishop obtained jurisdiction over others, he came to be called a metropolitan. Later the pattern was enlarged and one metropolitan obtained jurisdiction over other metropolitans and became a patriarch. The patriarchs were the bishops of the chief centers of the empire. At first there were Alexandria, Antioch, and Carthage. Later came Rome, Constantinople, and Jerusalem (again). The bishop of Rome was the only patriarch in the West, a fact that would have enormous importance in the coming centuries as the other patriarchs were slowly eliminated. But, of course, the most important changes had already taken place. The bishops had either taken by force, or had been given, the total power over all church functions. Very gradually the people surrendered their power to the priests, and then to the bishop.

> Renan, looking at the gradual development of the hierarchy out of the primitive democracy, from his secular point of view, calls it "the most profound transformation" in history, and a triple abdication; first the club (the congregation) continuing its power to the bureau or the committee (the college of presbyters), then the bureau to its president (the bishop).[16]

And, of course, from all bishops to a few—and finally, one.

Who Is Number One?

This last step, one bishop grabbing all the authority, was a big one, requiring hundreds of years of maneuvering, politics, and war. For, even as some bishops were increasing their local and personal power, they all recognized that bishops were equal in authority. None had universal authority over the whole church. Nobody in the church during its first four to five centuries was disposed to consent that any one bishop had a right to govern all other bishops.

In the second century, for example, Polycarp, bishop of Smyrna, and Anicetus, bishop of Rome, disagreed on when to celebrate Easter, and each church did so on different dates. Around AD 150 Polycarp visited Anicetus, but neither could persuade the other to change his doctrine. Apparently they agreed to disagree on this very important point and parted as friends, neither having any authority to overrule the other.

Such was the nature of the early Christian churches, each on its own. They might readily try to convince fellow bishops of one thing or another but had no authority beyond that. Some tried but could not impose their wishes by any authority they could dredge up from the past.

Victor, who succeeded Anicetus as bishop of Rome, was not nearly as tolerant as his predecessor. In an imperious and arrogant tome he commanded the Eastern bishops to abandon their different time for celebrating Easter. In an imposingly authoritative letter describing their position as being more correct, the Eastern bishops politely, but quite clearly, told Victor where he might take his opinions.[17] There the matter stayed. Victor has no authority to do anything else other than write unenforceable edicts.

In the third century, Bishop Callistus of Rome ruled that any guilty of sexual offenses could be forgiven and readmitted to fellowship. Tertullian roundly denounced him for such laxity. This was particularly ironic as Tertullian was one of those who had done so much to exalt the prestige of the Roman bishop. By such extolling, however, Tertullian had not meant the Roman bishop to rule the church.

Cyprian, bishop of Carthage in the third century, did much the same thing. He was willing to concede to the Roman bishop a high degree of prestige as the only Western apostolic (that is, founded by an apostle) church. But he vigorously opposed any right of jurisdiction for that church, asserting forcefully the equality and independence of all bishops. In the third century Cyprian and the other African churches opposed the Roman bishop (Stephen) on rebaptism of heretics. Stephen attempted to force them into submission, but they simply refused to change their own doctrines. No one blamed them for it. Indeed, they were supported by other bishops.

Stephen's successor finally negotiated a compromise under which each party could retain its own opinion. But significantly, the African bishops saw no need to obey Rome, as Rome had no authority to impose or regulate doctrine.

> But in carrying out this principle, even in persistent opposition to the pope, in whom he saw the successor of Peter and the visible centre of unity, Cyprian plainly denied the supremacy of Roman jurisdiction and the existence of an infallible tribunal for the settlement of doctrinal controversies, and protested against identifying the church in general with the church in Rome.[18]

In his letters to Stephen, Cyprian referred to him as "brother" and "colleague," aware of his own independence. He accused Stephen of error and abuse of his power. Of these protests he never retracted a single word.

So, in spite of opposing the Roman bishop and telling him off for meddling in his affairs, Cyprian was never reprimanded, considered a heretic, or in any way condemned. Why not? Because he was not opposing the head of the church, but simply disagreeing with a colleague. When some tried the same thing much later, after the Roman church had become the powerhouse of the world, the results were vastly different.

Perhaps the most telling evidence of the lack of any overall authority of the Roman church lies in the first and most important ecumenical council—that of Nicea. If there had been a church head, he would naturally have presided over that supremely important (in one church's view) meeting of bishops and church leaders. The Roman Catholic Church recognizes this and tries desperately to build a case for the primacy of Rome, feeling that such an event couldn't even have taken place without the instigation or cooperation of the Roman bishop. This, however, is restructuring history after the fact, and in the long run to no avail.

Constantine alone was the promoter of this transcendental event. The bishop of Rome was not consulted, did not preside (indeed, did not even attend), was not asked to confirm its rulings, and did not publish them to the world. The church of Rome played no part of any consequence at Nicea. The council was dominated by imperial power, and the decisions reached were based on the thinking of the Eastern churches. The Latin churches sent only a few bishops, and this first assembly of all churches decided on Catholic faith without the presence, voice, or influence of the bishop of Rome.

As a matter of fact, one of the decisions reached at Nicea was an attempt to set up a governing body within the church. The participants recognized that none existed.

The rather impertinent position of refusing to listen to the bishop of Rome continued through at least the sixth century. In 424, for example, a council of African bishops meeting in Carthage wrote Pope Celestinus a very firm letter repudiating Roman claims to the right of regulating officers of their churches. They plainly and simply urged him not to renew such claims again and sarcastically asked if the Holy Spirit illuminated only a single person and denied inspiration for all the large body of bishops.[19]

So, it is rather clear that Rome was opposed continually in its grab for power in the church—for the simple reason that no existing bishop recognized any such authority for anyone, let alone Rome. In the first centuries none of the other churches ever conceded any such authority;

quite the contrary, they continually fought against it. The whole history of the great disputes that ravaged Christianity during its first six centuries is clear proof of the lack of any universally recognized presiding authority to put the house in order.

The Fight for Supremacy

Clearly then, while many of the early church fathers did indeed honor Rome, they never conceded any authority to regulate doctrine or other churches; and in actual fact Rome did not rule during the first four to five hundred years of Christian history. Rome was an important Christian church, but only one of many; others claimed, and exercised, equal authority. Rome would become the leader of Christianity eventually by default.

Modern-day Catholic claims to a supremacy that never existed in the early church are based on wishful thinking, outright invention in some cases, and judicious rearrangement of history. That claim states that Christ "entrusted the government of the one Holy Catholic and Apostolic Church (outside of which there is no salvation) to one man alone or the earth, namely to Peter, the chief of the apostles, and to Peter's successor, the Roman pontiff."[20] For that claim (that is, that the Roman pontiffs were Peter's successors) there is not the slightest historical evidence. It is based on nothing more than admitted tradition which the church often esteems far beyond historical truth.[21]

The origins of the Christian community in Rome are murky and obscure and have been muddled even further by the strenuous efforts of Catholic historians to place Peter in Rome and make him a bishop there. What does the record show? The list of uninterrupted bishops supposedly succeeding Peter is pure guesswork. The Catholic Church admits that the names of the first bishops, the dates they held office, and even the order of sequence are confused and uncertain.[22] There was indeed a Christian community in Rome that dates from apostolic times. Who founded it is not known.

> The tradition that Peter came to Rome and was martyred under Nero has been challenged, but even non-Roman Catholic scholars incline to the conviction that it is dependable. It is highly unlikely, however, that he was the founder of the Roman Christian community.[23]
>
> Furthermore, the earliest fathers, with a true sense of the distinction between the apostolic and episcopal offices, do not reckon Peter among the bishops of Rome at all.[24]

As a matter of fact, there is no evidence that anyone ever claimed Peter was a bishop of Rome during the first three Christian centuries. Quite the contrary, in fact. The earliest such statement is not found until the year 354, when it appears in the Liberian catalog.[25] Interestingly enough, the nearer one goes back to Peter's time, the weaker is the evidence for the Roman claims, until finally, in the first century there is no worthwhile evidence at all.

Even Catholic scholars now publicly question any such claims. A recent study, "Peter in the New Testament," a collaboration by Catholic and Protestant scholars, concludes that yes, Peter was a prominent apostle, but by no means is there any evidence he was what today's church calls the "pope."

As a matter of fact, today's pope is a product of evolution and addition. There was no such office in the early church. "The term *papa,* 'father,' which became in English *pope,* was applied in the first three centuries to any Christian bishop."[26]

> The first attestation that one finds at Rome of its [the term pope's] application to the bishop of Rome, is in an inscription of the time of pope Marcellinus (died 304). . . . Previously no bishop of Rome is called *papa* although we have several letters addressed to bishops of Rome.[27]
>
> This title was not appropriated to the exclusive use of the holy see till the eleventh century.[28]

Now we can piece together the clues that indeed tell an interesting story. Again, there simply is no evidence in the first centuries that anyone tried to claim Peter as bishop of Rome, or that Roman bishops, the supposed direct successors of Peter, were rulers of the church. Even Catholic historians frankly admit that Jesus gave equal authority to all the apostles so that whatever power Peter had was shared with them.[29] They also admit that such titles as pope were shared by other bishops—Rome had no exclusive claim. At any rate, it was merely an honorary appellation they shared, not a title that automatically categorized someone as the predominating authority in the church. By the beginning of the fifth century, the papacy was still waiting to be born.

By the sixth century, however, efforts grew to reserve for the Roman bishop the previously shared title. By the eleventh century those efforts succeeded.

The pattern, then, is clear. Rome, in fact, was never the head of the early church. As the other main branches of Christendom declined, however, Rome increased her power and prestige until she did indeed control the church. This came about through political growth, ambition, and raw power. During the process, history was rearranged and invented so that a valid line of authority for the one "true" church would exist back to Peter as the first in a long line of Roman bishops holding power over all the churches. Such a line did not exist. It had to be invented.

Notes

1. Newman, 461.
2. Boulenger, Histoire generale de l'Eglise," Vol. IX, 431, in Barker, 624.
3. *Loc cit.*
4. Schaff, Vol. II, 148.
5. Lyon, 235.
6. Schaff, Vol. II, 134.
7. Durant, *The Age of Faith*, 63.
8. Gregory VII's letter to the Bishop of Metz, in Bettenson, 107.
9. Jacquin, "Histoire de l'Eglise," Vol. I, 399, in Barker, 317.
10. Gibbon, chapter 20.
11. Schaff, Vol. II, 144.
12. Funk, Vol. I, 56; Schaff, Vol. II, 129.
13. Funk 175.
14. Schaff, vol II, 128.
15. Lyon, 119.
16. Schaff, Vol II, 123.
17. Ibid., 216.
18. Ibid., 174.
19. Guignebert, 233.
20. *The Papal Bull against Elizabeth*, in Bettenson, 240.
21. Funk, Vol. I, 27–28.
22. Duchesne, Vol. I, 44–48.
23. Latourette, Vol. I, 95.
24. Schaff, Vol, II, 165.
25. Bainton, 40.
26. Durant, Caesar and Christ, 617.
27. Funk, "Lehrbuch der Kirchengeschichte, Vol. III, 749, in Barker, 637.
28. The Catholic encyclopedia, Vol. III, 749.
29. Funk, Vol. I, 59–61.

CHAPTER 17

The Rise of Rome

Rome, then, was not head of the church during the first six centuries. It did, however, become so during the subsequent centuries. This transition is one of the more interesting ones in history, and as we shall now see, a very natural one given the conditions of the time. It was the last step in an evolution that began with independent bishops and ended with one bishop consolidating all power. How did Rome accomplish this daring scramble to the top?

First of all, Rome was *important,* the only apostolic church in the West. That isolation not only increased its independence but also saved it from the non-Christian conquerors that poured over the eastern half of the kingdom. In addition, Rome's location, an important political city in the West, was supremely significant. The aura of the city would inevitably rub off on, and be associated with, the church, particularly during the times that Rome lacked a temporal ruler (as when the emperors made their capital in Constantinople). At such times, the Roman bishop could, and did, assume many temporal responsibilities and authority. So by geography alone, Rome had an early edge. In addition, she could claim two prominent apostles. Her neutral location made her a natural arbitrator for the warring factions in the East, where most of the action was taking place. The marbles, then, were slowly but surely accumulating in Rome's pocket.

Still, during the first centuries, it made little difference. Christian churches may have listened to Rome out of respect, but they then went on their own merry way. Leo, bishop of Rome from AD 440–61, was really the first to show signs of dominating the church. At one time he pressured the Emperor Valentinian III into issuing a decree stating that nothing could be done ecclesiastically without the consent of the Roman bishop.[1] As might be expected, the other strong bishops and the patriarchs ignored the decree. The beginning, however, had been made, and with it, the restructuring of history. As we shall see below, Valentinian's edict carried several outright inventions that apparently were beginning to be taken seriously by those pushing the Roman cause.

> Therefore, inasmuch as the pre-eminence of the Apostolic See is assured by the merit of St. Peter, the first of the bishops, by the leading position of the city of Rome and also by the authority of the holy synod, let not presumption strive to attempt anything contrary to the authority of that See. For the peace of the churches will only then be everywhere preserved when the whole body acknowledge its ruler. Hitherto this has been observed without violation; but Hilary, Bishop of Aries . . . has with contumacious presumption ventured upon certain unlawful proceedings. . . . By such presumptuous acts confidence in the Empire, and respect for our rule is destroyed . . . we decree, by a perpetual edict, that nothing shall be attempted by the Gallican bishops, or by those of any other province . . . without the authority of the venerable pope of the Eternal City. But whatsoever the authority of the Apostolic See has enacted, or shall enact, let that be held as law for all.[2]

Two things stand out here. First, the claim that Peter was a bishop; he wasn't. And second, that all churches had acknowledged Rome as their ruler; they had not. Wishful thinking of the parts of Leo and Valentinian, however, was becoming written history. The unremitting zeal of Roman bishops for acquiring temporal as well as spiritual power would eventually make supremacy a reality. Two decisive factors would give essential handholds to the top of the wall—forged claims to power and the rise of the Moslems.

Forgeries and Fallacies —Helping History Along

We have already mentioned how Constantine supposedly left temporal and religious power in the hands of the Roman pontiff. No trace of this story can be found before the eighth century, at which time it was invented. It came about as part of a larger forgery, the Pseudo-Isodorian Decretals, which appeared about the middle of the ninth century. The decretals were a mixture of forged documents intermingled with genuine canons and decretals. The whole set forth the following claims:

- The spiritual power of the Roman pope is superior to any power of emperors and princes.
- Bishops are subject to the pope.
- No general church action can take place without the approval of the pope.

These decretals were easily the most powerful support the papacy had for its claims to power. They have also been characterized as the boldest and most magnificent forgeries of history.[3]

Their falsity was proven by Lorenzo Valla in 1440; the Roman church accepted his conclusions as valid and admitted the fraud.[4] Why not? It was obvious, and by then it didn't matter, as the purpose of the forgery—establishment of papal supremacy—had been firmly nailed down.

Surely one must pause for a moment in the shadows cast by this ominous event. Must the church established by the New Testament Jesus use fraudulent papers and decrees from emperors to prove its supremacy over all other churches? In this case, do any means justify the ends? Does the supremacy thus established carry the moral and spiritual approbation of the Carpenter from Nazareth? Individuals may well be forgiven if they judge that such methods smack more of the base power of human manipulations than of heavenly principles.

The Rise of the Moslems—Survival as a Means to Power

At first glance, the rise of a major militant and competing religious power might seem inimical to all Christian interests. Indeed, it was for most Christians as they were suddenly overrun by the new Moslem surge from the deserts. For Rome, however, it proved to be an unqualified boon.

In the seventh century there existed five patriarchates, Alexandria, Antioch, Jerusalem, Constantinople, and Rome—all fighting for supremacy. Only Rome was in the Christian dominated West (where even the barbarians eventually became Christians). In 632 the Moslems took Palestine; in 638, Syria; in 640, Persia; and by 699 all of North Africa. These regions contained the strength and great bulk of the church. Only two Christian strongholds then remained, Constantinople and Rome, both competing for the leadership of the Christian movement. Constantinople, however, faced its powerful Moslem neighbors across the narrow Straits of Bosphorus. Moreover, Constantinople had lost its power base, since much of its influence was in the newly conquered territories.

Extreme rivalry then developed between these two bishops. Finally, they parted company after excommunicating each other, and Constantinople and the Greek Orthodox Church would ever after remain the weaker of the two. Rome had done its work well in six centuries, patiently building up her power in the West; when the chance came, she was ready. As the only powerful patriarchate left, she could move to take over most of what was left of Christianity. The maneuverings for all this had started much earlier, of course, but with competition out of the way, the road was finally open.

The Triumph of Rome

As we will recall, Leo the Great had started the ball rolling for papal supremacy and in collusion with Valentinian had made some far reaching claims for the papacy. Many of the claims were simply not true; but even falsehoods, if repeated often, can eventually become "fact."

The next "great" power was Gregory "the Great" (who became pope in 590). As with Leo, so with Gregory. Their fame is in no way correlated with towering spiritual stature, but rather with their political advancement of the papacy. Gregory faced some troubles in Rome (both the state and the church were in deplorable conditions) and asked the Emperor Maurice at Constantinople for help. Maurice was indifferent to his pleas. When help was not forthcoming, Gregory simply took things into his own hands. He assumed both ecclesiastical and political power in the West—even to the extent of conducting political negotiations with all of Western Europe. "During his pontificate he really established the Papal Kingdom, ruling as temporal governor at Rome, appointing generals and magistrates."[5]

Gregory also made one of the early attempts to root out some of the corruption that plagued the church throughout its history. He demanded that selection and ordination to church offices be carried out by established custom rather than by influence or bribery—both of which were now rampant in the church.

The reader may also recall that it was Gregory who eagerly saw to the spread of Roman Christianity as far as possible—including sending the famous missionary Augustine to England. In his zeal to build up the church, i.e., Rome, he instructed his missionaries to adapt the church to local customs and beliefs. That ploy, of course, enabled the church to extend her influence over vast numbers of pagans who might not want to accept Christianity as it was, and who wished to maintain at least some of their old beliefs. Adapting the gospel to the people was easier than the reverse.

In the century that followed Gregory, the papacy's power continued to grow. During this time, however, the popes faced continual problems with the Roman nobility. In the eighth century Pope Zacharias began the process that would protect the papacy from the ambitious Lombards, who had designs on the Roman pontiff's power. The key to the extrication lay in France. Pepin of France had his own designs on the Frankish throne and asked for Zacharias's blessing in taking it by force. Zacharias, who needed Frankish support against the Lombards, concurred, and his successor, Stephen II was able to crown Pepin king in 754.

Pepin was succeeded by Charlemagne, his son. Again, the Lombards moved against papal territory and the pope called on Charlemagne for help. The king thundered to the rescue and by conquering the Lombards added their territory (north and middle Italy) to his kingdom. Like his father, he also donated territory to the pope, who was now a very important real estate tycoon; in fact, the pope had become a temporal ruler in all respects.

Equally important, however, was the new combination: Charlemagne's realm and papal power molded into a Holy Roman Empire. In AD 800 (after a great deal of political maneuvering to keep himself in office) Pope Leo III crowned Charlemagne as emperor of that kingdom.[6] He had no authority to do so. He simply assumed it in a political vacuum and thus provided the papacy with its greatest weapon yet for advancing in power.

The "church" embraced Charlemagne with open arms. The occasion bore an uncanny relationship to an equally warm and incestuous reception for Constantine centuries earlier. In both cases the ideals and morals of Christ were severely twisted, tortured, compromised, and finally buried altogether. The church, seeking in both cases power and position, was willing to overlook any of the methods or the morals of its protector to get it. This new marriage with Charlemagne gave Rome legitimacy as the leader of the Christian church—something it was not about to pass up for any quibbling over morality and standards.

Alliance also gave it vast temporal power and in its grasp for that, the papacy was heedless of any associated moral or spiritual defects. If the kind of man Charlemagne was is any proof, the church of "Christ" had become content to make a deal with anyone who would advance its claim.

Here are some of the character traits of the man that church enrolled among its blessed (in 1165) for his support and leadership.

Charlemagne had four successive wives and five mistresses or concubines. This harem bore him eighteen children—eight of them legitimate.[7] "He was a man of unexampled ferocity, quick-tempered and sometimes treacherous . . . what he liked most of all was carousing with his numerous wives and mistresses, hunting, and waging war. As a war-leader, he was absolutely ruthless to the chosen enemy and nearly as ruthless toward his own people."[8]

For example, from 772 to 804 Charlemagne mounted eighteen campaigns against the Saxons on his eastern frontier. On one occasion he gave the conquered Saxons a simple choice—baptism into the Christian faith or death—and had 4500 of them beheaded in one day for making the wrong choice. The "defender of the faith" (a title awarded him by a subservient and grateful church) then calmly proceeded to Thionville to celebrate the birth of the Saviour.[9]

Let's make no mistake about Charlemagne. He was probably no worse than other rulers in his time, but that isn't saying much. He was everything opposite of Christ. That the church would choose as the price of power to marry itself to such a protector (and to praise him as an example of Heaven's anointed) is testimony to what the church had become. She happily submitted herself to her hero. During Charlemagne's reign, the empire ruled the church. He chose and deposed bishops at a whim. He made them vassals of the state and even considered the pope himself as such. This man of few morals ruled the church of "Christ" with a firm hand—a price the papacy was willing to pay.

Charlemagne's empire lasted for almost a century. At his death in 843, however, it was divided among his three grandsons, and from there splintered off into a number of little states. The breakup left Europe without a central political leader. The papacy, left on its own, sank into the depths of degradation.[10] From about 867 to 962 the papacy became simply and plainly the personal (and often immoral and political) tool and plaything of some powerful Italian families who used it as casually as any other weapon for personal advancement. They bought, sold, traded, and acted as pimp for its officers. It was a time of degradation and servitude for the supposed "vicar of Christ."[11]

During the tenth century, twenty-five men assailed, held briefly, and lost the papal throne. For the papacy the period was one of intrigue and corruption. The church itself had little control over who would set at its head—the papacy was the private fiefdom of avaricious and ambitious power brokers.[12] Finally, in 1059 Pope Nicholas invented the College of Cardinals in an attempt to regain control. Eventually, the plan would bring a little more control of the church into the hands of the churchmen. As we shall see, however, that did little to stop the corruption of the church and its leaders. It merely transferred the reins of power from one group to another.

Indeed, for the next seven centuries the papacy was degraded to a degree that is almost impossible to believe. If we didn't have valid historical records, we might easily conclude the accusations against the papacy originated from the perverted imaginations of its vilest enemies. The records, however, are clear. E. R. Chamberlain's "The Bad Popes" is but the most recent listing of papal ignominies and rascalities.

The Zenith of Papal Power

During this time, of course, the power of the popes advanced. To be sure, there were ebbs and flows, but in general the tides of papal power were straining to flood the known world of the time. Throughout the period, papal claims to absolute political and religious authority became even more frequent and aggressive. They claimed the right to authorize and interfere in the internal affairs of nations, rulers, and the lowliest subjects.

It became such that if, in the view of the popes, certain rulers weren't quite as obedient as the Vatican thought they should be, the popes encouraged and legalized rebellions and civil wars against them as heretics. The popes strained to find justification for this usurpation and arrogantly proclaimed their power over all and sundry, civil, religious, economic, and in any other way they deemed fit. Pope Gregory VIII, for example, during his fight with Henry IV of England, somewhat desperately wrote the following in 1081.

> Who can doubt but that the priests of Christ are to be considered the fathers and masters of kings and princes and of all the faithful? Is it not clearly pitiful madness for a son to attempt to subject to himself his father, a pupil his master?[3]

In their anxiety to gain control over everyone, the popes had a valuable and potent weapon and were not at all loath to use it. The sacraments, necessary for salvation, could be easily withheld.

> The pope had the power of excommunication and placing cities, provinces, or kingdoms under interdict. Excommunications were directed against individuals. The lesser excommunication deprived a person of the sacraments; the greater cut him off from all rights. If a king, his subjects were released from their oath of allegiance. Mass could not be celebrated in the presence of the excommunicate. Anyone who provided him with food or shelter incurred the penalties of the Church. Christian burial was denied him. The interdict was directed against a city, province or kingdom. The total interdict forbade public worship, the administration of the sacraments, and Christian burial. The churches were closed; no bell could be rung; no marriage celebrated; no burial ceremony performed. The sacraments of baptism and extreme unction alone could be administered.[14]

Here was a new twist to the gospel. Deny the blessings of "Christianity" to the people because the Vatican decided the ruler wasn't up to standard! A ruler might ignore any injunction against his own soul, but even kings trembled before this power withheld from the ignorant and superstitious masses. Using such methods in the eleventh century, Pope Gregory VII forced a German emperor to hurry to his side to humiliate himself. In the thirteenth century Pope Innocent III forced a French king to terms. In like fashion he forced John of England to his knees to beg forgiveness—and made him surrender England and Ireland to the pope. The pope then graciously returned them as a papal feudatory for which the English kings were to pay rent. That galling situation cost the church dearly when the same tactics failed later. When Henry VIII became king, the church no longer had its bullying power and Henry took the "rent" back for himself.

The Bull of Pope Paul III (1534) against Henry VIII for his sins railed as follows:

> That King Henry, his accomplices, etc. . . . together with the aforesaid descendants, be therefore void of civil rights and be not admitted to testimony, be unable to leave or make wills, codicils, or other dispositions, even among the living; and shall be incapable of succeeding to anything by will or from intestacy, and also incapable as regards jurisdiction, or the power of judging, the office of notary and all legal acts whatsoever (so that their processes or instruments and other acts whatsoever shall have no strength or validity); and none shall be held bound of right to make answer to the said Henry and the said other persons, in the matter of any debt or any matter, whether civil or criminal. . . . King

> Henry has incurred the penalty of deprivation of his kingdom and that they have been sundered forever from all faithful Christians and their goods. And if meanwhile he depart from this life we decree and declare, with the authority and fullness of power aforesaid, that he ought to be deprived of Church burial and we smite them with the sword of anathema, malediction, and eternal damnation.[15]

The ostensible crime was marrying another wife, a light request indeed in view of the immoralities of the church itself and of the many kings the church approved of doing much worse. But the real sin was refusing to knuckle under to the church's heavy hand of authority. The church of "Christ" had become vindictive and petty, and when it couldn't get its way, lashed out like a spoiled child in wild vengeance. By that time, however, it was all whistling in the dark on the part of the pope, as he no longer had the power to enforce such draconian decrees. Henry ignored him.

The popes reached their zenith of power during the thirteenth century; while their strength gradually declined during hundreds of years, they ruled with naked power and apparent lack of regard for humanity in the furtherance of their political aims—even embracing bloodshed and horror. Almost without hesitation popes would authorize a crusade against kings who dared to defy them. "To maintain the Italian interests of the papacy, men slaughtered each other in holy wars all over Europe."[16]

With supreme power in their firm grasp, the papacy launched and carried out two of the most incredibly anti-Christian acts to ever blot the name of Christ—the Crusades and the Inquisition, which we will study further in chapter 20. Suffice it to say now that this last arrogant abuse of authority carried with it its own seeds of destruction.

> It [the inquisition] co-operated with other influences in bringing the papacy into disrepute and effecting the papal captivity and schism; in causing the revolt of Germany against the papacy (under Louis the Bavarian, 1324 onward), of England (Wycliffite movement, 1360 onward); and finally, in bringing about the Protestant Revolution of the sixteenth century. The Christian consciousness was outraged by the Inquisition, and was sure to have its revenge.[17]

Unfortunately, popes abused their power in other ways as well. Pope Innocent IV (1243–54), for example, insisted that the clergy's duty was to obey the pope even if he should command anything wrong. He also decreed general ignorance for clergymen as well as laity. Bishops needed to know only the Apostles Creed—other clergymen needed to know no more than the common people.[18] Other popes encouraged and enforced ignorance for the masses—forbidding reading of the Bible itself. In 1864 Pius IX continued that policy in a syllabus *condemning* the errors of modern society, which included such "evils" as separation of church and state, freedom of worship, the neutrality of the state in religion, and "the right for all to manifest openly, and publicly all his thoughts and all his opinions."[19]

The popes and other leaders of the church fared no better than anyone else in handling absolute power. The humility and thoughtful consideration of Christ in his relationships with humanity, long forgotten in this new church, were replaced with the ordinary abuses of the tryanny of power.

Notes

1. The Edict of Valentinian III, in Bettenson, 22–23.
2. *Loc cit.*
3. Qualben, 149.
4. Funk, Vol. I, 288.
5. Case, 204–14.
6. Durant, *The Age of Faith*, 468.
7. Ibid., 471.
8. Payne, 219.
9. Durant, *The Age of Faith*, 462.
10. Lortz, 183.
11. Boulenger, "Histoire abregee de l'Eglise,109, in Barker, 579.
12. McSorley, 264–65.
13. Gregory VIFs letter to the Bishop of Metz, in Bettenson, 106.
14. Qualben, 183.
15. Bull of Paul III, dated 30 Aug. 1535, in Bettenson, 229.
16. Lea, A History of the Inquisition, Vol. Ill, 189–90.
17. Newman, Vol. I, 468–69.
18. Ibid., 517.
19. Boulenger, "Historia de la Iglesia," 807, in Barker, 509.

CHAPTER 18

And with Power . . . Corruption

In AD 400 the chronicler Ammianus related his surprise that the bishop of Rome "lived like a prince in the Lateran Palace and moved through the city like an emperor."[1] Popes had become emperors, in fact, and some took no pains to hide it. Giovanni Villani relates the story of a pope who would appear in the streets wearing a double crown, with heralds marching before him with uplifted swords crying, "I am Caesar! I am Emperor!"[2]

In name, of course, he was neither, but many of the popes had the equivalent power. Just like anyone else who abused such power, they often wallowed in the human corruption and degradation power so often brings.

The stories about papal corruption might be easily dismissed as biased attacks on humble servants of God, or if admitting any incidents at all, only as isolated aberrations. Neither is true. The pattern of moral corruption in a long series of popes, the "Vicars of Christ," is well documented and shows such a consistent and recurring pattern that this book cannot examine such corruption in full detail, but we will look at the overall record, an unenviable one to be sure. Over a period of hundreds of years, popes and cardinals lied, cheated, robbed (from each other as well as the rich and the poor); hungered insatiably for power, riches, and worldly glory; fought wars with the money, blood, and bodies of their subjects for their own aggrandizement; mocked and ignored the laws of sexual morality; murdered, tortured, and became gluttons.

Was there then no good at all? Of course, as there is in all humanity. But the times were not the best, and the church, rather than establishing standards, adapted to those of others, and the consistent pattern was negative. As historian Barbara Tuchman has mentioned, there simply was not much good to be found in the clergy of that time.[3] Examples? They abound.

Pope Sergius III (AD 905) was "malignant, unclean, ferocious." At his election the opposing faction had elected their own pope and Sergius was driven out of the city. Over the next twelve months, four more popes climbed on the chair, clung there precariously and briefly, and died violently. After seven years of exile, Sergius returned, backed by a private army that slaughtered his enemies—including the reigning pope. Sergius took as his mistress the infamous Marozia, daughter of Theodora. She bore him a bastard son who later became pope himself.

After the death of Sergius, Theodora (who rose to power during his reign) took direct control of the city and the papacy. Two of her nominees for pope were elected, served briefly, and died. Then she rather openly and cynically had her own lover, Bishop John of Ravenna, elected as pope. In the confused state of affairs that followed over the years, Theodora's daughter Marozia eventually gained power over the city and had Pope John killed.[5]

Pope John XII, coming along shortly after all this, was a dissolute sartyr whose "virtues" we have already summarized in the opening paragraph of chapter 1.

Also in the tenth century, an obscure priest named Boniface Franco murdered the reigning pope in order to gain that seat for himself. Forced to flee, he later returned and murdered another reigning pope and resumed his seat as Boniface VII.

Benedict IX (1032) squandered the wealth of the papacy on brothel upkeep, riotous living, banquets, and armies; rape and murder became commonplace under his rule and direction. Wanting to marry, he finally debased the papacy as low as it could get by selling it to the highest bidder—Giovanni Gratiano, for fifteen hundred pounds of gold in 1045.[6]

Benedict Gaetani, Boniface VIII (1249), openly accused the Holy Ghost of deceit in electing his predecessor Celestine to the throne. Boniface had Celestine imprisoned and Celestine died there shortly thereafter.

Boniface was also ruthless in his insatiable hunger for absolute power and shamelessly "plunged straight into the shabbiest of papal crimes, simony and nepotism," and didn't hesitate to use the weapons of the church in his private wars. On one occasion he desired Florence as part of his personal kingdom. He conspired with dissidents within the city and when the plots were discovered and his agents fined, he reacted viciously, eventually reducing the city with a papal army.[8] He seemed insensitive to Christian values.

> Sexual morality? Why—there is no more to going to bed with women and boys than in rubbing one hand against the other. Immortality? A man has as much hope of survival after death as that roast fowl on the dining table there—a remark made on a fast day at that, the shocked witness recorded. It was difficult to assess his true beliefs, but his orbirter dicta seemed all of a piece: the clever remarks of a learned man who was indifferent to, or even skeptical of, the inner mysteries of the religion he professed, the god that the world saw him worship was the god of power.[9]

Pope Alexander VI (Rodrigo Borgia, 1492) was an out-and-out monster. He not only survived in the jungle warfare of church politics of the time, but thrived on it. His huge income from church offices was used to indulge freely in his debauched appetite for sexual pleasures and the most exaggerated trappings of wealth. He also openly acknowledged his illegitimate children and loaded them with the wealth wrung from the church. To satisfy his greed he freely sold offices and pardons of every description. He rather shamelessly bought the papacy by bribing the cardinals whose votes he needed and after being elected ran delightedly through the streets shouting, "I am Pope! I am Pope!"[11]

And so on and on. Many so called Vicars of Christ displayed all the moral refinements of the raging Huns. Only in relatively recent times have popes consistently become men of any moral character. Up until then the list of papal sins deadens the mind. E. R. Chamberlain, in his excellent book *The Bad Popes,* chronicled in devastating detail some six hundred years of papal infamy and evil. Any who read the book or any of countless others (including those of Catholic historians) that attest the same thing can only be struck with the singular fact that this consistent behavior pattern has nothing to do with Christ—it is the very antithesis of what Christ taught. Indeed, even a casual survey of papal history easily inclines one to the thought that these men were totally active for the other side!

Pope Innocent VIII was the first of the popes to acknowledge his illegitimate children—and loaded them with riches. During his reign, "offices and pardons of every description were freely and openly for sale."[10]

The papal seat, far from exemplifying the full flavor of gospel morality and goodness, instead became an ugly, fetid blotch on Christian history—a depressing example of all that Christ had spent his life preaching against.

Naturally, with this kind of corruption, priestly offices quickly became sought after for their power and rewards. Those holding jobs would sell other jobs to finance their own private vices. Those outside would spend fortunes to buy a church office that would yield even greater fortunes. When, in 1474, Pope Sixtus IV died (and the news was received with joy by a long suffering populace), the people condemned not so much his selling of benefices to the highest bidder and extorting money in other ways, but rather on how he rewarded the boys who serviced his unnatural lusts with rich bishoprics and archbishoprics.[12]

> The world has probably never seen a more defiant disregard of all law, human and divine, than that displayed by both the Church and the laity during the pontificates of Sixtus IV, and Innocent VII, and Alexander VI. Increase of culture and wealth seemed only to afford new attractions and enlarged opportunities for luxury and vice, and from the highest to the lowest there was indulgence of unbridled appetites.[13]
>
> Simony . . . was the corroding cancer of the Church throughout the whole of the Middle Ages—the source whence sprang almost all the evils with which she afflicted Christendom. From the highest to the lowest, from the pope to the humblest parish priest, the curse was universal. Those who had only the sacraments to sell made a trade of them. Those whose loftier position gave them command of benefices and preferment, of dispensations and of justice, had no shame in offering their wares in open market, and preferment thus obtained filled the Church with mercenary and rapacious men whose sole object was to swell their purses by extortion and to find enjoyment in ignoble vices.[14]

The condition of the Christian clergy in the thirteenth century was horrendous and depressing.

> Preaching is regarded as disgraceful. All preferment and all sacerdotal functions are sold, as well as every episcopal ministration, laying on of hands, confession, absolution, dispensation; and this is openly defended. . . . As no examination is made into the lives of aspirants

> to the priesthood, but only as to their ability to pay the stipulated price, the Church is filled with ignorant and immoral men. Few are able to read. They haunt the taverns and brothels, consuming time and substance in eating, drinking, and gambling; they quarrel, fight, and blaspheme, and hasten to the altar from the embraces of their concubines. Canons are no better; since, for the most part, they have bought exemption from episcopal jurisdiction, they commit all sorts of crimes and scandals with impunity. As for monks, they specially avoid all to which their vows oblige them—chastity, poverty, and obedience—and are licentious and undisciplined vagabonds. . . . As for the nuns, modesty forbids the description of the nunneries, which are mere brothels, so that to take the veil is equivalent to becoming a public prostitute. We might suspect this to be the exaggeration of a soured ascetic if it were not the unanimous testimony of all who describe the condition of the Church from the thirteenth century on.[15]

Oddly enough, the Catholic Church no longer makes any real effort to cover up all such sins. Somehow they can swallow them whole and still claim that the organization that spawned and encouraged such immorality truly represents Christ, that Christianity survived hale and hearty in their organization. That, after all is minor league chutzpah. In 1870 the church stood before the world to announce that all popes, even those moral misfits we have described, were made of such fine stuff doctrinally, that they were, and always had been, infallible. Caesar Borgia, for example, was a monster, but in bravely defending church dogma had done all that was necessary. Since the Nicean council the church has always been more concerned with dogma and its definition than in morality and ethics. In that respect, we're told, popes are incapable of making mistakes. Alas, even that weak reed is false, as we shall see.

Infallibility and the Redefinition of History— The Strange Contradictions in the See of Peter

In March of 896, Pope Stephen VII had the body of his predecessor (Formosus) drug from his tomb, dressed in sacerdotal robes, propped in a chair, and brought to "trial" for papal mistakes. His real crime? Having belonged to a rival faction that was still fighting Stephen's gang for the depraved office of the papacy). Stephen provided the corpse with defense lawyers, but they remained prudently silent while Stephen ranted, raved, and screamed insults at his dead peer. The convened synod obediently condemned Formosus as guilty in this travesty of a madman's trial; the hapless corpse was stripped, its three fingers of benediction were hacked off, and the body was thrown to a mob in the streets.[16]

A subsequent pope reinstated Formosus among the blessed and condemned Stephen. A few years later, Pope Sergius III overturned that judgment. The final result, apparently, was that the lunatic trial of Formosus was therefore correct after all.

Today the Catholic church clasps all her popes firmly to her bosom with the claim of infallibility—that is, they were simply incapable of making doctrinal mistakes, which in the case of Stephen and Formosus presents a moral conundrum worthy of the finest shady church politics. If Stephen was infallible, then Formosus must indeed have been a rascal and therefore dead wrong—especially dead. But then, what about the pope who reinstated Formosus among the blessed, and what of Sergius who found that judgment fallacious and Stephen right after all? All of which, since Formosus was also a pope, most certainly makes any claims for infallibility for this series of bumblers specious at least, and as full of holes as any broken ship at the bottom of the sea.

As we shall now see, the doctrine of infallibility, invented in the nineteenth century, followed the same development as many other church doctrines. It was a charade, conceived in arrogance by a pope who thought he could be the judge of what the world should believe. Ever since then the church has had to squirm under the weight of historical reality and has had considerable trouble covering up the facts that make the claim ludicrous. And that's just on the point of infallibility in doctrines, let alone personal worth in morality or any other troubling point.

The concept of infallibility originated, of course, far back before the actual date of adoption. The church, having lost most of its political power after the fourteenth century, still had plenty of clout left to keep a steady thumb on most of its people. By the fifteenth century, however, it was no longer enough. The world in general had suffered enough from church abuse and corruption, and the reformation was in full swing. Groups within the church also wanted reform. From the sixteenth to eighteenth centuries popes and councils bickered with each other to see which held the real power in the church. The popes, naturally, always maintained that they held full control. Various councils, however, ruled that *they* (the councils) had full power to make changes in the church and were the final authority.

It was in this context that Pope Pius IX finally brought matters to a head. He set the stage with his first broadside in 1854, a one-sided declaration of the immaculate conception of Mary. That theory had been opposed, and Pius simply decided about the doctrine on his own and pushed it through. After that he was ready for bigger game—and the other prelates knew it. When the Vatican Council of 1869 was announced, everybody knew infallibility would follow. Not disappointing them, Pius proceeded with his claim; the Roman pontiff, when speaking in discharge of his office as pastor, defining a doctrine regarding faith or morals, is infallible.[17]

The claim was extended to state that the pope had full plentitude of jurisdiction over the whole church. Pius was careful to state that only the Roman church was indefectible, and he built his office up to a powerful position. "His feet only shall be kissed by all princes; he may depose the emperors; he himself may be judged by no one; the Roman church has never erred, nor will it err in eternity."[18]

The decree aroused instant and fervid opposition in the council. Catholic historians have tried to pass off the story that the decree was almost instantly and universally accepted by clergy and public alike. It was not. Sharp opposition broke out within the Catholic ranks (and still continues today). Almost immediately the council was divided into two camps. A sizeable majority of 140 opposed the doctrine, arguing that it had foundation in neither history nor scripture.[18] As a matter of fact, some of the bishops proceeded to demonstrate the very "fallibility" of popes. The overall vote of the time, however, decided that the traditions of the church—their own construction of the past—were to be preferred over truth and history.[20]

And so, infallibility was adopted and the opposition steamrollered, excommunicated, or pressured into accepting or being eased out of the church. That's how popes became infallible—even retroactively, and even though many of them quite obviously had made serious mistakes and many had contradicted each other.

We must study this curious doctrine from two points of view. First, plainly and simply, was it true? No. There are well established and flat contradictions of the doctrine. Second, how can we admit that some of the immoral miscreants who became popes could in any way define—infallibly or any other way—moral doctrine for others, supposedly in the name of Christ? The thought is appalling.

Here, we have examined very briefly some of the moral tackiness of various popes. If one chooses to believe such men could have infallibly defined church dogmas, that point is theirs. The evidence suggests that immoral men and infallibility are incompatible, but beyond that we can't go. We can, and will, however, examine a few historical examples plainly demonstrating that popes weren't really infallible at all. Quite the contrary, in fact.

Fallible Infallibility

During the Arian-Athanasian controversy, Bishop Liberius of Rome had been banished (355) because he refused to subscribe to the Arian creed then enjoying success in the church. Surely then, this "stalwart example of principle" would be one the church would point to with pride. Not so; principles soon melted to the consistency of liquid Jell-O as banishment took its toll. Liberius, unable to bear the fruits of his principles, finally caved in, decided that Arianism wasn't so bad after all, and changed his mind.[21] By thus giving in to reigning politics—and accepting a doctrine today considered heretical—Liberius was restored as bishop of Rome. (As a matter of historical interest, his predecessor, Bishop Julius, had been Athanasian. Liberius became the opposite.)

His return, however, created further problems for infallibility, as there were then two bishops of Rome, Felix and Liberius. Felix didn't last long under the pressure and soon died. Not long after these particular events, Constantius died also, and within a short time Valentinian became emperor. Now was Liberius's chance to switch back, and he lost no time in once more changing sides. He again became Athanasian (his belief all the time anyway), thus rejecting his previous doctrine which had replaced the doctrine before it. Strange events indeed for somebody incapable of making a doctrinal mistake.

Bishop Vigilius of Rome also mired himself helplessly in similar fashion in the later fight over monophysitism. He managed, under pressure from different groups at different times, to compromise himself no less than four times, as he readily caviled to whatever political wind was blowing at the time.[22]

Thus, the endless controversies over the nature of God neatly sucked under these two candidates for infallibility. In the seventh century they swallowed one more. Bishop Honorius of Rome, making the mistake of backing the wrong party, had supported the belief in monothelitism (one will). For his foolishness, he was anathematized by the eventual winners of this particular doctrinal contest, at the third council of Constantinople in AD 680.[23] Until the eleventh century, Honorius was openly admitted as a heretic.

> The condemnation of the unfortunate Honorius was inserted in the confession which every newly elected pope had to sign down to the eleventh century, and which is embodied in *Liber Diurnus,* i.e., the official book of formulas of the Roman Church for the use of the papal curia.[24]

Only later, under the increasing demands for infallibility, did the church desperately try to explain away the facts—resulting in a great deal of squirming and wriggling. All to no avail. The fact remains that poor Honorius was plainly and openly condemned as a heretic by the church itself. Only under later pressure did it reverse that decision.

Some similar squirming resulted from a curious item called the *Filioque* controversy—yet another assault by the "nature of God" controversies on claims of infallibility. The *Filioque* clause was an addition to the Nicene Creed. No one really knows just when, how, or by whom the clause "and from the son" was added. The best guess for where is Spain, during the sixth or seventh century. From Spain it spread, and the Roman bishops at first opposed it. Pope Leo III (795–816) widely promulgated the original text that didn't include the *Filioque.* Politics reared its ugly head, however, and Charlemagne embraced the clause—not as a treasured truth from heaven—but as an excuse for aggression against Eastern "heretic" Christians who wouldn't accept it or Charlemagne's rule. That kind of pressure the popes understood, and they withdrew their objections to please the emperor. In 1014 the creed was solemnly accepted in a St. Peter's ceremony.[25]

What one Roman bishop could do, another could undo.

And so the long list of fallible men and doctrines continued. In the fourth century Bishop Innocent of Rome condemned Pelagianism, a raging controversy of the day. His successor, Zozimus, defended the same doctrine Innocent had condemned. The emperor, Honorius (no relation to Pope Honorius), supported the other party and quickly corrected Zozimus, who then changed his mind and decided that Pelagianism wasn't so great after all.[26] In 1278 Pope Nichola II approved the proposition of one faction of the warring Franciscans; that is, that Christ and his apostles had possessed no property and therefore the Franciscans shouldn't. Perhaps seeing the danger of renouncing property for the church, Pope John XXII pronounced Nicholas's proposition false; one pope overruling another.[27]

In the fourteenth and fifteenth centuries the church warred further against itself (and infallibility). The popes had finally lost their supremacy over the rulers of Europe and the question was, who was to rule the church: the pope, or the councils? This battle struck one of the severest blows of all against claims of infallibility. Benedict XII (1334–42), a French pope, constructed a papal palace in France, and church policies were controlled by the French kings.

After seventy years, the Italians, ever arrogant in their feelings that only Italian popes were fit to rule the church, revolted. In 1378 they elected their own pope. Thus, there were then two popes, one in France and one in Rome. That spectacle, of course, led, and leads, to some interesting questions for the papacy.

Finally, in 1409, a general council of the church assembled in Pisa to try and close the maw of this monster that threatened to swallow the church whole. The council deposed both current popes and elected another, supposedly the only authorized one. That only opened the mouth wider and made the teeth sharper. Both of the deposed popes refused to recognize the authority of the council or the new pope! Lo and behold, there were now three popes. Desperately, then, yet another council was called in 1414 to resolve this ludicrous bickering over power, this time with more luck. Two popes were deposed and one resigned. The depositions stuck this time, and in the new pope, Martin V, the church again had a single head but was left with a record more suited to the most bumbling banana republic O. Henry could have invented.

That did not end the long list of mistakes made by supposedly infallible men, but enough. The samples are proof of the pudding. Infallibility was an invention, a deliberate attempt to restructure history into what it had never been; an attempt that even some Catholic historians have openly admitted as a fraud.[28] The real surprise of the whole affair is not that a pope would have the gall to claim infallibility with this kind of record (that fits in rather well with the nature of the church and what it was throughout history). The amazement comes that so many have swallowed it all, surely one of the more artful, convincing jobs in history.

Curious, indeed, is this doctrine of infallibility. It took 1800 years for the church to discover and officially promulgate the doctrine that its leaders couldn't make mistakes; seemingly a long time to decide on such a transcendental event. The doctrine has no basis in history or scripture—the opposite, in fact, as we have seen—and the original founders of the church never dreamed of making such a claim.

Again, this all ties in. Once the original church was lost, the physical remains of that church began a reorganization from the bottom up, rather than what had gone before from the top down. The bishops grew in power, and one bishop began to dominate all the others. The final step in this march to glory was to declare that bishop as perfect and all powerful. Power had now been absolutely centralized into the hands of one man. Development could go no further.

Christ versus the Christians—Setting the Record Straight

We have now spent considerable time in studying the weaknesses of those men who proclaimed themselves as the vicars of Christ on earth. How does their record square with what was taught by the man from Nazareth? Not at all well. Compare what we have learned of popes and bishops, for example, with a few items from the book given them for a guide.

> This is a true saying, If a man desire the office of bishop, he desireth a good work. A bishop then must be blameless, the husband of one wife, vigilant, sober, of good behavior, given to hospitality, apt to teach; Not given to wine, no striker, not greedy of filthy lucre; but patient, not a brawler, not covetous; One that ruleth his own house, having his children in subjection with all gravity; (For if a man know not how to rule his own house, how shall he take care of the church of God?) (1 Timothy 3:1–5)
>
> And whosoever shall exalt himself shall be abased; and he that shall humble himself shall be exalted. (Matthew 23:12)
>
> Feed the flock of God which is among you, taking the oversight thereof, not by constraint, but willingly; not for filthy lucre, but of a ready mind; Neither as being lords over God's heritage, but being examples to the flock. (1 Peter 5:2–3)
>
> He that saith, I know him and keepeth not his commandments, is a liar. (1 John 2:4)
>
> Know ye not that the friendship of the world is enmity with God? (James 4:4)
>
> And whosoever would be chief among you let him be your servant. (Matthew 19:27)

Even without scriptural help, however, we can draw certain conclusions on our own. Clearly, the immorality, lust for power, and all too plain love of worldly things exhibited by many popes and other church leaders is the exact opposite of what Christ taught. The reader can readily see the problem. Can those representing the very antithesis of all the New Testament Christ taught be his representatives? And can the church boasting of such low quality leaders be the one representing Christ to the world?

Catholic apologists argue yes, and with reasons that seem more than a little doubtful to most. They reason that we can readily separate morality from the act of "guarding the faith." That is, a man can be a moral misfit but can still guard the dogma of the church with inspiration. The Catholic historian Mourett, for example, argued that in spite of being an evil man, Caesar Borgia was a faithful caretaker of the faith and that under his pontificate "the faith of the Roman church remained immaculate."[29]

Such arguments may well please philosophers, but the doublemindedness required for such distinctions is a heavy price to pay for accepting Roman claims of succession to all that Christ was. For most of us it will fall short. Everything that Christ taught argues exactly the opposite. Leaders must be examples in *all* things. They are required to be humble, moral, principled, more attached to the divine than the worldly, and in all things righteous. They are even required to have a family and rule it well in order to qualify to rule the church of God. Perhaps this is all best summed up by Christ himself when he explained that "ye shall know them by their fruits" (Matthew 7:16).

In James we find the ideal of religion as taught in the original church:

> But be ye doers of the word, and not hearers only, deceiving your own selves. . . . But whoso looketh into the perfect law of liberty, and continueth therein, he being not a forgetful hearer, but a doer of the work, this man shall be blessed in his deed. . . . Pure religion and undefiled before God and the Father is this, to visit the fatherless and widows in their afflictions, and to keep himself unspotted from the world. (1:22, 25, 27)

In view of what Christ and his followers taught and the realities of much of Christian history, the anamolous position of the "Christian" church is difficult to reconcile with Jesus. History offers cold comfort to the inheritors of the papacy, as the record clearly denotes the office as an invention of the times having little to do with Jesus Christ. The first bishops of Rome made no effort to control the church nor could they have. Only with time and political developments did Rome realize she could become the leader of all, and then popes bent their efforts to that purpose. The ensuing power built gradually. It was perhaps neither good nor evil, simply a power group like any other at the time. Its sin, if any, is in representing itself as a direct link with heaven. Its effect on the office holder was simply a reflection of the power politics, personal corruption, cruelty, and capaciousness of all leaders of the times.

The mistake, then, is to ascribe direct heavenly connections and approval for the organization thus generated. From the appearance of history, the church became just another political kingdom, and popes were temporal princes—a quite human organization and one unrelated to the goals Christ left for his followers. The popes, then, behaved not much differently than any other rulers of the day.

One *might* accept a single exception to the moral principles established by the New Testament. However, repetitive moral dissolution by church leaders can only make us pause and wonder.

It is senseless to argue that such corruptions were rare aberrations, isolated vignettes that displayed occasional venal weaknesses of a few individuals. The corruptions were consistent, in fact common, all through the ages. This consistent and continuing pattern is one of the fundamental evidences of the loss of the original church. It is difficult—if not impossible—to reconcile this very *active* involvement in earthly riches, power, and immorality with the pattern laid down by the New Testament Jesus. Something doesn't mesh. Either Christ and his message were not what they seemed, or the message was changed.

Many have tried to prove the former; using the obvious and abundant evidence of corruption, bloodshed, chicanery, and rascality at all levels on the part of priests and bishops. Those individuals say, in effect, "If this is of Christ, then even the original is distorted legend," since those moral principles expressed in the New Testament are the very opposite of those practiced by church leadership through the ages. The churches themselves, of course, don't like to mention these things at all and come up with various rationalizations, including not even accepting the historical facts at all and preferring church tradition.

There is, however, a more logical—and historically valid—explanation of Christian anomalies. That is, the idea expressed in this book that the original church did not survive at all. That which we know as "Christianity" today is not what Christ established, but a human directed agency—and thus, naturally, displaying human traits; in each time frame, consequently, "Christianity" reflected the prevailing morality.

Neither those who wish to expose Christianity as a sham nor the

Christian churches themselves are eager to accept such ideas—each for very pressing reasons. The evidence for it, however, is abundant, as we have seen. The primary evidence lies in the lives of Christian officials and what they have represented.

Notes

1. Durant, *The Age of Faith*, 51.
2. Payne, 382.
3. *Atlantic Magazine*, December, 1975.
4. Chamberlin, 31.
5. Ibid., 43.
6. Ibid., 76.
7. Ibid., 98.
8. Ibid., 105.
9. Ibid., 113.
10. Ibid., 169–70
11. Ibid., 172.
12. Lea, *A History of the Inquisition*, Vol. III, 639.
13. Ibid., 209.
14. Ibid., 624.
15. Ibid., 630–31.
16. Chamberlin, 30.
17. Bettenson, 273.
18. Qualben, 160.
19. Boulenger, "Histoire de Feglise" Vol IX, in Barker, 623.
20. Wilken, 11.
21. Shotwell and Loomis, 557, 583.
22. Schaff, Vol. III, 771.
23. Jacquin, "Histoire de l'Eglise," Vol. II, in Barker, 407.
24. Schaff, Vol, IV. 505.
25. Zaehner, 95.
26. Durant, *The Age of Faith*, 69–70.
27. Ibid., 794.
28. Barker, 623.
29. Mourett, "Histoire generale de l'Eglise," Vol. V, in Barker, 694.

CHAPTER 19

"By Their Fruits Ye Shall Know Them"

The Abuses of Christianity

"The problem with Christianity," a Lutheran acquaintance once told me, "is that after any study at all of its history you can conclude only that either Christ was an imposter or else the Christianity of history has nothing to do at all with Christ and what he taught."

Such sentiments are not unusual for anyone who has taken a serious look at three special events in the background of descendant Christian churches: the Inquisition, the Crusades, and the sundry collection of abuses called the Dark Ages. In its wake as it evolved through the ages, Christianity left behind a cluttered and unsavory trail.

Many, seeking desperately for some key to explain away this glaring inconsistency between what Christianity is and what it should be, have used the curious and deeply unsatisfying argument (Paul Johnson's *History of Christianity* is one of the most recent) that without Christianity the Dark Ages would have been much worse. As we have seen, however, this may have been only a pseudo-Christianity at best, a human accretion of philosophy only faintly related to the original. If genuine Christianity had really survived, the Dark Ages might not have been what they were at all.

The reverse of the old argument is probably true; the Dark Ages were so bad *because* of Christianity, which greatly contributed to its abuses. The

"Christianity" that reigned in that dreary bit of history deliberately cultivated ignorance, suffocating all attempts at educating the masses, fought tenaciously against freedom of thought, and disallowed any questioning of dogma. That ruthless suppression was backed up with naked force. The tools of enforcement were often torture and bloodshed.

> The Albigenslan heresy was quenched in blood; Wyclif's followers were suppressed; John Huss was burned and a holy war declared against his followers; even the attempts to reform the church by the general councils had failed . . . the doctors of Paris had tried to force the adoption of reforms in these general councils, but "The popes succeeded in ridding themselves of the councils, in remaining masters of the church, and in bringing about no reforms."[1]

The bloody, agonizing, and incredibly cruel Inquisition was the final stage of this debased Christianity. Christianity was also the driving force—the direct cause really—of the equally bloody and cruel Crusades, against Christian "heretics" as well as unbelievers.

The church also introduced the charade of indulgences—buying off God's punishment by those with sufficient cash to do so—and thus creating an open atmosphere of cheating, immorality, and cynicism. Within her orders, the church reaped the harvest of all this, as rampant immorality stained the whole body of the church.

It is not that "without Christianity the Dark Ages could have been worse." They could not have been much worse than they actually were had the bloodiest savages ruled. Things were so bad precisely because of the contributions of what was then labeled Christianity. "The world has probably never seen a society more vile than that of Europe in the fourteenth and fifteenth centuries."[2]

> Christianity was practically a failure. Mankind had scarce grown better under the New Law. Vices and passions were as unchecked as they had been before the coming of the Redeemer. The Church itself was worldly and carnal; in place of elevating man it had been dragged down to his level; it had proved false to its trust and was the exemplar of evil rather than the pattern of good.[3]

The Values of Ignorance

I suppose we needn't say too much about the unsavory aspect of ignorance officially promulgated by the church in the Dark Ages—other than to describe it briefly. That the church actively supported all efforts to suppress inquiry, learning, and knowledge speaks succinctly for what it had become.

The typical picture we may have of the middle ages is that of a humble monk huddled over his writing table dutifully copying out precious bits and facts; preserving precious knowledge; somehow carrying civilization through the chaotic middle ages. Some of that may be true, but the opposite is more likely the general rule. The church forbade reading, writing, investigation, and knowledge, and most monks participated very little in learning processes. Others invested huge amounts of time in endless dogmatic quarrels and a subtle splitting of theological hairs. One feels, as historian Henry Lea expresses it, more pity for these rather than awe.

> The other tendency was the insane thirst which inflamed the minds of the schoolmen for determining and defining, with absolute precision, every detail of the universe and of the invisible world. . . . The inquirer who disturbs the dust now happily covering the records of these forgotten wrangles can only feel regret that such wonderful intellectual acuteness and energy should have been so woefully wasted when, if rightly applied, it might have advanced by so many centuries the progress of humanity.[4]

However, this kind of fussing was about the only thing the church permitted. All the defining and speculation, however, was built on a shaky scaffolding of pure conjecture, a very few facts, and large doses of tradition and "approved" tests. The church frowned on *learning* (she didn't mind arguing over minute details) and on any book that didn't uphold her point of view.

Translation of the scriptures into the vernacular was forbidden. In spite of that, parts were translated and books were written and circulated. Once the Inquisition geared up to full production, such books and their authors were prime targets; inquisitors were directly empowered to seize and burn all such writing.[5]

Of course, it wasn't long before the printing art burst upon the world, and that fortuitous technology was the beginning of the end for the church-preferred rigorous mind control for all—adherents or not. Freedom of choice was simply not a part of the medieval church's makeup. In 1515 Pope Leo X issued a bull with a feeble swipe at praise for the values of printing. The good pope then recited a list of complaints about printers actually printing and selling books translated from all sorts of foreign languages as well as Latin and the vernacular. Since these contained many "errors of faith" and "libels on persons of dignity," they were not to be tolerated.

> Therefore forever thereafter no one should be allowed to bring any book or writing without a previous examination, to be testified by manual subscription, by the papal vicar and master of the sacred palace in Rome, and in other cities and dioceses by the Inquisition, and the bishop or an expert appointed by him. For neglect of this the punishment was excommunication, the loss of the edition, which was to be burned, a fine of a hundred ducats to the fabric of St. Peters, and suspension from business for a year. Persistent contumacy was further threatened with such penalty as should serve as a warning deterrent to others.[6]

The warning came too late. People did indeed continue to defy any such fetters and the church grew desperate, even perhaps a bit hysterical. Soon, people began paying for their search for knowledge with their lives, as succeeding popes lashed out wildly in their attempts to control the masses.

> In accord with Pope Paul IV . . . Philip II ordered, September 7, 1558, that all those who would buy, sell, or read prohibited books, such as the Holy books in the vulgar tongue, should be condemned to be burned alive.[7]

As contrasted to the original church, the new church felt that she must kill any who would read, or wanted to read, the scriptures.

The Council of Trent (1545), obstensibly called to reform the abuses of the church, failed. Interestingly enough, however, they didn't feel any need to correct this particular part of the church. They actually reaffirmed the church goals of ignorance for the people and prescribed very rigid regulations "forbidding the reading of the scriptures by the people."[8]

But it was all too late. Freedom and the human spirit had blossomed, and not all the might of the church could crush the millions of fragile and struggling flowers popping up all over her kingdom—but she certainly tried, and not with the gentle compassion Christ taught.

One Catholic apologist argues that "had there been no medieval church there might well have been no Renaissance, and the history of modern Europe would have been a very different affair."[9]

That might well be true, but not in the way its author intended it. The church created the Renaissance by its corruption and suppression. The movement was a direct response to the efforts of the church to keep all thoughts and freedom under rigid control.

> There is little doubt that if the church had corrected itself in time, it would have avoided the Reformation. This interior and voluntary reform of the church, that some of its most illustrious doctors (Saint Bernard, Gerson) had demanded, was constantly postponed or refused by short-sighted popes, concerned more with temporal than spiritual affairs.[10]

The Renaissance emphasized individual initiative, creative thinking, original research, and freedom of the human soul. The church had taken a stand against them all. The celebrated case of Galileo was symptomatic. Galileo simply stated the truth as he discovered it through research and observation. The church clung desperately to her version of the "truth," (which, as all now know, was actually false). Her attitude was that the tradition of the past was sufficient and there was no need to observe or explore any further. That was official policy, supposedly divinely installed through this one and only true church, which refused to admit she could be wrong. The answer? Ruthlessly suppress Galileo and his ilk for seeking answers on their own rather than accept tradition.

Catholic apologists think of various arguments to avoid charges of anti-knowledge, but they only dig the hole deeper. One states that the church "was actuated as usual primarily by a desire to safeguard revealed truth."[11] That puts the church in an awkward position. If she was "acting to safeguard revealed truth," where was the truth—which was false—revealed from?

Such was church policy, however, and it wasn't restricted to ancient times. In 1948 the official organ of the Jesuits, *La Clvilta Catholica,* stated:

> The Roman Catholic Church, convinced through its divine prerogatives, of being the only true church must demand the right of freedom for herself alone. . . . As to other religions . . . she will require that by legitimate means they shall not be allowed to propagate false doctrines. Consequently, in a state where the majority of the people are Catholic, the Church will require that legal existence be denied to error [as defined by the Catholic Church]. . . . In some countries, Catholics will be obliged to ask full religious freedom for all, resigned at being forced to cohabitate where they alone should rightfully be allowed to live.[12]

The church has always been intolerant and judged herself as the only one capable of defining what is acceptable to believe. In the sixteenth century Ignatius of Loyola wrote his "Rules for Thinking in the Church," a list of do's and don'ts for his new order, the Jesuits. The long list of restrictions is very interesting and enlightening, and offers clues to the church's attitude and how she wanted people to think. One in particular sheds great light.

> That we may be altogether of the same mind and in conformity with the church itself, if she shall have defined anything to be black which to our eyes appears to be white, we ought in like manner to pronounce it to be black.[13]

Interestingly, the Roman church seems never to have lost that desire for absolute thought control, only the raw power to enforce it. In 1952 Cardinal Segura of Seville, Spain, protested even rudimentary freedoms for Protestant groups in Franco's Spain. A chorus of horrified U.S. Roman Catholic leaders broke forth in objection, arguing that such views were anachronistic and not part of the church today. Rome set them and the record straight, and the Vatican backed the Spaniard's interpretations as correct.[14] That simply corroborated the fact that Roman Catholicism tolerates freedom of religion only because it has to. Given a choice, Catholicism would suppress all religions.

U. S. Catholic leaders continued their protests, arguing that in their country, such goings on would simply never be tolerated. That is probably true (and not due to the church, but the country) but is simply no answer to the *official* stand of intolerance espoused by the Catholic Church. Many religions have been intolerant in their formative years, but this particular religion has never relinquished the idea.

Indulgences—Heaven on the Installment Plan

We have now seen that popes eagerly pounced on any idea at all that would reinforce their power and extend their jurisdiction. One of the greatest of these tools, enabling them to manipulate huge masses of people and money to carry out their ambitious plans, was the theory of indulgences.

Early on in the evolution of the leftover Christian churches appeared the doctrine of confessing sins to a priest. This created some discomfort for all parties because of the obvious problem—how could man forgive sins that supposedly only heaven had authority to forgive? In the fourth century a new theory evolved to answer the problem simply stated that the priest could not indeed forgive all sins, because God held personally in his control certain punishments to inflict on the sinner after his death. Augustine then proposed the doctrine that there was special place reserved for the punishment God meted out, called purgatory. Gregory the Great extended and greatly developed the idea into a caveat. By the tenth century it was fixed doctrine.[15] The church elaborated on the ferocity and horror of purgatorial punishment, so much so that people trembled at the thoughts of dying and entering purgatory to pay off their load of accumulated sin.

So, all parties were faced with unhappy dilemmas. The people were bound for unimaginable suffering in purgatory, and the church, which had created the horrible place, was now stuck with it; they couldn't get sinners out, thereby losing an important public relations battle. In today's terms, it was a no-win situation for all parties. All the church would preach was hellfire and damnation, offering nothing positive except some vague holdout of happiness on the other side after ages of suffering.

The reward was nebulous, while the punishment had been described in vivid and excruciating detail. The negative was the forte of the medieval church.

But let it not be said that the church was helpless in such a contretemps. If doctrine were lacking, invention and imagination could supply the needed items.

A new theory evolved to answer the problems created by the first two solutions. This is how it worked. The good deeds of Christ, Mary, and the other saints, the church explained, far outnumbered their evil ones. Indeed, so much so that there were plenty left over after those worthy had graduated from—or simply passed rapidly through—purgatory. In other words, a good, average, hardworking saint generated so many good deeds that he or she need use only a small portion of them to boot himself or herself out of hell.

What happened to all those leftover good deeds? What indeed? You and I could be forgiven for thinking that those individual performances would be valid only for the individual who performed them. Not so, said the church. Those excess "sin payments" went into a special bank, termed the "Treasury of Merit"; a sort of Interheaven Monetary Fund for sinners. Deposits could be loaned or bought. Like all banks and funds, there must be a banker or a loan officer, and this one was no exception.

By now it will come as no surprise to discover that the banker was the pope. The end result was a storehouse of other people's good deeds that one man could arbitrarily transfer to someone else—regardless of the new person's worthiness. With that, the pope gained access to an unprecedented bonanza and tool for control of nations and people. When granting a loan from the Treasury of Merit—an indulgence—the pope, or his agents, exacted a price. To escape the rigors of a horrible hell (which the original gospel knew nothing about) people would do almost anything. Even, if necessary, accept a loan of somebody else's good deed. But it wasn't free.

Two popes granted indulgences in the ninth century, and from then on business boomed and the trade-offs began. Some of the items used were simply silly or sacrilegious, such as the remission of sins for trotting around Rome's basilicas as mentioned in chapter 12.[16]

> All Christians, of both sexes who duly confessed and having had communion, will visit the same day or on several days the basilicas of St. John Lateran, of Saint Peter of the Vatican, of Saint Paul on the Ostian Way, of Saint Mary Maggiore on the Esquiline and will recite three Paters, Aves, glorias, plus another Pater, Ave, Gloria "*a nos intentions,*" to which he will add a credo in each basilica, we grant mercifully in the name of the Lord, a plenary indulgence from all punishment which their sins have merited.[17]

Happy thought. Run around the churches, mumble some words, and presto—receive instant forgiveness. No need for all the fuss of genuine repentance and forsaking of sins that Christ had taught.

Other indulgences were infinitely more dangerous and degrading. Need some heretics burned out? Grant indulgences to those who will do the dirty work of murdering their fellow man. For forgiveness of purgatory (not to mention the chance of looting) an army could easily be found to kill and plunder those who would oppose the church. The Crusaders, of course, were only an extension of that. Rape, murder, thievery, or excess of any kind was allowed on a Crusade, since the participants were being forgiven for everything.

But, if such a tool could be used for suppression or growth in power, could it also be used to enrich the church more directly? It could indeed. What more logical step than to sell the loans directly as well as using them for an indirect form of control? A practice of doing just that soon developed. For a certain fee a person could buy a share of the treasury and thus be assured of passing up the pleasures of purgatory.

Pope Clement was perhaps the most blatant at it, using the money to help pay for the construction of the church of St. Peter at Rome. He empowered agents to travel the kingdom and gather in money for this purpose. This particular scandal would be the final one in a long list that would fully ignite the Reformation—an event personified by Martin Luther.

One of the pope's agents for peddling indulgences was a Dominican named John Tetzel. Undoubtedly Tetzel greatly abused his office and exceeded his authority. The point remains, however, that he was still empowered directly by the pope to sell forgiveness of sins (with other folk's good deeds) for money. His enthusiasm for the task carried him far beyond even that grotesque parody.

The people of the town of Wittenberg—a singularly important town only because of Luther—were hearing rumors that the forgiveness business was much better where Tetzel was operating. Better indeed. Through Tetzel, one could buy forgiveness of sins not even committed yet, and no confession need be made after the committing of sins (which left the future an open door for whatever earthly pleasures one might seek).

Interestingly, indulgences had been sold for years in Wittenburg with no protest from Luther. Only these very obvious and extreme perversions drove him to rebellion. And rebel he did, with far reaching effects we will study shortly.

Like so many other doctrines of the evolved churches, indulgences and the Treasury of Merit were pure inventions of later times, unknown in the original gospel, the scriptures, or the church of the early fathers, and in addition completely contrary to any doctrine that can be found in the Bible. They were artificial practices invented to satisfy the avarice of the church and had nothing to do with character growth through service, dedication, or positive living habits that the original gospel had taught. They lessened personal responsibility; salvation no longer rested on individual worth but on what somebody else had done.

The vilest sinner, the murderer, the criminal, and the immoral, could purchase easy access to heaven at the last moment of life. Crusaders and heretic hunters could indulge in virtually any sin or outrage against their fellow man with the blessed assurance of forgiveness. The whole emphasis of religion came to be not service, a good life, and other positive acts, but rather how to avoid punishment for sins. Negative values replaced the positive ones.

Catholic apologists have been saddled rather heavily with the indulgence issue. Modern writers try to dodge a little by saying that indulgences didn't really pardon the sin (a function of heaven), but only freed the sinner from the penalty. That rather meaningless sophistry meant even less to the sinner of the day than it might to us.

> The popular mind did not stop to make the fine distinction between guilt and punishment, and, if it had, it would have been quite satisfied to be made free from the sufferings entailed by sin. If by a papal indulgence a soul in purgatory could be immediately released and given access to heavenly felicity, the question of guilt was of no concern.[18]

The indulgences of the middle ages were an unmitigated evil that convinced participants they could buy their way to heaven on the coat-tails of those who had managed to live by more positive values. Indulgences encouraged corruption and well deserved ridicule for the church that promulgated them. The worst evil of all, however, was not personal, but the tryanny indulgences exercised over those who would dare to disagree with the church. This tyranny took three forms: crusades against heretics, crusades against infidels, and the Inquisition. It is important to remember that all of these bloody campaigns were deliberately instigated and encouraged by a church that supposedly guarded the values Christ had entrusted to the world.

Notes

1. Malet, "Histoire de France," Vol. I, 289, in Barker, 692.
2. Lea, A History of the Inquisition, Vol, III, 642.
3. Ibid., 16.
4. Ibid., 551.
5. Ibid., 612–13.
6. Ibid., 614.
7. Mourett, "Historie generale de TEglise," Vol. V, 513, in Barker, 613.
8. Mosheim, Part I, chapter 1, 25.
9. Zaehner, 165.
10. Malet, "Histoire de France," Vol. I, 289, in Barker, 692.
11. Zaehner, 165.
12. *Time Magazine*, June 28, 1948, 70.
13. Bettenson, 260.
14. *Time Magazine*, Aug. 3, 1953, 41.
15. Durant, *The Age of Faith*, 523.
16. Payne, 382.
17. L'Anne Sainte, brochure, in Barker, 555.
18. Schaff, Vol. V, part 2, 757–58.

CHAPTER 20

Crushing the Infidels—The Crusades

From about the fifth century on, pilgrims to the holy city of Jerusalem acquired a special status—making that trip was the surest way to wipe out the worst of sins. Again, not through any real positive values, but purely by the physical act of visiting a certain city. In the tenth century that road to virtue abruptly ended as Palestine fell to Moslem conquerors.

The church didn't like it, and, as a matter of practical politics, wanted this handy tool back. The pope, then, became a warlord, one of the most powerful of all Europe. Pope Urban II initiated the first Crusade with an open invitation to the dregs of Europe to kill for Christ.

> You, oppressors of orphans and widows; you murderers and violators of churches; you robbers of the property of others; you, who like vultures are drawn to the scent of the battlefield, hasten, as you love your soul, under your Captain Christ, to the rescue of Jerusalem. All who are guilty of such sins as exclude you from the Kingdom of God, ransom yourselves at this price, for such is the will of God.[1]
>
> They granted plenary indulgences to all who would go. This involved forgiveness of past sins and the forgiveness in advance, of any sins they might commit while engaged in crusading, with the assurance of freedom from purgatorial pain. The prisons of Europe were thrown open and the worst criminals were encouraged to join the crusading hosts on the same generous condition.[2]

Six hundred thousand eager volunteers applied for this happy prospect. They received an open invitation for killing, looting, raping, and whatever else they cared to try, and had the assurance of the pope himself that they were not sinning. Anything went. Some, of course, may have been motivated by genuine piety, but even the best of morals broke down under the conditions of the Crusades.

> It was a motley and disorganized host. Freed by their plenary indulgence from all moral obligations and compelled to support themselves to a great extent on the population through which they moved, they carried devastation everywhere.[3]

(Reasoning that Urban had dispatched them to slaughter infidels, they quickly included Jews in their charge and dispatched them wherever they could find them. At Cologne, 10,000 died where they had taken refuge in the archbishop's palace.)

Restrained by moral forces at home, the sin-liberated crusaders degenerated into mobs. "For a while no woman was safe; peasants who in feudal France and Germany had been compelled by priest and lord to lead the most moral lives, now indulged in an orgy of rape."[4]

The survivors of the first crusade finally conquered Jerusalem in 1099—and promptly and mercilessly massacred the inhabitants, including women and children. That massacre has long been reckoned among the greatest crimes in history.[5] Estimates vary, but it seems clear that the crusaders for Christ killed at least 40,000 people, the great majority of which were unarmed civilians.[6]

The sins of the first crusade were multiplied by the subsequent eight during three long centuries of atrocities and bloodshed.

> A similar point of view is also expressed by Professor Arnold Toynbee . . . when he lumps together the crusades with the Spanish Inquisition, the English slave trade, the plantation in the American South, and the genocide of Jews by Nazis, as all belonging to the "catalogue of Western atrocities."[7]
>
> It is notorious fact that the Crusades were responsible for an immense amount of bloodshed, and the appalling massacre of the people of Jerusalem is enough to discredit the Crusades as "holy wars" forever.[8]

Some subsequent justifications offered for this squalid blotch on humanity (enrichment from mixing cultures, genuine piety, and faith in some of the crusaders) fail to mitigate the example of "Christianity." Reduced to bare essentials, the stark reality is that the supposed representative of Christ deliberately set loose an unrestrainable rabble to conquer Jerusalem at whatever cost to humanity—and the costs were dear indeed.

When a fanatical twelve-year-old raised an army of children to invade Jerusalem, Pope Innocent III, rather than try to end such an inevitable tragedy—and travesty—announced that "the very children put us to shame"[9] and encouraged it. Thirty thousand children marched forth under the blessing of the pope to suffer and die of hunger and thirst, drown, and to be sold into slavery. Twenty thousand more, setting forth from Germany, suffered much the same fate.

The end result of the Crusades was to decimate Europe's population and to concentrate the wealth and power of Europe "in the hands of the church and the heads of state."[10]

Crushing the Heretics—The Other Crusades

The power of indulgences had been harnessed and used to control the power of Europe and send hundreds of thousands to chase a dream (or more worldly pleasures) at the beck of a pope. Such power could also be used for even more basic purposes—to ruthlessly stamp out any who dared disagree with the power and right of the Roman church at home, and many did not care to play the power games of Rome and did indeed disagree. These began to compare the Roman power, wealth, and corruption to New Testament ideals. They rightly concluded that something was rather rotten indeed, and bravely tried to do something about it. This early reform movement, then, actually began long before Martin Luther appeared on the scene. Luther was only the first to succeed. The movements of the eleventh century were unsuccessful. They were suppressed by raw force, as the popes offered the same indulgences to any who would stamp out heretics at home as those that undertook crusades abroad.

> The Church of Rome defended by violence the empire which she had acquired by fraud; a system of peace and benevolence was soon disgraced by proscriptions, wars, massacres, and the institution of the holy office. And as the reformers were animated by the love of civil as well as of religious freedom, the catholic princes connected their own interest with that of the clergy, and enforced by fires and the sword the terrors of spiritual censures. In the Netherlands alone more than one hundred thousand of the subjects of Charles V are said to have suffered by the hand of the executioner.[11]

Popes and priests wanted no competition of any kind. From the eleventh century on, there were official crusades against the Waldenses, Albigenses, Hussites, and Cathars. These are strange names to most of us, as compared to Lutherans and Calvinists, but their lack of fame is easily explained. They failed, crushed by a ruthless and vindictive church. Thousands suffered and died as the church, with supreme wisdom and "truth," decided that as heretics their lives were of no value. The crusades "were accompanied by the indiscriminate massacre of the helpless populations in the regions involved."[12]

In 1028, for example, a group known as Cathars had developed and grown extremely strong. "They were a quiet, friendly people, dedicated to purity, teaching that there was only one God. . . . They regarded God, not the pope, as head of the church. It was observed that these people possessed an enviable serenity and gaiety."[13] Common people and nobility alike were taken with the simplicity of the Cathar faith. Obviously, such a threatening group had to be removed. "The church was in danger."[14]

> Pope Innocent III pronounced against the heretics, saying they were worse than the Saracens. On March 10, 1208, Innocent III had already delivered sentence of death on the heretics. He called upon the northern nobility to crush the south, offering both indulgences and land to the crusaders in the army dedicated to the destruction and final obliteration of the heresy.[15]

The crusaders' first fruits blossomed in Beziers, where the leader of the crusade, Simon de Montfort, demanded the city hand over its 222 known Cathars. The city refused and the crusaders massacred the entire population—20,000 men, women, and children.[16]

> For thirty-five terrible years the crusaders brought fire and sword to the south of France. The treachery of the crusaders was as remarkable as their cruelty. In the summer of 1210 the citizens of Minerve offered to surrender on the condition that their lives were spared; the instrument of surrender was drawn up and solemnly signed; and de Montfort's troops went on to butcher some hundreds of heretics who had thought that the promise of the crusaders would be kept, while the pope's legate looked on.[17]

The Albigenses of southern France were crushed with cruelty and bloodshed in the same fashion; the Waldenses the same. In the fourteenth century John Wyclif of England preached boldly against the abusive powers of monks and denounced the corruption of the church. In spite of persecution he survived to die a natural death, but the church's petulant and pitiful vengeance extended beyond the grave. Wyclif's bones were later exhumed and burned.

Wyclif's ideas survived, however, and were spread in Europe by John Huss. Huss was not as fortunate as his mentor. A church council in 1415 found him guilty of heresy, and he was burned to death for his beliefs, but it was to no avail, as the beliefs survived and spread. The Hussites, however, like all other dissenters, were mercilessly persecuted and killed by the church for daring to believe differently.

One is particularly disturbed to realize that these "heretical" groups were not wild-eyed fanatics calling for blood, fire, and revolution. Their movements were usually simple, calling for a return to New Testament standards of humility, faith, and moral rectitude, particularly among the clergy. They did not insist on overthrow, simply a reform movement to purity—and most often simply to be let alone. They were indeed a dagger at the throat of the rich and powerful princes of the church. These latter correctly saw that such preaching was a direct danger; they were intolerant of any criticism of the church, which "heretics" and their kind represented. Rather than allow the new movements peace and freedom to live their conscience, the church decided they must be annihilated.

The pattern was repeated wherever the church held power. No one was allowed to disagree with officially defined dogma, policies, or politics. Those who dared, risked their lives. The church was ruthless in suppression and defined as heretics any who disagreed with her. With that simple device she removed all rights to enjoy property, freedom, or even life itself for her opponents. That rather ugly and ominous power gave rise to the equally ugly atrocities of history.

The Purging of the Heretics—Free Will and the Church

The descendant church did not become intolerant only in the eleventh and twelfth centuries, of course. She had acquired that attribute early. As soon as Constantine made Christianity legal, the then warring churches lost no time in eagerly persecuting the pagans. By the fourth century the use of force and coercion by the church was finding a happy and permanent niche. Augustine concluded "that the church, being the spiritual father of all, should have a parent's right to chastise an unruly son for his own good."[18] "Augustine never failed to defend the laws of coercion and to point out their happy influence."[19]

In that century the church promulgated the theory that "errors in religion, when maintained and adhered to after proper admonition, were punishable with civil penalties, and corporeal tortures."[20]

In the thirteenth century, Thomas Aquinas, justifying the evils of the unjustifiable—the Inquisition—argued that those who opposed the "true" church "deserve not only to be separated from the Church by excommunication, but also to be shut off from the world by death."[21] His reasoning was that if forgers or other criminals could be put to death, then how much more so heretics.

The Inquisition

The church did not like dissent. We have already traced the early evolution of using force to suppress it. Eventually this evolution led to one of the ugliest blotches of all against the church—indeed against all mankind—the Inquisition. The church instituted an integrated program for forcing men to believe—or at least to publicly confess a belief—in church doctrine. To assure that end, torture and killing were condoned and even encouraged.

The Inquisition got its start at the Council of Verona (1184) when bishops were empowered for a witch hunt and directed to root out heretics in their districts and have them punished by secular power (nothing wrong with using the state to carry out church judgments!). The powers and the methods of the Inquisition grew steadily worse.

By 1229, Pope Gregory IX made heresy a capital offense. He furthermore insisted that all heads of state must aid the church in seeking out heretics and inflicting punishment on them. All the kings of Europe promptly fell into line and agreed to make heresy punishable by death. One's imagination staggers a bit at the contrast between the gentle humility of Jesus and his early church and this new church that asks the state to murder those who disagrees with it.

Within a few years, however, Gregory found that the bishops were a little soft—not applying extreme measures nearly severely enough. In 1233 he organized a papal inquisition and put the task of hunting down heretics in the hands of professional head hunters, the Dominicans, who could now work altogether independently of the bishops.

> The abuses compounded. Obstinate heretics were condemned to the stake; those that recanted were to be imprisoned for life; those that relapsed were to be executed; the property of heretics was to be con-

> fiscated; houses of heretics and their friends were to be destroyed and never rebuilt; the lands of civil rulers who should neglect to purge them of heresy were to be open for occupancy by any Catholic who would extirpate heresy therefrom. . . . The civil authorities were required to act in entire subserviency to the inquisitors and to have lists of all heretics made out, to be read three times a year in public. The local inquisitors were to receive a third of the proceeds of confiscations and fines, the cities a third, and the bishops the other third. . . .[22]
>
> As evidence must be found for the conviction of suspected heretics, torture in its most exquisite form was employed in order to compel confessions of personal guilt and betrayal of accomplices. Skilled cross-questioners were employed to use every device for betraying the victims into damaging admissions, and false promises of favors were often made to secure confessions.[23]

Torture? Death? Persecution? Today the perpetrators would be classified as war criminals and condemned by all; but they proclaimed they were doing it in the name of Christ! The Inquisition was a travesty on the name of the individual who was the supposed founder of this church. On this item alone it seems a painfully clear revelation that the church had little to do with Christ and the principles he taught.

Augustine had argued that there existed an *unjust* persecution (against the church) and a *just* persecution (that of the church against heretics).[24] In simpler words, it was all right for the church to kill, maim, and torture, since it was for a good cause. The church welcomed such reasoning.

Catholic historians, in attempting to explain away the Inquisition, admit only that it went to extremes, and apologize by saying that it was the "spirit of the times."

> The Inquisition was a dreadful institution. It was responsible for the shedding of much innocent blood, and for much cruelty. *But only an unhistorical process of thought will attempt to place all the blame on the church.* The "guilt" lies rather in the viewpoint of that time, which in many ways was still barbarous, in the vital union of religion and politics, and not least in the lofty conception then held of the true faith, which is the greatest good in this world, not to be compared with anything else, even with life itself.[25]

Curious argument. It wasn't the church's fault; it was the times. The Catholic Church wants always to be known as the only church of Jesus Christ, that it stayed intact through all time, and that it made infallibly correct decisions. Yet they admit that the church, the "true" representation of Jesus, could sink to the very depths of barbarity and argue that it merely reflected the "times."

One would certainly think that *the* church of Jesus would not have a changing morality that ebbed and flowed according to how cruel and monstrous the world around it was. One hesitates further with this thought. The church, as the most powerful institution of the times, *set the standards of the times,* and they invented the Inquisition; the world around it did not. The Inquisition was not foisted off on the church by the times. A closer look might indeed show that the reverse of the argument is true, that the barbaric times were actually caused by the actions of the church. On top of all this, however, one searches in vain for any reference from Jesus stating that the church should adapt to the world, or use torture to force its message on a suffering populace.

Historian Henry Lea summarizes what the Inquisition was and what it accomplished for Christ.

> A few words will suffice to summarize the career of the medieval Inquisition. It . . . rendered the administration of penal justice a cruel mockery for centuries. It furnished the Holy See with a powerful weapon in aid of political aggrandizement, it tempted secular sovereigns to imitate the example, and it prostituted the name of religion to the vilest temporal ends. . . . Thus the judgment of impartial history must be that the Inquisition was the monstrous offspring of mistaken zeal, utilized by selfish greed and lust of power to smother the higher aspirations of humanity and stimulate its baser appetites.[26]

Notes

1. Newhall, 38.
2. Newman, Vol. I, 461.
3. Ibid., 459.
4. Treece, 105.
5. Zoe, 137.
6. Ibid., 140.
7. Treece, 80.
8. Zoe, 552.
9. Treece, 235.
10. Zoe, 584.
11. Gibbon, chapter 16.
12. Newman, Vol. I, 461.
13. Payne, 297.
14. Ibid., 300.

15. *Loc cit.*
16. Ibid., 301.
17. *Loc cit.*
18. Durant, *The Age of Faith*, 68.
19. Batiffol, le Catholicisme, Vol, III, 335, in Barker, 505.
20. Mosheim, Cent. IV, Part II, chapter 3, 16.
21. St. Thomas Aquinas, in Bettenson, 134.
22. Newman, Vol. I, 464–65.
23. Ibid., 466–67.
24. Batiffol, Le Catholicisme, Vol, III, 329, in Barker, 505.
25. Lortz, 236; italics added.
26. Lea, *A History of the Inquisition*, Vol. Ill, 650.

CHAPTER 21

Enough Is Enough—The Move to Reform

Catholics may feel discriminated against in this book, as not much has been said about Protestants. That is not from any particular pleasure derived from illustrating the Catholic position but for something much simpler. The Catholic Church emerged from the seething chaos of the confusing post-apostolic years; that is, what was left over after the original church was gone. Therefore, it is the inheritor of all the changes of a man-made institution—the mistakes, additions to, and corruptions of the original Christian church ended in today's Catholicism. Therefore, any book looking at Christian history must focus on that inheritor.

Whatever else they are, the Protestants are also legitimate children of the Catholic Church. The Protestant churches are also inheritors but in a different way; they are secondary heirs. Simply put, they exist because they thought to reform the corruptions and excesses of the Catholic Church. They base their particular claims to the truth on that thesis. In order to justify their existence, they must accept the legitimacy of the Catholic Church as the genuine (at one time) inheritor of the original Christian church. That is, the Protestants could not have reformed something that was false from the beginning. They therefore must accept that the Catholics inherited the truth, corrupted it through the ages, and then they, the Protestants, reformed it (each one into its own particular version of the "truth").

As we have seen, however, that basic claim is precarious. The Catholic Church had little to do with the original church. It was simply the winning party that stalked out of the smoking ruins of the original church many hundreds of years later. The Protestants are descendants of that particular organization, *not of the original church.* In effect, we have a dead limb breaking off from a dead branch. And that is why we have spent so little time on the Protestants. They are secondary in this particular problem. In order to make their claim valid, the Catholic claim must be valid. That, as we have seen, is highly dubious.

This corruption of the Catholic Church that the Protestants sought to reform is interesting. Catholics admit some of their leaders were pretty rotten but rationalize it away with various sophistries. They have never come to grips with the essential contradiction of morally bankrupt men representing the morals and ethics of Christ.

The Protestants have their own problems in this regard, but historically neither group's claim has much validity. People all through the ages have seen that, and from the twelfth century on, the common people saw it clearly without any benefit of the sophisticated history we can study today. The New Testament spoke of humility, service, morality, love and consideration for mankind, and other ideals. The people of the dawning age saw immorality, arrogance, church-approved bloodshed and torture, wealthy prelates, and endless arguments over dogma. Europe was just beginning to emerge from the feudal system; from their impoverished state the people saw the impossible contradictions between the church in their age and the principles espoused by Christ and his followers.

Thus began the Reformation. Not with Luther, but, as we have seen, much earlier, with the Cathars, Albigenses, Hussites, and Waldenses. Their movements spread for the simplest of reasons—people, tired of the hypocrisy offered by the controlling powers, yearned for a less complex and more honest faith. The early movements failed, for reasons we shall examine shortly. The ideas, however, spread until Martin Luther appeared on the scene.

The Protestors of Christendom

In 1973 an eminent body of Catholic and Lutheran scholars ended an eight-year study of issues that divided the two groups. The effort, published as *Peter in the New Testament*, revealed some surprising discoveries; there is remarkably basic agreement between the two churches.[1] And with good reason. Martin Luther never intended—at first anyway—to establish a new church. He was a Catholic and believed in Catholic doctrines.

The Lutheran church was born because of a series of accidents of history, afterthoughts, and political influence—not as any kind of plan. Luther was simply caught up in events and rolled with them. The reason for the close agreement today with Catholics is that Luther really changed very little of the dogma—simply the authority and a few other items. Originally he didn't intend even that.

Today we imagine, and are taught, that Luther's posting of his ninety-five theses on the door of the Castle Church in Wittenburg as a dramatic exclamation point of history, a sweeping, courageous act of defiance. It was neither. Such a procedure was a normal, regular feature of university life, the equivalent of a student poster on today's bulletin board.[2] Luther was no hot-headed firebrand calling for an end to the church and replacement with his own version. He was not even protesting indulgences themselves (he accepted their validity!) but the abuse in their traffic by Tetzel. Of his theses Luther later said:

> There is much in them concerning which I am doubtful; much else that I do not understand; other things of which I am not persuaded, and nothing that I stubbornly adhere to; *for I submit everything to the holy church and her judgment.*[3]

This was no wild-eyed revolutionary eager to tear the church to pieces but a loyal son who fully expected the pope to support his efforts to end the abuses of indulgences, not indulgences themselves.

> Luther had no intention of founding a church. He merely wished to start a reform within the Catholic faith. But public excitement over his dramatic defiance stirred controversy all over Europe. In defending himself, Luther broadened his position and challenged many Catholic practices. Finally, after years of debate and armed warfare, the German princes threw off allegiance to Rome and organized Protestant churches on Luther's model.[4]
>
> Luther and Calvin set out to reform, not to re-create, and still less to destroy, the existing Catholic church in the West, its doctrines and institutions. They believed that church to be of divine origin, and they drew on its traditions and the theologians in advocating their own positions.[5]

The reformers actually retained most of the chief dogmas of the church they were trying to change. Luther himself maintained that it was no new church that came into being at the Reformation. In no case among the reformers was any revelation given or claimed from heavenly sources for their movements. They were acting on their own, accepting the foundation of the Catholic Church as true, and the churches they founded were their own.

How to Succeed in a Reformation without Really Trying

Ironically, the earlier twelfth century groups, who genuinely wanted to completely reform the church or begin new ones, failed completely, while Luther, who wanted to reform a single item and keep the church, succeeded so dramatically. There was good reason for the success, however. The previous movements had only their good intentions to arm them against a merciless and powerful foe. Luther had Prince John of Saxony, eager to rid himself of papal domination. By himself Luther would have had no more chance than previous reformers and, like them, would probably have been ground into dust by the remorseless might of the church.

But the world had been changing. Politics now became the key to the new Christian movement just as they had for the earlier Christian formations. Even popes now had to pause against the almost equally potent power of princes who were beginning to shift the heavy shackles of Rome, ready to throw them off altogether at the first chance. Before, the church always had the power of excommunication and denial of all church rites (marriage, baptism, etc.) and even civil existence, but now the rebellious political leaders had their own churches, and the threats were empty. While the church might rant and rave and call upon other powers to crush the heretics, it was to no avail if the other princes weren't interested. And they weren't. All saw the glimmer of hope of freedom from the church and weren't about to let it go.

Just as the Catholic Church had become a pawn of politics, the Protestant movement eagerly jumped into the same pit. Did Lutheranism grow and flourish for its own righteousness, its one-man war against abuses, its fight to establish an alternative to Catholicism? Not at all; neither did the previous reformers. Lutheranism succeeded because Prince John had a quarrel going with the pope, and the establishment of a new church seemed a politically wise move in the power struggle. The founder of Lutheranism was not Martin Luther, and certainly not God, but Prince John.

John had his friend Melanchthon and Luther draw up the form of worship, set up a church government, and decide on the duties and salaries of the clergy. The reformers happily pitched into their task. Ordinances were performed, sermons preached, and people's religious activities directed by the "Church of Prince John of Saxony"—called the Lutheran Church.

In Scandanavia the kings latched onto Lutheranism in similar fashion. They stripped Catholic bishops of authority and by their own authority established a new religion as official religion of the land.

Calvin and the Swiss Reformation

John Calvin led the reform movement in Switzerland, and his church had about the same authority that Luther's did. He and his coworker Farrel recommended certain changes to the civil government (council) of Geneva. This body took over the religious authority of the Catholic bishops and effected the change to Protestantism.[6] The council then proceeded to civilly enforce religious observance. This, then, was the "Church of the Council of Geneva," and Calvin's movement would eventually spawn a whole host of further protesting children who formed their own churches in turn.

The town council of Zurich performed essentially the same service for Zwingli and his reform movement. That church was in essence the "Church of the Town Council of Zurich."

The Church of Henry VIII—Or, Anything for a New Wife

Henry VIII's formation of the English brand of Protestantism is perhaps the most blatant example of how new churches were formed—not from heavenly revelation or guidance from God—but from historical accident, rebellion, and political maneuvering. Luther, Calvin, and Zwingli may not have had the very personal reason Henry did, but their movements were essentially of the same nature.

We could call it the "Gee, as long as I've gone this far and have a political protector, why don't I form a new church while I'm here" syndrome. Henry was a special case of that. Ironically, the origin of English Protestantism and all subsequent break-offs from it that provided so much religious heritage for the world came about not because of moral protests against Roman corruption but from finances, politics, and sex.

Early in his reign, Henry was completely unsympathetic to Luther and the other rebels. In 1521 he wrote a tirade against Luther and thus won from Pope Leo X the title "Defender of the Faith!" Irony upon irony. Henry seemed content with English religion, but he chafed under the financial and political connections to the pope. And then came the crunch.

Henry wanted to change wives. He appealed to the pope for a divorce. If the pope had possessed a little vision, he could have seen the disastrous results of denying Henry. He didn't, however, and Henry's appeals fell on deaf ears. (Popes could overlook hundreds of years of immorality among themselves and those kings they favored but weren't about to tolerate any sign of rebellion from a king showing signs of independence.) Only then did Henry rebel and become a reformer—so that he could get what he personally wanted. Church property was seized and in 1534 the English Parliament—not God, a prophet, or some other heavenly authority—declared that the very earthly and un-Christlike Henry was the supreme head of the Church of England. The wording of their ruling is revealing.

> Be it enacted by authority of this present Parliament, that the king our sovereign lord, his heirs and successors, kings of this realm, shall be taken, accepted, and reputed the only supreme head in earth of the Church of England . . . and that our said sovereign lord, his heirs and successors, kings of this realm, shall have full power and authority from time to time to visit, repress, redress, reform, order, correct, restrain, and amend all such errors, heresies, abuses, offenses, contempts, and enormities, whatsoever they be . . . to the pleasure of Almighty God, the increase of virtue in Christ's religion.[7]

It seems hard to imagine Henry being able to "increase the virtue of Christ's religion," but that's what they said.

After Henry's death, Catholic fortunes rose under Queen Mary, but the Protestant cause finally became firmly rooted under Elizabeth.

Religion by Whim and Politics

And so it went. Churches began to proliferate, coming into being by politics, further rebellion, or personal whim of some strong leader and his followers. Protestant churches today can almost all be traced back to one of these four reform movements of the sixteenth century (Luther, Calvin, Zwingli, and Henry). Baptists, for example, entered the world when two Englishmen, John Smyth and Thomas Helwys, fled to the Netherlands to escape persecution and founded a new church in 1609. They and their followers were rebelling against the Church of England, which the rebellion of Henry had established. They didn't like the way the "old" church was being run; but the authority to found a new church was their own.

Calvin's protest eventually produced the French Huguenots, the Dutch Reformed Church, the Church of Scotland, and English Puritans.

The American Presbyterians descended haphazardly from the reform elements from all nations. The English Puritans split off another group in America called the Congregationalists.

A man named Francis Asbury established and organized the first Methodist churches in America independent of all foreign connections. The move infuriated the founder, Wesley, who had intended that Methodist societies stay within the Church of England.

Mary Barker Eddy, of Christian Science fame, had no thought of forming a new or separate church. She really intended her movement to work *within* established churches. It was only later on that Mrs. Eddy saw the possibilities and organized yet another new church.

Hundreds of churches stemmed from the Catholic Church, each convinced their way was the right way, and each spawning further protest children in turn who disagreed with her. A hypothetical Mr. X decided that Mr. Y's way of running a church was wrong. X formed a new group. One of his flock, Mr. Z, decided that both X and Y were wrong and then started his own group. And so it went.

In the United States today such movement is becoming chaotic as thousands shy away from organized religion altogether and form countless local groups who seek their own religious definitions. Those groups may eventually lead to even more churches.

Splitting off began very early in the history of Protestantism. The German princes who supported Luther, for example, were disturbed when they saw that the reformers could achieve no unity of belief or practice. Expecting one strong reform religion opposing Rome, they were naive to hope to control the evolution of the many new churches. Once the splitting began, it was impossible to halt the determined fragmentation.

The irony and contradictions never end in this affair. All the reformers denied revelation, so they could not get a personal message from heaven to start a new church. At the same time all claimed *inspiration* in interpreting scriptures. So they couldn't receive revelation because it didn't exist, but things could be revealed by inspiration. We may be forgiven, perhaps, if we don't entirely understand this strange way of saying that what couldn't happen really could happen.

There is more, however. Each reformer claimed his own inspiration was correct and true but couldn't agree with the others. And since they were rebelling against the Catholics, reformers had to prove them false (Catholicism still had to be *originally* true to establish the legitimacy of the reformers in reforming it) but at the same time be able to justify themselves and their new doctrines. This led to some fast footwork.

Luther, for example, believing the Catholic Church had valid priesthood authority, had to get it to himself, a rebel against that authority. He was perfectly aware that he couldn't claim it after being excommunicated. To overcome the problem he created the priesthood of all believers. He concluded that the priesthood was bestowed on all baptized people—men and women—within a congregation. The congregation could not use its priesthood individually but delegated its tiny share to the pastor, who then possessed enough to exercise it in their behalf.

Too often we look at the reformers as heroes, which they were, but don't look at the fundamental weaknesses and contradictions of their new religions. In truth they occupied the same lifeboat as the Catholics. They all descended from one church, and the doctrines they adopted or invented were just as contradictory to the original church as their parent.

Luther, who had rebelled against an authoritarian and intolerant church, quickly picked up those characteristics for himself. He began to insist on his own interpretations as the only correct ones. He was especially fond of Paul, for instance, and readily judged other New Testament writers who didn't measure up to what he (Luther) thought they should be. The letter of James, for example, he simply dismissed as "straw epistle,"[8] because James dared to preach faith without works is dead in apparent contradiction to the favorite, Paul.

And, even if that prized apostle wrote something that Luther didn't agree with, then Paul was wrong, certainly not Luther.[9] Luther "was intensely biblical; yet he interpreted the Bible by Augustine rather than Augustine by the Bible."[10]

> Few religious leaders ever expressed greater devotion to the scriptures than Luther, and in controversy with the Romanists he made the scriptures the only rule of faith and practice. Yet we shall see that even the scriptures must adapt themselves to his theories or suffer the penalty of decanonization.[11]

Luther had other problems. He believed the state had to support the church, forcing it on the people if they didn't like the idea; he supported civil leaders in opposing more freedom for the masses.

The other church leaders were not much better. The English Church, progenitor of so many Protestant groups, mercilessly persecuted, tortured, and killed those who wanted freedom for their own ideas. This church faced two groups: Protestants who objected to its (still) Catholic doctrine and Catholics who objected to Henry as head of any church. All this led to a particularly grotesque event in 1543.

> Accordingly, on July 30, 1543, the strange sight was seen in Smithfield of six simultaneous executions, three burnings for heresy and three hangings for denial of the royal headship of the church.[12]

Neither Zwinglians, Calvinists, or Catholics had any tolerance for other religions. As a matter of fact, an almost predictable pattern emerged. A particular church would form in protest of its mother group and be brutally persecuted. The new group would grow and establish itself elsewhere and just as brutally attempt to persecute any who dared to disagree with it.

So, in the great names of the Reformation, Calvin, Zwingli, Luther, and even Henry, we find an incredible intolerance of other ideas and blithe acceptance of evolved Catholic doctrines that were nowhere to be found in the early church or the scriptures; for example, Augustine's predestination, harsh repression of dissent, the Greek philosophical definition of God first defined at Nicea, and so on.

But all this was only natural. The reformers did not claim to have any authority by revelation. The churches belonged to them personally, or their patrons. It was the church of Luther, or Calvin, or of the method (Congregationalists), or the single doctrine chosen as a weapon of truth (Baptists and Seventh Day Adventists). Many of the newer Protestant groups hang by a single doctrine from the New Testament and drape other ideas around it as ornaments.

Several major and formidable circumstances prevent the new churches from doing much better than the parent they condemned so heartily. First, they erroneously assumed that the Catholic Church, up until the eighth or ninth century, really did represent the Christianity established by Jesus. They therefore adopted, for the most part, that churches' doctrines that had in reality been invented after the third century.

Second, they assumed that they could take the priesthood upon themselves or have it delegated to them by the congregation.

Third, the churches were saddled with the Nicene concept of a philosophically defined God in contrast to the very personal one of the Bible. Their final problem, faced also by the early church, was no revelation. Revelation had been the foundation of the original church. Since, however, it ceased when the Apostasy began, ministers and priests ever after declared it dead; a dangerous restriction placed on a God whom they believed all powerful and never changing. After reading the New Testament carefully, it seems impossible to imagine the church of Jesus operating without this critical factor.

Recall, however, that the *churchmen* declared the heavens sealed. The New Testament made no such drastic promise.

Logically, the acts, teachings, and doctrines of modern churches (and their past) should agree both in spirit and fact with that taught and emphasized by Christ and his followers. In fact they do not. Christ and the apostles taught the futility of contention. Yet popes, priests, ministers, and pastors have engaged each other and the world in harsh, intolerable, acrimonious, and vindictive arguments—often ending in bloodshed.

The halls of history ring with the battles of different groups trying to outshout their fellows, gunning down anyone opposing them, and establishing themselves as the only legitimate heirs of Christ. The winners of the first battle, the eventual Catholics, were no better, and probably worse, than the pagans. The Protestants were no better in their turn. The push for ecumenical harmony in recent years is just that—recent. For the greater part of their history most churches have been bitterly at odds with each other.

Rationalizations have been attempted and Catholic and Protestant writers have for years tried to explain away the differences between what their churches actually are and what the original was, what Christ and the apostles intended. It is the constant theme of religious history books, as if by writing and interpolating enough one can justify the changes that have been made.

The Catholics argue that they have descended from the original intact. The Protestants are in reality Catholics under a different name, as they believe they reformed the original "Catholic" church into whatever branch of interpretation of that original model they belong to. The original Protestant fathers took pains to establish the legitimacy of the Catholic Church, knowing their descendancy depended on having a genuine church to descend from. History supports neither claim. Both are at best attempts to preserve what was left over from original Christianity and the historical evidence for loss of the original, and consequent substitution, is abundant.

Subsequent to the reformation, many Protestant churchmen took great glee in using the abundant evidence of the Apostasy to try to shoot down the Catholics. What they didn't recognize (as the first reformers did) was that by torpedoing the Catholic ship of state they likewise sunk their own ship in the backwash. Like it or not, the Catholic Church is the root of all Protestant religions. It was never the Church of Jesus Christ but merely a pickup organization that came along much later, as history suggests. The Protestants share the same origins.

The Catholics have also participated in the game by saying in essence just what we've mentioned above. They have used their share of the evidence to shoot down the Protestants. Both are correct in shooting at each other, but neither has put the two together, as they have spent most of their ammunition building up their own stock and tearing down the other.

Neither side, as a group, has been willing to use all the evidence that proves both parties wrong. A few individual scholars have, but too often in academic studies. And even then they are still hesitant to call a horse a horse, preferring something like "a four limbed ambulatory creature feeding on graminaceous crops and used as a supporting adjunct for human travel." Most religious scholars are a bit myopic, spending so much time explaining why their church is radically opposed to and different from the original doctrines of Christ that they may not want to state the obvious because of the dangerous and demoralizing implications. Nonetheless, the evidence comes thundering down throughout the ages in clear and unequivocal terms. The apostasy was complete.

Apostasy—normally a word applied to some errant backslider but now seen as a process for the whole of what we know of as Christian history. Apostasy *of the* church, not *from* the church. The events of history simply reflect the reality of the fall.

Recognizing that an apostasy took place instantly clarifies history. Instead of wading through a murky mix of mud and clay, one is swimming clear. The many contradictions of history dissolve. Catholics and Protestants are simply remnants of the original church, and the original disappeared. It did not descend by tradition into Catholicism or by reform movements into Protestantism. It was gone and those organizations picked up the pieces, each in its own time.

Once the apostles were gone, what was left over pushed, pulled, stretched past the breaking point, and finally flopped into the slot as the "Catholic" church, a new church formed sometime around the fifth century but really evolving all through the Middle Ages into the form we know today. In the process it invented offices, ideas, and doctrines never known in the original church. By selling itself to civil power, it became so powerful—and corrupt—that groups began protesting its corruptions. From this grew official groups and churches, the Protestants of today.

Notes

1. *Time Magazine*, Aug. 6, 1973, 54.
2. *The Ninety-Five Theses*, 1517, in Bettenson, 185.
3. Robinson, Vol. II, 57–59; italics added.
4. Spence, 44.
5. Zaehner, 118.
6. Barker, 746–47.
7. Henry VII, "Statutes of the Realm," in Bettenson, 227.
8. Barker, 698.
9. Schaff, Vol. Ill, 37.
10. Newman, Vol. II, 6.
11. *Loc cit.*
12. Clarke, 288.

CHAPTER 22

You Can't Get There from Here

We have spent considerable time detailing the unsavory past of the Christian churches. The criticisms and revelations are not merely those of the author but have simply been gleaned from the pages of history, where they abound in great detail. They are brought together here in a unique way. Lumped together in this fashion, they present some obvious, and perhaps unwelcome, contradictions.

For example, those professing to be leaders and representatives of Christ clearly ought to reflect on the moral and ethical principles he handed down, and the churches representing him ought to adhere closely to the doctrine he left. Neither has been true. Some would like us to accept the churches as true anyway, arguing that the clergy have only been human and therefore subject to human weaknesses. But that doesn't wash too well in light of history. Weaknesses yes, but not wallowing in war, plunder, immorality, simony, avarice, chicanery, hunger for power, and all the rest we have discussed here.

It seems more logical—if perhaps more unwelcome—to conclude that those guilty of such behavior were not representing Christ at all but were simply leaders of an ordinary human organization protesting representation of Christ, form without substance. That organization has been, through its history, at times good, yes, but also at times corrupt, immoral, indifferent to human suffering and welfare and higher thoughts, and often concerned only with the aggrandizement of its highest officers.

Is this the inheritance of the man from Galilee? If so, then he was less than that book implies he was. But if we accept the New Testament description of Jesus and his teachings, it quickly becomes obvious that the history of Christian churches has little to do with the original model. Of course, descendant Christianity has had good men and women and good and worthy acts, but so have other institutions of man *once in a while.* One feels impelled to believe that the church representing Jesus would be good all the time (or at least with very minor—not wholesale—infractions) and never have such heavy sins hanging over the heads of its leaders. Perhaps we could accept one, once in a while, on the basis of human weakness, but can we do so consistently and throughout long periods of history?

The evidence is clear. Many of the Catholic Church's doctrines, practices, and offices are entirely different from those of the original church. Catholic and Protestant writers alike offer abundant evidence for this. The Catholic writers, of course, spend a lot of time explaining why not. The Protestant writers simply use the evidence to shoot the Catholics down. As mentioned earlier, however, neither side seems willing to put both sides together and state the obvious. That is, that both churches are man-made organizations, pickup institutions left over from the original.

That admission is so painful because it makes eighteen centuries of Christian history rather empty, and few are willing to brave that fire. Yet, that explanation erases the overwhelming contradictions of history, contradictions that had the church of Jesus murdering, scheming for power, and assuming all the worldly ambitions of any petty dictatorship or the vices of a backstreet gangster. The alternative fits better—the churches responsible for all that were not churches of Jesus at all.

The churches involved, naturally enough, would like to glide smoothly past these historical skeletons in their closets and proudly point out their many modern accomplishments and good deeds; but the skeletons are real and chatter loudly as a counterpoint to modern pride and satisfaction with the status quo. Those churches must recognize their roots and realize that their organization and dogma are only slightly related to the original church and doctrine. However, they have been reluctant to do so. First, they are all rather involved with internecine warfare with each other and therefore not likely to admit to any fault even if knowing it. They have also ignored, obfuscated, denied, and rationalized, never coming to grips with fundamental contradictions.

Knowing what we now know, we must have great sympathy with those who have studied history and have concluded that "if this is of Christ, I want nothing to do with it." The church has always labeled such as heretics and when it could do so, beat, tortured, killed, and shamed them. The dissidents have been correct in their feelings, however. What they saw was ersatz Christianity, not the real thing. Some readers have carried this even further. Judging by the record of "Christianity" in history, they have attempted to debunk Christ and Christianity altogether. If the record is so bad, they argue, then the founder was a charlatan.

But debunking Christ on the basis of the corruptions of descendant churches is not really quite fair. In that we judge him by the very ordinary and human organizations that put together a patchwork quilt of religion only remotely related to him. Christ and his followers predicted that their organization would be lost and that those that followed *would not* be theirs. This puts a very different light on the matter. The original was valid. It was removed, and the leftover parts would never again equal the whole—as some theologians have admitted. Discovery of ever more ancient manuscripts is showing us a picture of an ancient church totally unlike anything conventional churchmen had ever imagined; scholars are having to admit basic contradictions more and more.

Thousands of ordinary individuals, faced with an apparently inexhaustible supply of Christian churches clamoring for their allegiance, have come to the same conclusions.

A Babble of Churches

The result of eighteen hundred years of Christian history is a seething and restless mass of hundreds of "Christian" churches. Most loudly claim to be the one true church—and obvious and impossible contradiction. Faced with that, churches and people have unhappily, but necessarily, adopted a cop-out. It doesn't really matter what church you belong to, we're told by some; we're all Christians and going to the same place. All this, of course, while still claiming for themselves the truth and anxiously snaring any stray from another congregation or a heathen wherever they can be picked up.

Hans Kung, in his book *On Being a Christian*, has shown how the Catholic Church used to claim that everybody who was not Catholic was doomed to hell. Now they rationalize that very harsh standard by stating that everybody is really a Catholic anyway, even if not a member of the church!

In light of the exclusiveness and narrow interpretation Jesus placed on his doctrine, these strange contradictions waver uncertainly on the horizon. Nonetheless, churchmen continue to justify *all* Christian faiths.

> Today, in America, no one has far to go to find religious expression. As long as there are religious edifices on almost every street, in one of which you and I, and the scholar, the ignorant, the literalist, the liberal, the rich, the poor, may worship and witness in his own sincerity, there will be inspiration and solace for everyone who yearns for a religious experience. That, in itself, makes every organized religious accent important.[1]

It was religion made to fit the consumer's preferences and biases, rather than absolute standards and doctrines as originally established.

The Baptist church is a good example of the frenzied and crazy-quilt fandango Christianity dances to. In reality there is no Baptist *church*—there are only Baptist *churches.* Instead of one unified body with the same doctrine, Baptists are split into a myriad of groups—all theoretically the church of Jesus, all practicing and teaching different doctrines! They recognize "no human founder and no human spiritual authority,"[2] yet their division upon division purely and plainly demonstrates the human cussedness of forming a new church when dissatisfied with the old. Each congregation is its own law and enacts its own doctrine.[3]

Such ideas are not only contrary to New Testament teaching, they are actually condemned. The tormented cry wrung from Christ in Gethsemane was unity—not division. The apostles pled in their epistles for unity of faith—not separation. In spite of that, every Baptist decides for himself what God is saying in the scriptures. The upshot of such a system is a chaos of opinion and doctrine—the antithesis of the original church.

Although the Baptists are perhaps the extreme, they are not alone. Some ministers obtain a consensus among their flocks and preach that common opinion—a fairly amazing twist. In effect, they judge morality, ethics, and so forth by majority vote—which constantly varies. As soon as someone no longer agrees with the group, he or she retires—perhaps to start a new church. Some scholars and churchmen have argued that such diversity is good and healthy, because everyone is allowed to express their religious feelings as they wish. That perhaps may be, although such systems anywhere else eventually lead to chaos, but all we are saying here is that those ideas have nothing to do with the original gospel.

The whole history of Christianity since the reformation has been constant division into further fragments. At the very beginning of the reform movement, many well-planned schemes were laid to unite the Protestant groups. All failed, as the leaders jealously guarded their interpretations of the scriptures and refused to accept others. Those who disagreed with the founders started winging it on their own. It still goes on today. A 1975 news item discussed a group of clergy and laymen who opposed women's ordinations and were laying plans to secede from the United Presbyterian Church, a capsule summary of Christianity. A new idea is invented; a group opposes it and parts company to form a new church. There is nothing here about God ordaining it (he can't, since the churches maintain there is no revelation); it comes about through internal argument.

The poem "The Blind Men and the Elephant" by John Godfrey Saxe is a powerfully accurate description of Christianity through the ages. In his poem Saxe describes six blind men chancing upon an elephant. One grabs the tusk and decides the elephant is like a spear. Another takes hold of the trunk and loudly proclaims the mighty elephant is like a snake. And so on, "each in his own opinion, exceeding stiff and strong, though each was partly in the right, and all were in the wrong."

Descendant Christians have apparently been similarly blind about the nature of the original church. They don't know much about it, and while they grope about and feel parts here and there, they seem content with that fragment they have found and immediately begin to wail they have truly described this particular elephant.

"Disputing loud and long," as Saxe describe it, is something Christians have been fond of—and skilled at—throughout their history. The result is hundreds of Christian churches, "each in his own opinion, exceeding stiff and strong."

It is clear that something is wrong with modern Christianity when we consider Paul's words: "For God is not the author of confusion, but of peace" (1 Corinthians 14:33). An obvious conclusion from that is that it isn't God who is responsible for the confusion that beats on our senses from this mad cacophony from hundreds of Christian churches.

Progress in the Church —From "Primitive" Unity to Early Modern Confusion

It's not surprising that the churches are wading through a morass of confusion. So were the early churches after the original disappeared. Once that model was removed, later churchmen could only grope around in the dark feeling bits and pieces here and there. One reason for so much confusion today is that some parties in those early churches decided to change the original fragment they found to conform to what they thought the church *ought* to have been. Robert Wilken, in his book *The Myth of Christian Beginnings*, delves deeply into past Christian history and exposes the plain fact that Christian scholars have used history for their own purposes. They quite often have manipulated history to explain away the contradictions between their churches and the original. One of the first uses of this technique was to explain why there was a church at all.

Early church fathers were aware of the earlier predictions that Christianity would be lost. However, something labeled Christianity survived. Rather than admit that it was something less than the whole gospel, churchmen danced rather nimbly around earlier predictions and with some judicious rearrangement of history, created a continuum from Christ down to themselves. Competing versions of Christianity also juggled things around to make their side look better, and as often as not destroyed the competitor's documents. The first complete history of Christianity that we have was written by Eusebius in the fourth century. That worthy said, in essence, "Let's destroy all texts that don't agree with us, since we know we are right."

> The gravest of the ecclesiastical historians, Eusebius himself, indirectly confesses that he has related whatever might redound to the glory, and that he has suppressed all that could tend to the disgrace, of religion. Such an acknowledgement will naturally excite a suspicion that a writer who has so openly violated one of the fundamental laws of history has not paid a very strict regard to the observance of the other; and the suspicion will derive additional credit from the character of Eusebius, which was less tinctured with credulity, and more practised in the arts of courts, than that of almost any of his contemporaries.[4]

Throughout Christian history there has been no shortage of those who would "correct" history to make it look better. Origen (AD 185–243) complained about it early.

> Today the fact is evident that there are many differences in the manuscripts, either through the negligence of certain copyists, or the perverse audacity of some in correcting the text.[5]

Most of the "heretical" writings were burned along with their authors, and very little has survived. Those that we have today have generally been edited and rewritten.

An example of the process was the book of Enoch. Largely unknown today except by scholars, it was respected and loved, and in widespread use in the early church.

> How could a book of such long-standing influence, authority, and veneration possibly have become lost? Very simple: it ran afoul of ideas held by the doctors of the Jews and Christians alike after those worthies had fallen under the influence of the University of Alexandria.[6]

The book was banned by such as Hilary, Jerome, and Augustine, who readily admitted that earlier leaders held ideas quite different from their own. But never mind, they knew best what was scripture and what wasn't. Enoch was not to be trusted, and it fell into disuse. Today it is being slowly rediscovered, as fragments and versions appear here and there. "Recently some of the oldest and most important fragments of Enoch have turned up among the Dead Sea Scrolls, and far more important ones are still being held back by their uneasy Christian editors."[8]

The result of refusal to accept the original ideas and dogmas (and changing them to fit the changing circumstances) was a constantly changing church that was formed by, rather than forming, its environment.

> Indeed, the one sure thing that we learn from Christian history is that Christianity is always changing, in spite of the protestations of Christians to the reverse.[9]

Owen Chadwick, in his book *From Bousset to Newman*, clearly shows that the greatest changes in the Catholic Church, in ancient as well as modern times, have been in doctrines—the fundamental ideas and regulations of the gospel. The rule has been constant change.

> The controversies in the history of Christianity are less a testimony to the perseverance of an original faith, as Eusebius would have it, than they are to the place of novelty, change, and innovation. The new has been, on balance, more acceptable to Christians than the old, even though they have claimed otherwise.[10]

So, what are we to do now? The gospel plainly was not supposed to change, but change it did. Rather than accept the implications of that, or the fact that the loss of the church had been equally plainly predicted, subsequent Christian scholars and historians began to look for justifications for the changes. Anything, it seemed, rather than admit that the whole crazy-quilt mess could be wrong altogether. Better find some way to make it look good. The attempts look like desperation plays from eighty yards out with five seconds go and no time outs.

John Henry Newman's theory of doctrinal development has been one of the most welcomed (by the prelates) attempts to explain away the mind-boggling contradictions in modern Christianity. In perhaps one of the most widely known rationalizations, Newman admitted that there was indeed discrepancy between the original church and every variety of modern Christianity. But, increase and expansion of Christian creeds and doctrines were necessary. Why? They required time to develop in the fertile bed of human minds and hearts.[11] As these were imperfect, it would take a while to experiment, evolve, and develop them to where they should be.

That's the answer many wanted. What Christ gave was only kind of a seed. The ideas needed more thought to come to full fruition (along with the mayhem and corruption that accompanied them). The gospel has to grow up with men, like a plant or a puppy.

Churches have latched on to this particular explanation as if it were a long lost rich cousin. "The tenacity of Newman's theory among Christian intellectuals of every confessional stripe is a testimony to its success in dealing with the new problems posed by historical thinking."[12] More simply put, that means they like it because it explains away the overburdening contradictions of history.

But does it? That explanation implies that the end product, eighteen years of shame, corruption, bloodshed, and argument, was necessary to develop the gospel that the supposedly perfect Christ had given. What Jesus deeded to the world needed the improvements and developments the world has added.

> Other arguments are usually based on variations of Newman's theme. The apostolic faith is capable of development, or unfolding. What is obscure may be made clear; what is implicit may become explicit; but no new revelation is ever added.[13]

Interestingly, churchmen have to argue that Christ, the Son of God, whom they supposedly worship, was "obscure," and men have made his gospel "clear." However much some may protest in that vein, it doesn't add up, and the arguments become clear for what they are: desperate attempts to explain away the difference between what Christianity was *supposed* to be and what it is as practiced today. The church hasn't gone from the obscure to the clear or any such thing—rather the opposite. It grew from accretion of all too worldly elements that have caused the great confusion of Christian fragments today.

A more sophisticated application of this line of thought was outlined by Robert Wilken in *The Myth of Christian Beginnings.*

> As a first step in constructing a new historical picture of Christianity I would suggest that we turn the whole history of Christianity on its end. Instead of viewing Christian history as a movement away from something—an original perfection—why not view it as a movement *toward* something? Perfection lies, if anywhere, not at the beginning, but at the end.[14]

In essence Wilken argues that the first Christianity, the one established by Christ and the apostles, was only a crude model. It then had to evolve into something more sophisticated and perfect through association with man.

At first glance these ideas have some compelling logic. After all, times, people, and customs do change and the church must change with them to meet modern standards. Such ideas also certainly do save the church—in a weird sort of way. The excesses of blood, bitterness, and tyranny of the Christian past can be explained away because the church was evolving towards full development of perfection.

Paul Johnson's *History of Christianity* explains it just that way. He argues that indeed the history of the world caused by Christian ethics has been pretty awful. He concludes, however, that no matter how bloodthirsty and perverse Christianity became, civilization would have been much worse off without it.

We can surely question that. A glance at history suggests that Christianity was the direct cause of much of the mischief and abuse, not a victim of it. "Christianity" didn't help civilization much and probably did it a good deal of harm. The point, of course, was whether it really was Christianity at all. Had the original intent and purposes of Christ survived, they might well have benefited civilization immensely—we'll never know. What did survive, however, was only a humanly directed device, and its effect on history is all too clear.

These sophisticated arguments, far from answering the many conflicts and incongruences in Christian history, throw a gloomy pall over it. If we buy the arguments presented, we must conclude that what Christ gave was not at all something well formed. He says to us, in essence, here's my doctrine, see what you can do with it.

That thought is depressing indeed. We must then accept that Christ intended the eighteen hundred years of power politics, contentions, money, immorality, and so forth that we have detailed in this book (or else the equally disturbing thought that Christ did not have enough prescience to foresee that all this would happen). We must also believe that the perfect form of the church (or at least what we have of it to this point) is this hopeless confusion of hundreds of Christian religions clamoring to be heard as the only legitimate voice of the Savior; that is, that this endless bickering and raging confusion was *supposed* to happen, as part of the evolution and development of what Christ gave.

Faith, for those who have it, and reason stare at that kind of explanation. One wonders if the churchmen and scholars who have so openly and desperately accepted such arguments realize the implications. Perhaps they do. All other historical institutions (governments and such) have evolved just as Newman and Wilken argue, that is, from a rough primitive form to more sophisticated entities through the years. But was Christ and what he founded like any other institution—or something different? Rather than Christ the perfect Son of God, must we allow him only as one more muddled-headed reformer who really didn't know where his doctrine would go or end up?

The New Testament declares that Christ is not only the Son of God but also perfect. To a believer, then, this has serious implications. It simply means at the very minimum that what Christ gave and ordained was *better* than what men could do. His ideas, if practiced, could indeed lead to the rewards he promised. Newman's and Wilken's ideas contradict that by saying the gospel had to evolve into something better than it was or be interpreted better. But, if ordinary men changed (by interpretation of helping along the evolution) Christ's gospel, it would be less, not more, than what it was in its purity.

If churchmen accept the arguments for evolution and development, then they must, consciously or subconsciously, downgrade Christ to a human level. If they admit to Christ being divine, they stand condemned by arguing that men could improve on that doctrine; they are in essence saying that Christ was indeed only a man; one with good ideas, ideas that needed the further development men could give them. But if Christ was only another man, why have churches built up to him at all? Why try so desperately to pin themselves on Jesus and search so intensely for the original truths?

Sticky questions indeed.

The attempts to explain away the Christian past have been straw clutching of the most desperate nature. Churchmen have been trying to justify the unjustifiable. History provides a much clearer, although perhaps unwelcome answer. Christian history cannot be reconciled with Christ. Therefore, what Newman and Wilken and others have argued is true—but for the wrong organization.

Notes

1. Spence, p. XII
2. Ibid., 23.
3. Ibid., 24.
4. Gibbon, chapter 16.
5. Barker, 14.
6. Nibley, *Ensign*, October, 1975, 81.
7. *Loc cit.*
8. *Loc cit.*
9. Wilken, 185.
10. Ibid., 175.
11. Ibid., 135–37.
12. Ibid., 139.
13. McSorley, xiii.
14. Wilken, 192.

CHAPTER 23

Lost—But Gone Forever?

The Emperor Has No Clothes!

It is strange, and somewhat troubling, that virtually every book on Christian history (and there are many) has easily seen, detailed, and admitted the atrocities, inconsistencies, and immorality of the Christian past; and having admitted it, most cast desperately about for some way to justify it. We simply are unwilling to admit that the Christian past may not have been real Christianity at all. We accept the soundness of the original message, and since there seems to be no other answer, that gospel must have continued regardless of its shady record. So, no matter how repellent, all that unsightly material has to be explained away somehow. All sorts of rationalizations have been proposed.

We have presented a different, much more logical answer, though perhaps harder to accept. What has been called Christianity was simply man-made stuff. Christ was what he said and meant what he taught. He did not preach a religion to be accommodated to the weaknesses of men, but one that would elevate weak men to high moral standards. But he and his apostles knew that the original gospel would be lost. They predicted the Apostasy and the long night of spiritual darkness; a substitute organization would take over and corrupt the original. History has amply born that out. Is it not preferable to accept this than try to justify eighteen hundred years of blood and horror and account for all the atrocities committed in the name of Christ?

At first blush, all we have presented in this book may seem hopelessly pessimistic. The church of Jesus was lost, and what's more seems to be unfindable again. Scholars despair at encountering the original faith and gospel, as well they might. Nineteen hundred years of searching have yielded only doubt, disaster, and division. New discoveries of ancient manuscripts, occurring all the time, only add further to the gloom and dismay. They more than ever point out the yawning gulf between what Christianity originally was intended to be and what it eventually became—the contradictions mount up.

Is there, then, any hope at all of finding the original faith? Yes, if we accept once and for all that there is no requirement that the gospel stay on the earth intact from Jesus' time until now. Descendant churches have fought tenaciously for that continuous survival. To do otherwise, and accept the record of history, would mean an admission too enormous to allow.

Modern Christianity, disturbed by new discoveries of old manuscripts because of the message they hammer out so loudly, wants to keep those manuscripts quietly in the scholar's corner where they won't disturb things. Like the fable of the emperor's new clothes, no one wants to point out that the descendant churches really have nothing on at all. The old manuscripts point out some of the nakedness.

The Dead Sea Scrolls, for example, are extremely disturbing to modern churchmen. They reveal a pre-Christian people who had a knowledge of the principles of Christianity. That should have been impossible, according to church dogma, which states that the gospel was first revealed by Jesus during his lifetime. Or does the evidence of the scrolls, then, which is firm and definite, imply that Jesus was a plagiarist—that he simply lifted the principles he taught from this group of people and passed it off as his own? This in turn casts doubt on everything.

No wonder there is so much consternation in the Christian churches. Their own dogma has backed them into a corner from which there is no escape. Admit they are wrong about the first appearance of the gospel with Jesus and the whole edifice built on that premise crumbles into powder. Admit that Jesus borrowed his religious ideas and the result is equally devastating. Or so we would think. The churchmen, however, in the face of obvious evidence, are finding ways to change their beliefs without admitting they were wrong.

Interestingly enough, the first church fathers never had the idea that the first and only appearance of the gospel was with Jesus. Quite the contrary. Irenaeus wrote plainly and clearly about four separate dispensations of the same gospel, being lost and restored again on different occasions.

> Thus were they perfected who knew one and the same God, who from beginning to end was present with mankind in the various dispensations. . . . For this reason were four principal covenants given to the human race. . . . Man having been lost, God worked to save him progressively, giving him in succession the four testaments from Adam to Noah, from Noah to Moses, from Moses to Jesus Christ, and the New Testament by our Lord Jesus Christ.[1]

Eusebius and other church fathers taught the same thing.

> The teaching of Christianity was neither new nor strange. . . . It had been followed centuries before them by Abraham and Moses and later prophets; and the religion of the patriarchs was identical with that of the Christians. . . . The student of church history will have little difficulty in recognizing that this teaching is in the direct line of Justin Martyr, Aristides, Clement of Alexandria, and Origen.[2]

Jesus came to *restore* the gospel, not to *reveal* it for the first time. Those closest to Christ in time and to the original message of Jesus understood the church was like the moon, coming and going.[3]

In light of the early church teachings, it is easy to understand how the Dead Sea Scrolls could write of gospel principles two hundred years before Jesus. Some of the principles had been kept intact from previous dispensations. The idea of a single dispensation was yet another invention of later churches, created to establish an artificial succession that didn't exist, from Christ to their church.

Jesus, then, was not forming a new religion; he was restoring what had been lost. In that light it is easy to imagine it could be lost again . . . and restored again. Both of those ideas were predicted by Christ, the apostles, and the early church fathers. The loss itself is indirectly attested to by the towering mountain of history that tells us what Christianity became, obviously not what Christ intended. History, then, merely informs us of the progress of something *called* Christianity, but that something was foreign to the genuine item. It went merrily along its way, inventing new doctrines, outraging the spirit of the gospel, and trampling the principles its author held sacred.

Rather than having to accept this humanly created version of Christianity, might we not accept what Christ and the apostles said (and the early church father corroborated) about an apostasy? The Acts of the Apostles talk of a restitution of all things at some future date (Acts 3:19–21); Paul spoke of another dispensation, the dispensation of the fulness of times (Ephesians 1:9–10); John saw in the future an angel flying in heaven with the gospel to preach to those on earth—presumably because they didn't have it (Revelation 14:6–7); and we have already mentioned the feelings of the early church fathers.

The original gospel would have to be restored, apparently in the same fashion in which is has been done in the past. In spite of churchmen telling us that God has given up talking to humanity, restoration would apparently have to come about through heavenly messengers of some sort, revelations, and yes, even prophets. To believe anything else is to deny the entire history of the Old and New Testaments. Our modern sophistication may lead us to doubt or dislike those implications, but that doesn't make them any less probable.

In this book we have studied the fallacies of both Catholic and Protestant positions in history. It seems unlikely that the New Testament Jesus would work through an organization with the record of the Catholic Church. If not the Catholics, then certainly not the Protestants, who are of the Catholics; if the Catholics are wrong, then the Protestants are wrong with them. Protestants did a good and noble thing by reforming the church—and inadvertently restoring freedom to mankind. But again, their power and authority was political and personal. They never claimed that God had asked them to do the thing they did—it was a series of personal movements. None claimed any revelation or restoration, nor can they, since by their own admission revelation ceased long ago.

All of this is not to deny any good for those churches, or for the many worthy souls they have produced. On the contrary. The purpose here is simply to point out the anomaly.

Thousands of years ago, prophets lived and received revelations and wrote them down into what we today call scriptures. All through recorded time God has worked through this one consistent system. But suddenly, after the death of the last apostle, at least according to the churches today, the system abruptly stopped. God no longer talked to man *and would never do so again.*

That happened only later in the history of the church, however, as the first churches after Christ grasped desperately for revelation, knowing it to be the foundation of the gospel. Only when it became obvious that they couldn't and weren't receiving revelation was it banned. They were flailing around in the dark like a man suddenly gone blind. Therefore, they began saying that nobody else could see, or ever could, just because the couldn't.

Without revelation, so basic to the original church, is it surprising that Christianity declined? Dr. Harry Emerson Fosdick described very well the condition of modern Christianity.

> A religious reformation is afoot, and at heart it is the endeavor to recover for our modern lives the religion of Jesus as against the vast, intricate, largely inadequate and often positively false religion about Jesus. Christianity today has largely left the religion which he preached, taught, and lived, and has substituted another kind of religion altogether. If Jesus should come back to earth now, hear the mythologies built up around him, see the creedalism, denominationalism, sacramentalism, carried on in his name, he would certainly say, "If this is Christianity, I am not a Christian."[4]

Roger Williams, the founder of the Baptist church in America and the pastor of the oldest Baptist church in this country at Providence, Rhode Island, refused to continue as pastor because there was no regularly constituted church of Christ, on earth, nor any person authorized to administer any church ordinance, nor can there be until new apostles are sent by the great head of the Church, for whose coming I am seeking."[5]

The message of this book is a simple one. So-called Christianity today, as proven by its historical record, cannot be the organizations that represent the Christ of the New Testament. A close look at the Bible indicates that Christ and the apostles knew what would happen, but even knowing that, remained optimistic. Why? Just as had happened in the past, they knew the gospel, full and intact, would be restored again at some future date. Roger Williams was just one of millions who have recognized the necessity of such a restoration.

Granted all we've said about historical "Christianity," what should we do about it?

It seems pretty clear that Christ promised a return of his church in a new "dispensation" at some future date—much as it had come and gone throughout history.

If that is true, it seems that at the minimum we ought to keep our faith strong, continue in our worship, and look for the true meaning of Christ in our lives.

And maybe, keep our hearts, our minds, and our eyes open. Perhaps that restoration will happen. Maybe it has already happened and we don't know about it; and therefore we ought to be looking.

It was promised. Think about it.

Notes

1. Irenaeus, "Against Heresies," III, Ante-Nicene Fathers.
2. Barker, 59.
3. Nibley, *The Passing of the Primitive Church*, 145.
4. Richards, 29.
5. *Loc cit.*

SELECTED BIBLIOGRAPHY

Ancient Christian Writers. *The Works of the Fathers in Translation.* Johannes Quasten and J. C. Plumpe, eds. Westminister, Maryland: the Newman Press; London: Longmans, Green and Co., 1961.

The Ante-Nicene Fathers. *Translations of the Writings of the Fathers Down to AD 325.* Alexander Roberts and James Donaldson, eds. 23 vols. Edinburgh: T & T Clark. 1866.

Bardenhewer, Otto. *Patrology: The Lives and Words of the Father of the Church.* Translated by Shahan. St. Louis: Herder, 1908.

Bainton, Roland H. *Early Christianity.* D. Van Nostrand Company, Inc. 1960.

Barker, James L. *Apostasy from the Divine Church.* Salt Lake City: Deseret News Press, 1960.

Bettenson, Henry. *Documents of the Christian Church.* Oxford University Press, 1974.

Case, Shirley Jackson. *Makers of Christianity.* New York: H. Holt and Co., 1934–37.

Chadwick. O. *From Bousset to Newman.* Cambridge University Press, 1956.

Chamberlin, E. R. *The Bad Popes.* Signet Books, New American Library, 1969.

Clarke, Charles Philip Steward. *Short History of the Christian Church.* London: Longman's Green and Co., 1928.

Deissman, Adolf. *Light from the Ancient East*. Grand Rapids: Baker Book House, 1965.

Duchesne, Louis. *Early History of the Christian Church*. Translated from the 4th ed. London: John Murral, 1931.

Durant, Will. *Caesar and Christ*. New York: Simon and Schuster, 1944.

Durant, Will. *The Age of Faith*. New York: Simon and Schuster, 1950.

Eusebius Ecclesiastical History. Translated by Christian Frederick Cruse. Grand Rapids, Michagan: Baker Book House, 1974.

Foakes-Jackson, Frederick John. History of the Christian Church from the Earliest times to AD 461. 6th ed. Cambridge: Deighton, Bell and Co. 1942.

Foakes-Jackson, Frederick John, and Kersopp Lake. *The Beginnings of Christianity*. 5 Vols. London: MacMillan Co., 1939.

Funk, Franz Zaver von. *A Manual of Church History*. 2 vols. Translated by Luigi Cappodelta. St. Louis: Herder Book Co., 1939.

Gibbon, Edward. The Decline and Fall of the Roman Empire. Abridged by D. M. Low. Harcourt, Brace and Company. New York.

Guignebert, Charles. *Christianity, Past and Present*. New York: The McMillan Co., 1927.

Hennecke, Edgar. *New Testament Apocrypha*. Wilhelm Schneemelcher, ed. Vols. I–II. Philadelphia: The Westminister Press, 1963.

Hiers, Richard H. *The Historical Jesus and the Kingdom of God*. University of Florida Humanities Monograph Number 38. Gainesville, 1973.

Historians History of the World. Henry Smith Williams, ed. London: The History Association, 1905.

Jonas, Hans. *The Gnostic Religion*. Boston: Beacon Press, 1963.

Johnson, Paul Henry. *A History of Christianity*. New York: Atheneum, 1977.

Kung, Hans. *On Being a Christian*. Translated by Edward Quinn. Garden City, New York: Doubleday & Co., 1976.

Latourette, Kenneth Scott. *A History of The Expansion of Christianity*. Vol. 1. New York and London: Harper & Brothers Publishers, 1937.

Lea, Henry C. *A History of the Inquisition*. Vol. III. New York: The McMillian Company, 1922.

Lea, Henry C. *The History of Sacerdotal Celibacy in the Christian Church*. New York: Russell & Russell, 1957.

Lightfoot, J. B. *The Apostolic Fathers*. Grand Rapids, Michigan: Baker Book House, 1967.

Lortz, Joseph. *History of the Church*. Milwaukee: Bruce Pub. Co., 1939.

Lyon, T. Edgar. *Apostasy to Restoration*. Salt Lake City: Deseret Book, 1960.

Marshall, R. P. and M. J. Taylor. *Liturgy and Christian Unity*. Englewood Cliffs, New Jersey: Prentice Hall, 1965.

Mackaye, William R. "The Selling of Mother Seton," *The Washington Post; Potomac Magazine*, Sept. 14, 1975.

Mathew, Arnold H. *The Life and Times of Rodrigo Borgia., Pope Alexander VI*. New York: Brentano's, 1912.

McSorley, Joseph. *An Outline History of the Church by Centuries*. Rev. ed. B. St. Louis: Herder Book Co., 1957.

Mosheim, Johann Lorenz. *Institutes of Ecclesiastical History, Ancient and Modern*. Translated by James Murdoch. London: Simms and M'Intyre, 1848.

Newhall, Richard Ager. *The Crusades*. Rev. ed. New York: Holt, Rinehart and Winston, 1963.

Newman, Albert Henry. *A Manual of Church History*. 2 vols. Revised and enlarged. Philadelphia: The American Baptist Publication Society, 1953.

Nibley, Hugh. *The Passing of the Primitive Church*. Church History. 30:131–54. June, 1961.

Nibley, Hugh. *Since Cumorah*. Salt Lake City: Deseret Book, 1973.

Nibley, Hugh. *When the Lights Went Out. Three Studies on the Ancient Apostasy*. Salt Lake City: Deseret Book, 1970.

Payne, Robert, *The Christian Centuries*. New York: W. W. Norton & Co., Inc., 1966.

Qualben, Lars Pederson. *A History of the Christian Church*. Rev. and enlarged. New York: T. Nelson, 1958.

Quasten, J. *Patrology*. 3 vols. Spectrum Publishers. Utrecht-Antwerp, 1966.

Richards, LeGrand. *A Marvelous Work and a Wonder*. Salt Lake City: Deseret Book, 1972.

Religious Movements in Contemporary America. I. I. Zaretsky and M. P. Leone, eds. Princeton University Press.

Robinson, James Harvey. *An Introduction to the History of Western Europe.* 2 Vols. Revised Ed., by James T. Shotwell. Boston: Ginn and Co., 1902.

Schaff, Philip. *History of the Christian Church.* Vols. 1–7. New York: Charles Scribner's Sons, 1930.

New Schaff-Herzog Encyclopedia of Religious Knowledge. Samauel Macauley Jackson, ed. New York and London: Funk and Wagnalls Co., 1908–12.

Sperry, Sidney B. *Paul's Life and Letters.* Salt Lake City: Bookcraft, 1955.

Shotwell, James T. *An Introduction to the History of Western Europe.* 2 Vols. Rev. ed.

Shotwell, James T. and Louise Roper Loomis. *The See of Peter.* New York: Columbia Univ. Press, 1927.

Spence, Hartzell. *The Story of America's Religions.* New York: Holt, Rinehart and Winston.

Talmage, James E. *The Great Apostasy.* Salt Lake City: Deseret Book, 1973.

Wegner, G. S. *6000 Years of the Bible.* New York and Evanston: Harper and Row, Publishers, 1963.

Wilken, Robert L. *The Myth of Christian Beginnings.* Garden City: Doubleday & Company, Inc., 1971.

ABOUT THE AUTHOR

It is hard to believe that anyone could have had as happy a childhood as Dr. Packer had, being raised in the southeastern corner of New Mexico in the 1930s in a town called Carlsbad. At the time, it was an economically deprived area, a dry, dusty little town with few chances for career development. To a ten-year-old-boy with a bicycle, the usually full Pecos River, and miles and miles of area to explore—it was heaven! The vagaries of trying to raise a crop in the desert or deal with the hassles of butting heads with hard-headed eastern companies attempting to extract potash in that bone dry desert bothered little boys not at all.

Living in that paradise was hard for Dr. Packer, but further horizon beckoned. In 1945 his family packed up and headed for Peru—where a different kind of paradise, and where for him, future choices had to be made.

After many travels and experiences, Dr. Packer earned BS and MA degrees at the University of Utah, and his PhD at Utah State University. While working on his PhD in entomology at Utah State University (completed in 1970), his thesis committee challenged his determination to take a beginning journalism course as a waste. His professor in that course further guaranteed an "A" to any student who published writing from that class. Dr. Packer published all three of the articles he wrote for that class and never looked back. Since then, he has published extensively in many magazines, including *The Ensign*, *American Heritage*, *Smithsonian Magazine*, and *Family Circle*, on topics such as archaeology of the Book of Mormon, a variety of scientific articles, and gunshot wounds in the Old West.

That initial journalism experience also led him to a career as the managing editor of a major scientific organization, editor of scientific journals and in scientific publishing, which further led to teaching journalism courses at the university level. He also served as the Director of Communications for the Senatorial Campaign for Elder V. Dallas Merrill in Maryland. While in Maryland, he taught in the LDS Church "Know Your Religion" series all over the Midwest and the East Coast from Virginia to Canada.

Academically, Dr. Packer has been recognized in his studies by the Ford Foundation for early Admissions, a Rockefeller Foundation Fellowship, and a Fulbright Lectureship in Colombia (which he reluctantly had to turn down).

He and his wife lived in Central America for several years, where he served as a department head and taught scientific courses at an agricultural college—in Spanish. Dr. Packer lived and worked in South and Central America for about twelve years. After Central America, he and his wife and family settled down in Maryland for the next thirty years and raised their five daughters there. During their thirty years in Maryland, Dr. Packer rose to the level of executive director of several national nonprofit organizations.

He has served the Church twice as district president, twice as bishop, and as a counselor in the Silver Spring, Maryland, stake presidency. He served his mission in Argentina, has been a temple ordinance worker, Church Institute of Religion instructor, and served on the high council for many years. While living in Maryland, he taught the Gospel Doctrine course for approximately sixteen years.

Dr. Packer is now retired and resides with his wife in Salt Lake City. They attend the Ridgedale Ward, where he currently teaches the Gospel Doctrine course as well as teaching the High Priests once a month.

0 26575 51371 4